About the editors

Kees Koonings is Associate Professor of Development Studies in the Faculty of Social Sciences, Utrecht University. He is the author of books and articles on development issues, ethnicity, and militarism and violence in Latin America.

Dirk Kruijt is Professor of Development Studies in the Faculty of Social Sciences, Utrecht University. He has published on poverty and the informal sector, military governments, and issues of war and peace in Latin America.

They are Coeditors of two previous Zed Books titles:

Societies of Fear: The Legacy of Civil War, Violence and Terror in Latin America (1999)

Political Armies: The Military and Nation Building in the Age of Democracy (2002)

KEES KOONINGS & DIRK KRUIJT | editors

Armed actors

Organized violence and state failure in
Latin America

Zed Books

LONDON | NEW YORK

Armed actors: organized violence and state failure in Latin America was
first published by Zed Books Ltd, 7 Cynthia Street, London N1 9JF, UK
and Room 400, 175 Fifth Avenue, New York, NY 10010, USA in 2004.

www.zedbooks.co.uk

Editorial copyright © Kees Koonings and Dirk Kruijt, 2004
Individual chapters © individual contributors, 2004

The rights of the editor and contributors to be identified as the authors
of this work have been asserted by them in accordance with the Copyright,
Designs and Patents Act, 1988.

Cover designed by Andrew Corbett
Set in FF Arnhem and Futura Bold by Ewan Smith, London
Index: ed.emery@britishlibrary.net
Printed and bound in Malta by Gutenberg Press Ltd

Distributed in the USA exclusively by Palgrave Macmillan, a division of
St Martin's Press, LLC, 175 Fifth Avenue, New York, NY 10010.

A catalogue record for this book is available from the British Library.
US CIP data are available from the Library of Congress.

ISBN 1 84277 444 1 cased
ISBN 1 84277 445 X limp

Contents

Introduction | 73 The cocaine industry: production and trafficking | 74 The growth of the drug industry: major conditioning factors | 75 The industry and its entrepreneurs | 78 Business practices in the drug industry | 82 Conclusions | 84

Abbreviations

ABIN	Agencia Brasileira de Inteligencia (Brazilian Intelligence Agency)
ACCU	Autodefensas Campesinas de Cordoba y Urabá (Self-Defence Forces of Cordoba and Urabá)
ARENA	Alianza Republicana Nacional (National Republican Alliance)
AUC	Autodefensas Unidas de Colombia (United Self-Defence Forces of Colombia)
CAD	Comité de Autodefensa y Desarrollo (Committee of Self-Defence and Development)
CADEG	Consejo Anticomunista de Guatemala (Anti-Communist Council of Guatemala)
CDC	Comités de Defensa Civil (Civil Defence Committees)
CGT	Confederación General de Trabajadores (General Confederation of Workers)
CNE	Consejo Nacional Electoral (National Electoral Council)
COFAVIC	Comité de Familiares de Víctimas de 27 de Febrero (Committee of the Relatives of the Victims of 27 February)
CRAG	Comité de Resistencia Anticomunista de Guatemala (Committee of Anti-Communist Resistance of Guatemala)
CRS	Corriente de Renovación Socialista (Socialist Renovation Current)
CUFAN	Comando Unificado de la Fuerza Armada Nacional (Unified Command of the National Armed Forces)
CVDC	Comités Voluntarios de Defensa Civil (Voluntary Civil Defence Committees)
DECAS	Defensa Civil Antisubversiva (Anti-Subversive Civil Defence)
ELN	Ejército de Liberación Nacional (Army of National Liberation)
EMDN	Estado Mayor de la Defensa Nacional (National Defence Staff)
EPL	Ejército Popular de Liberación (Popular Liberation Army)
ESA	Ejército Secreto Anticomunista (Secret Anti-Communist Army)
FADA	Fuerza de Acción Armada (Armed Action Force)
FAFERJ	Federação de Favelas do Estado do Rio de Janeiro (Federation of Favelas of the State of Rio de Janeiro)
FANO	Frente Anticomunista del Nororiente (Anti-Communist Front of the North-East)
FARC	Fuerzas Armadas Revolucionarias de Colombia (Armed Revolutionary Forces of Colombia)
FEA	Frente Estudiantil Anticomunista (Student's Anti-communist Front)
FEDECAMARAS	Federación Venezolano de Cámaras y Asociaciones de Comercio

	y Producción (National Federation of Chambers of Commerce and Industry)
FGR	Fiscalía General de la República (Public Prosecutor's Office)
FMLN	Frente Farabundo Marti de Liberación Nacional (Farabundo Marti National Liberation Front)
FRG	Frente Republicano Guatemalteco (Guatemalan Republican Front)
GALGAS	Guerrilla Acción Libertadora Guatemalteca Antisalvadoreña (Guatemalan Anti-Salvadoran Liberating Guerrilla Action)
IML	Instituto de Medicina Legal (Institute of Forensic Medicine)
IUDOP	Instituto Universitario de Opinión Publica (University Institute of Public Opinion)
MANO	Movimiento de Acción Nacionalista Organizada (Movement of Organized Nationalist Action)
MAS	Muerte a los Secuestradores (Death to Kidnappers)
MINUGUA	Misión de las Naciones Unidas para Guatemala (United National Mission for Guatemala)
MP/PP	Milicias Populares del Pueblo y para el Pueblo (Popular Militias of the People and for the People)
MP/VA	Milicias Populares Valle de Aburrú (Popular Militias of the Valle de Aburrú)
MRTA	Movimiento Revolucionario Tupac Amatu (Revolutionary Movement Tupac Amaru)
OPS	Organización Panamericana de Salúd (Pan-American Health Organization)
PAC	Patrullas de Autodefensa Civil (Civil Defence Patrols)
PDVSA	Petroleos de Venezuela SA (Venezuelan Petroleum SA)
PMA	Policía Militar Ambulante (Mobile Military Police)
PNC	Policía Nacional Civil (National Civil Police)
PRI	Partido Revolucionario Institucional (Institutional Revolutionary Party)
PRN	Proceso de Reorganización Nacional (Process of National Reorganization)
PROVEA	Programa Venezolano de Educación-Acción en Derechos Humanos (Venezuelan Programme of Action-Education in Human Rights)
PRT	Partido Revolucionario de los Trabajadores (Revolutionary Workers Party)
SIC	Servicio de Investigación Criminal (Criminal Investigative Service)
SIN	Sistema de Inteligencia Nacional (System of National Intelligence)
SNI	Serviço Nacional de Informações (System of National Intelligence)
UP	Unión Patriótica (Patriotic Union)

Acknowledgements

In June 2003, we organized at Utrecht University a two-day seminar where the authors of the thirteen contributions brought together in this book discussed the draft versions of their chapters. We are very grateful for the willingness of our colleagues from Latin America, Europe and the USA to prepare papers on the basis of our designated framework to facilitate both conceptual convergence and comparative country studies. The workshop in Utrecht was facilitated by the Department of Cultural Anthropology and the CERES research school for development studies. During the preparation and the aftermath of the seminar, Kootje Willemse and Mari Mar Azofra provided wholehearted and efficient organizational and logistical support. Between June and October 2003, the authors accepted our rather strict deadlines for redrafting their contributions. We express our appreciation to Mario Fumerton and Simone Remijnse for, respectively, the rapid and proficient translation of three papers originally presented in Spanish, and valuable editorial support during the final stage of completion of the manuscript. As on previous occasions, the team from Zed Books, especially Robert Molteno, coached us smoothly and pleasantly through the process of editing the text and producing the book.

Utrecht, December 2003
Kees Koonings and Dirk Kruijt

Introduction

KEES KOONINGS AND DIRK KRUIJT

The inspiration to dedicate a volume to the issue of armed actors and organized violence in Latin America has come from the apparent failure of many of the so-called 'new democracies' in this region. This failure reflects the inability to guarantee one of the core functions of democratic states, namely the legitimate monopoly over the collective means of coercion. Of course we are familiar with the state terrorism, guerrillas and conventional civil wars of the 1960s–1980s period. Organized social and political violence in Latin America prior to the recent wave of democratization was based on politico-ideological conflicts between authoritarian states and more or less well-defined armed and unarmed opponents. As a result, state conceptions of the use of the legal means of coercion were embedded in a militaristic logic of internal warfare that was consecrated by pseudo-legal formulae derived from national security doctrines. With the onset of democratic transitions, it was widely expected that elected civilian governments would restore the rule of law and would espouse peaceful, non-violent means of interest representation and mediation. The strengthening of civil society, nurtured by opposition to military rule and active involvement in democratic transitions and peace negotiations, was expected to offer a durable social and cultural foundation for democratic consolidation.

However, after more than two decades of democratization, state and non-state violence continues to mark social and political life in many Latin American countries. In the recent literature labels and concepts such as 'extralegal violence', 'uncivil movements', 'unrule of law' and 'ugly' or 'illiberal' democracies have been introduced to pinpoint what seems to have become a structural characteristic of post-authoritarian Latin America. At the beginning of the twenty-first century, the problem of organized violence, dubbed the 'new violence', appears to be enduring. One of the noteworthy characteristics of contemporary Latin American societies is the coexistence of formal constitutionalism, electoral democracy and a nascent civil society on the one hand, and the use of force to pursue economic or political interests by a variety of 'armed actors' on the other. These armed actors may be directly or indirectly state related or linked to political opposition or economic and criminal interests. Often, these elements are interconnected.

The result is the permanent erosion, delegitimization or collapse of the formal violence monopoly of Latin American nation-states. We refer to this phenomenon as (partial) 'state failure'. Much of the literature on 'failed' or 'collapsed' states deals with scenarios of near-total disintegration of state institutions and the widespread proliferation of intra-state armed conflict. The testing ground for these concepts has been predominantly Sub-Saharan Africa. The situation in Latin America is different. The formal institutions of the state endure, albeit with varying legitimacy and effectiveness. Notions of nationhood and citizenship continue to be supported by broad sectors of the population. The ideal of rights and the rule of law are still widely supported even in violence-battered countries such as Guatemala, Colombia or (parts of) Brazil. Hence, organized violence does not affect national societies in a uniform way. The impact of violence varies considerably within countries between towns and countryside, from one region to the next, or within specific areas of the large conurbations. In fact, we are faced with so-called contested spaces in a geographic, institutional and socio-cultural sense. Particularly in the metropolitan areas, the phenomenon of 'divided cities' has changed large parts of the urban peripheries into virtual no-go areas where drug lords, violent political entrepreneurs and gangs of disenchanted youths rule supreme. Yet to many inhabitants of better-off neighbourhoods, these realms of violence, misery and uncivility appear mainly in the morning paper or on the evening news: the violence could just as well be taking place on another continent. In a country such as Colombia, the contestation of space and the division of geographical and social domains have become nationwide phenomena.

However, this violence and the armed actors associated with it are not insulated; many-stranded linkages exist between this domain and the core institutions of the political and legal order. As a result, there is a generalized sensation of – maybe sometimes partial – state failure that interacts with organized violence of this 'new' variety. In turn, this may lead to the installation of uncivil societies that overwhelm the process of democratic consolidation in Latin America. State failure results not only in so-called 'governance voids' – spaces or domains in which the legitimate state is effectively absent in the face of armed actors that abide by the rule of force – but also in the internal erosion of the capacity and willingness of state agents themselves to abide by the rule of law. In some cases this may lead to the (re)-installation of authoritarian regimes guided by political armies. More frequently, it results in the spread of state violence (for example, by the police) or in the proliferation of shady agents such as intelligence services and paramilitary groups. Currently this is not only an important scholarly but also a political and public concern in the region.

In this book we propose to analyse and compare some of the key notions and issues with respect to armed actors, violence, state failure and uncivility in Latin America. The authors discuss key concepts and general trends and examine empirically contemporary cases of armed actors and violence scenarios. After a brief conceptual exploration by Kees Koonings and Dirk Kruijt in Chapter 1, the next three chapters discuss the institutions that constitute the domain of the means of coercion of the state: the military (analysed by Dirk Kruijt and Kees Koonings in Chapter 2), the police (discussed by Piet van Reenen in Chapter 3) and officially sanctioned civil defence organizations (surveyed by Mario Fumerton and Simone Remijnse in Chapter 4). These chapters show that different logics of violence – open civil war, problematic post-war pacification, and democracies with increasing levels of social and criminal violence – produce a cohabitation of these formal institutions with less visible armed actors. These actors arise to deal with internal security, public order and law enforcement issues in ways that are at odds with legitimacy and probity. Chapter 5, by Menno Vellinga, moves to the explicit domain of organized crime and crime-related violence. Boosted by the expansion of the narco-economy, the corruptive and coercive capacities of large criminal networks deeply affect the economy, social relations and politics in Latin America.

The following two chapters offer case studies of organized violence and the involvement of key armed actors on a national scale. Colombia, analysed by Francisco Leal in Chapter 6, offers the most extreme and enduring case of conflicting armed actors with profound repercussions for the fragile democratic and legal order. Venezuela, in contrast, appears recently to have been moving away from its stable bipartisan civilian democracy. As Harold Trinkunas shows in Chapter 7, the Chávez administration installed a regime that combines growing political involvement of the military and stepped-up political violence with passionate mobilization of both supporters and opponents of the current government.

The next three chapters explore with great empirical detail the nature and consequences of divided cities in Argentina, Brazil and El Salvador. The recent economic crisis and growing social exclusion in Argentina have transformed greater Buenos Aires into a vast zone of social disintegration, rising tensions and criminal violence. Marcelo Sain shows in Chapter 8 that a variety of gangs and criminal rackets occupy the spaces left by a systematically deficient police and justice system. Alba Zaluar shows in Chapter 9 how poverty, exclusion and local governance voids in Rio de Janeiro have created virtual urban battlefields dominated by the confrontation between drug gangs and unsavoury police forces. Wim Savenije and Chris van der Borgh refer, in Chapter 10, to

3

the same problem of social exclusion as the key backdrop to the proliferation of violent youth gangs in the poor districts of San Salvador.

The book concludes with two chapters that pursue the wider significance of violence and armed actors in the region. Luis Alberto Restrepo, in Chapter 11, reflects on the ambivalent assimilation of enduring violence and uncivility in everyday life in Colombia. In the Epilogue, Patricio Silva brings together a number of explanations for the current wave of violence and insecurity in Latin America. He argues that this poses an urgent challenge for the state, politics and civil society with respect to the preservation or recovery of a legitimate order and a non-violent society.

1 | Armed actors, organized violence and state failure in Latin America: a survey of issues and arguments

KEES KOONINGS AND DIRK KRUIJT

Democracy and violence

Democracy is about citizenship rights and the structures and mechanisms to put these into practice. Citizenship means the incorporation of individual agents or groups in the modern nation-state in order to realize civil, political, social and cultural participation. A democratic social and political order therefore means the mutually reinforcing coexistence of civil society, political society and the state. A democratic state, citizenship rights and civil society presuppose the rule of law. The rule of law presupposes the effective monopoly of the collective means of coercion in the hands of the state. Democracy stands as a condition for the legitimacy of this violence monopoly. These notions have gained widespread attention and support in Latin America over the past two decades among political and social agents, scholars and the public at large (Domínguez and Lowenthal 1996; Linz and Stepan 1996; Diamond 1999). Still, the track record of democratic consolidation in the region has been far from spotless. A large body of scholarly literature on democratization has shed light on the various aspects of the Latin American democratic deficit. This debate has become increasingly urgent in recent years now that the initial optimism with respect to democratization has subsided. Among the contemporary obstacles to the deepening and quality improvement of democracy in the region, the following problems are highlighted (Agüero and Stark 1998).

First, there are the manifold flaws in the design and functioning of political democracy and governance. These range from issues related to institutional design (electoral systems, state apparatus, decentralization, among others) to problems in accountability and political culture (O'Donnell 1999). Second, there is the deep-seated problem of social inequality and exclusion. Popular mobilization before and during the democratic transition has consistently pressed for democratization of society and not just politics. Hence, political democracy is seen not only as an end in itself but also as a condition for enhancing citizenship rights and promoting social justice (Alvarez et al. 1998; Castañeda 1996; Foweraker 2001). Although throughout the twentieth century citizenship has been limited mostly to social rights and integration of selected

5

social groups and classes (Roberts 1996), with the demise of the institutional dictatorships and the democratic transition, citizenship and civil society have taken centre stage in public and political discourse, mobilization strategies and academic research (Jelin and Hershberg 1996). During the 1980s and 1990s, social movements and civil society have been challenging the structures and practices of social exclusion. But in doing so, they have been facing the proliferation of neo-liberal adjustment policies, the withdrawal of the state, and the progressive impoverishment and informalization of Latin American societies (Kruijt, Sojo and Grynspan 2002). Finally, we witness the tenacious problem of social and political violence. Two decades of democratic consolidation have shown that contemporary violence is not just a leftover of the dictatorships and civil wars of the 1960s–1980s (Koonings and Kruijt 1999). Initially, it was supposed that the progress of democratization could be measured *inter alia* by the degree to which repression and extra-legal violence have been hemmed in by the forces of the law and by the degree to which social and political antagonism came to be channelled through consociational, nonviolent arrangements. Up till the present, however, social and political violence in Latin America has appeared to be enduring, despite the consolidation of formal (political, electoral) democratic systems. Violence has acquired greater variation and new dimensions beyond the conventional state and insurgent violence of the past. As a result of this 'new violence' (a concept to which we will return below), one of the most noteworthy characteristics of contemporary Latin American societies is the de facto coexistence of formal constitutionalism, (electoral) democracy and an often vibrant civil society on the one hand, and the use of force to stake out power domains or pursue economic or political interests on the other. The violence that underlies this is not only extra-legal in the sense that it is pursued by state agents that overstep the boundaries of legality or by non-state agents that seek alternative ways of imposing 'justice' (Huggins 1991). It is also 'uncivil' in the sense that it undermines the constitution of citizenship as a principle based on non-violence and the rule of law. As such violence undermines the very foundations of democracy and bears witness to the failure of the state to uphold the rule of law and citizens' security. In the literature on Latin America, this problem has led to qualifications as the 'unrule of law' (Méndez et al. 1999), 'uncivil movements' (Payne 2000), and 'ugly' or 'illiberal' democracies (Pereira 2000; Diamond 1999). At the core of this syndrome lies the notion of 'new violence' to which we can now turn.

State failure, uncivil society and 'new violence'

Not only have modern states been grounded upon violence (Giddens 1985), but also there is the permanent fragility of the state's monopoly of legitimate force. This means that the coercive capacity of the state runs the risk of being 'unharnessed'. This can come about if the state uses violence without consented legitimacy (as happens with dictatorships, state terrorism and dirty warfare). It can also result from decentralized or atomized state-related actors that use parts of the coercive resources of the state for other ends. Finally, the state as a structure and effective power arena may break down in part or in full. We can call this governance voids (Kruijt and Koonings 1999: 12), state failure or, in its most extreme manifestation, collapsed states (Zartman 1995). In Latin America we see the hand-overs and leftovers of political conflict and violence of the recent past: authoritarianism, repression, counter-insurgency, political militarism and security doctrines, police violence, etc. This violence has been changing in the new context of formal democracy, but continues to constrain the consolidation of the rule of law and citizenship rights.

Apart from the problem of state failure with respect to its legitimate violence monopoly and the rule of law, civil society also has its dark side. According to Keane (1997: 63–4) the space offered by the anonymous freedoms within civil society also facilitates the mobilization of agents against the legal order, using coercive rather than legal-institutional means.[1] Herewith we can define 'uncivil society': agents or groups that force their interest upon the public domain on the basis of coercion and violence, in such a way that the legitimate aspirations of other groups or sectors in civil society are jeopardized and the rule of law is fragmented or shattered. In effect, this is a further aspect of state failure in the sense that the state is effectively incapable of countering coercion and violence by non-state agents. It should be added that, in fact, state violence very often recruits or provokes non-state violence (paramilitary, hidden, informal) to do the dirty work or to occupy the spaces created by the delegitimization of the legal order and the impunity that goes with it. In the combined instance of the failure of legitimate statehood and its control of violence and the rise of uncivil society we see what Méndez, O'Donnell and Pinheiro (1999) have labelled the 'unrule of law'. However, unrule of law is a mild manifestation, suggesting that contemporary violence by state and non-state actors is a governance problem, something that can be restored through concerted public action. More intense manifestations are 'societies of fear', and societies in which the so-called 'new violence' seems to have become endemic. Such appears to be the case in many parts of Latin America.

Earlier, we argued that post-authoritarian violence should be distinguished from the violence of the 'traditional order' and the violence of the authoritarian regimes of the 1960s–1980s (Kruijt and Koonings 1999). Pereira and Davis (2000: 4) observe that contemporary violence in Latin America should not be seen as the continuation in new forms of the historically established patterns of violence in the region, as 'new moves in an old game'. They point at the rise of 'citizens-on-citizens violence', as well as at the blurring of the boundaries between state and society owing to the confluence of such things as repressive crime fighting, social cleansing, criminal racketeering, and the elimination of political opponents by state, pseudo-state or non-state actors alike. One could try to pinpoint the new violence by noting its increasing variety both in form and in the nature of its perpetrators (Kurtenbach 2003). Newness may also lie in its purpose. Whereas the 'old violence' revolved around defending or challenging the power of the state and the position of certain regimes, new violence entails in a way its 'democratization' in the sense that a variety of social actors pursue a variety of objectives on the basis of coercive strategies and methods (Kruijt and Koonings 1999: 11).

Perhaps the principal dimension of newness is the manifest contrast between the persistence and proliferation of violence and the simultaneous adoption of democracy, citizenship and the rule of law as norm and goal in Latin America. Precisely for this reason, the new violence does not aim at conquering state power or changing or defending a regime per se. New violence instead occupies the interstices of the fragile and fragmented formal legal, institutional and political order. As a tentative definition we therefore suggest that 'new violence' is socially or politically organized to wield coercion by evading or undermining the legitimate violence monopoly of formally democratic states. This implies the permanent 'uneasy coexistence' of the legal democratic order and the new violence in a parallel logic that is at the same

---

Box 1.1 Fuzzy realms of democracy and violence in Latin America

Rule of law: human and citizenship rights	Unrule of law: violence, fear and insecurity
Citizenship and civil society	Armed actors and uncivil society
Legitimate and effective empowerment	The politics of coercion
Decent states and public policies	State failure, arbitrariness, rule of the jungle

time antagonistic and complementary in present-day Latin America (see Box 1.1). This represents, in fact, a hidden form of state failure: on the surface the institutions and practices of democratic politics, civil society and the rule of law hold sway; at the core, these very notions are undermined by violence.

The proliferation of armed actors

With the rise of this new violence, post-dictatorial Latin America had to cope with the presence of a variety of armed actors, most of them non-legitimate. We can at least distinguish the following typology of armed actors (Koonings 2001: 403–5).

First, we have the expanded legitimate security sectors or the formal armed actors within the public domain: the military, the security and intelligence forces, and the police. In the Weberian ideal of the modern rational-bureaucratic state, these forces are the tools of legitimate coercion against extraterritorial military opponents or internal violent or terrorist infractors of the rule of law. These state-related actors, however, were instrumental in the 1960s to 1980s as the backbone of Latin America's 'national security' dictatorships (Kruijt 2001: 413–14). The crusades against communism, the internal wars and the campaigns against internal terrorism coincided for the most part with heavy-handed governments, whose instrument of power was the unique combination of the legitimate security sector and an array of connected services: military intelligence, the security bodies, the controlled police forces. As the brain and backbone of the confrontation with real or imagined insurgents and terrorists, the intelligence and security systems expanded to such a degree that their official and unofficial functions became difficult to distinguish.

The monopoly on violence implied another, even more enviable monopoly on intelligence and information. Even after the military regimes ended and the reduction of the armed forces set in, military intelligence controlled, for years after the regime transitions, the civilian cabinets as imposed advisers on matters of national security and development. The de facto military predominance over the police forces generally reinforced the power of the security and intelligence services delivered by the military. The police, in many Latin American countries, are still prone to arbitrariness while targeting social enemies, rather than upholding the rule of law (Chevigny 1995; Glebbeek 2003; van Reenen, this volume).

In the second place, there is the expansion of legal violence to extra-legal violence in the name of law and order. In many cases a murky symbiosis has developed between the official security forces and vigilante forces or private police forces. This was clearly the case during the decade of the Peruvian *pax fujimoricana* in the 1990s when even within the Sistema de Inteligencia Nacional (SIN), led by Vladimiro Montesinos, there existed a parallel service for blackmail and wet jobs. At the same time the armed forces, corrupted by drug money and equipment frauds, acted as the executive arm of the civilian regime. Other examples are the proliferation of special forces, extra-legal task forces, paramilitary commandos, para-police forces, death squads, etc., especially in the case of the prolonged civil wars in Colombia and Guatemala. In the specific case of rural self-defence bodies (*rondas* and *patrullas*) and sometimes urban *serenazgos*, a peculiar combination of subordination to state terrorism, particularism of local power holders, and more or less justifiable instances of community defence have emerged in countries such as Guatemala and Peru (Fumerton 2002; Remijnse 2003; Fumerton and Remijnse, this volume).

Third, we have old and new forms of guerrilla movements that still employ violence as a coherent working and negotiating strategy. Conventional cold-war-era guerrilla groups have become scarce in post-cold-war Latin America (Wickham-Crowley 1992; Gaspar 1997). The two Peruvian guerrilla groups of the 1980s and the 1990s (Sendero Luminoso and Tupac Amaru) have been more or less dissolved after being crashed by counter-insurgency operations involving peasant *ronderos* (self-defence patrol members). After the peace accords and the regime transitions in El Salvador, Guatemala and Nicaragua, all former Central American guerrilla organizations have been transformed into political forces, acting as peaceful actors in electoral instead of insurgency campaigns. The first post-cold-war guerrilla movement is the Mexican EZLN. This movement has indulged in hardly any fighting, however, displaying a high political profile at the negotiating table. Pursuing a series of social and political reforms, it won the hearts and minds of the Mexican popular and middle classes. Only in Colombia do 'regular' left-wing guerrilla forces still wield considerable military power to resist the state and paramilitary strength. As shown in Box 1.2 below, however, the state-related security forces, the guerrilla and the paramilitary act as 'macro-forces' at the national level. At the regional and local levels the proliferation and fragmentation of second-generation armed actors is absolutely astonishing.

In the fourth place there is the phenomenon of 'uncivil society' already referred to above. Sometimes, social and political movements tend to radicalize. Their 'speaking rights' in the political arena are in some cases directly derived from their use of force to back up their economic and social claims. The tactics of Ecuador's indigenous movements in the 1980s and 1990s and of the Brazilian landless workers' movement are examples of the weapon of coercive pressure to reinforce a negotiating position (Hammond 1999). It is therefore not surprising that these kinds of movements are targeted by the military and police forces as new and post-cold-war security threats. in countries such as Brazil, Colombia, El Salvador, Guatemala and Nicaragua, however, it was typically right-wing violence which nurtured uncivil society. The smooth ties between local and rural elite sectors and the local police forces offer a ready instrument for reactionary violence, applied often in connivance with private armies and security providers.

Finally, there are the small-scale and larger criminal organizations, linked to the international drug trade or local racketeering. These criminal gangs have managed to mount parallel systems of violence and enforced order on a national scale in countries such as Colombia and Mexico, and, to a lesser degree or on a more localized scale, in Argentina, Brazil and Suriname. In the case of tiny Suriname, a former Dutch colony granted independence in 1975 and tormented by military rule in the 1980s, a parallel economy based upon drug trafficking, gold exploitation and timber export amounts to 60 per cent of the official national economy. This economy was the financier during a 'forgotten' war between 1987 and 1992, when the regular army, insurgent *bosneger* (former Maroon – descendants of runaway slaves) groups and a variety of paramilitary forces were engaged in guerrilla and counter-insurgency campaigns. At the same time, the leaders from both sides were cocaine business partners during the truces and the peace negotiations. Drug bosses and their gangs in the slums, in Argentina's *villas*, Brazil's *favelas* and Colombia's *barrios* and *tugurios*, have reproduced this kind of national war scenario in urban territorial disputes. It is even estimated that around six thousand child and adolescent soldiers in Rio de Janeiro operate as warriors in drug gang wars, a number comparable to those in the individual Sub-Saharan African conflicts in the late 1990s and early 2000s (Dowdney 2002). The involvement of youth is not a specific South American phenomenon: in the Central American countries of El Salvador, Honduras and Guatemala, the *maras* or criminal youth gangs are the principal national security threat (Savenije and van der Borgh, this volume).

This typology, however, becomes blurred, as most ideal types do, in the analysis of real situations. In countries such as Colombia and Guatemala, for instance, where a *desborde de la violencia* (spill-over of violence) has been institutionalized during the last couple of decades, most analytical distinctions become unfocused or confused when day-to-day situations bring about a systematic interaction between the armed actors involved, particularly in local configurations. In Box 1.2 we summarize the complicated set-up of urban paramilitary and extra-legal armed actors in the city of Medellín, Colombia, during the 1980s and 1990s.

*Box 1.2   Colombia's national armed actors and local proliferation
in Medellín during the 1980s and 1990s*

Describing the complicated Colombian scenario, Pécaut (1999) introduced the notion of the 'banality of violence'. The protracted internal conflict transformed the country into an array of war theatres where a variety of armed actors and power players interfere. At the national level one can distinguish between the security forces, the FARC (Fuerzas Armadas Revolucionarias de Colombia) and the ELN (Ejército de Liberación Nacional) as armed actors of the left, and the AUC (Autodefensas Unidas de Colombia) as the unified paramilitary forces, product of the initiatives of the landed elite and the representatives of the clandestine economy commissioned to protect their interests. Behind this macro-configuration are the links between officialdom and the hidden forces, between the security forces of law and order and the forces of disorder, between the paramilitary and the death squads, between the official economy and the clandestine one. Translating this structure to the local level reveals a striking fragmentation: Escobar (2002) shows the articulation of changing alliances between local partners and national actors. Avilés (2001: 43–7) mentions more than a hundred paramilitary associations, unified during conferences and meetings in the 1990s in institutions such as CONVIVIR, a grouping of vigilante-type movements financed by rural entrepreneurs, of several hundred local self-defence committees and local *serenazgos*. Ceballos Melguizo (2001: 115–24) provides an extraordinary analysis of the fragmentation of violence in Medellín in the 1980s and 1990s. In this microcosmos of violence operate criminal consortia such as *bandas de la pesada* (gangs of heavies), networks of businessmen, smugglers and authorities together with the occasional criminals who undertake the dirty work, *oficinas* (offices). Groups of followers of the mafia heads act as intermediaries between demand for and supply of death contracts and criminality, *galladas* (youth gangs) gather around the cocaine trafficking, and the occasional *sicarios* (young murderers) commit murders on command. So-called *chichipato* gangs (small gangs without even decent weaponry) rob stores, homes, vehicles and pedestrians in the poor *barrios*, using *bazuco,* a potent coca base, as their daily stimulant. A variety of *protectores* (protectors) and social cleansing groups carry out summary executions, alongside massacres by fragmented paramilitary forces and crimes by local militia groups. The lower-class militia groups are a hybrid of leftist guerrillas and common criminals, organized into gangs. The drug trade was a catalyst. Entering the 'protection market' in the 1990s, they acted as adversaries of the right-wing death squads and social cleansing groups. Presenting themselves as 'armed power groups of the *barrios*', they started exterminating criminals, drug and *bazuco* dealers. The first organized groups had names such as the Milicias Populares del Pueblo y para el Pueblo (Popular Militias of the People and for the People, MP/PP), Milicias Populares Valle de Aburrá (MP/VA), and the América Libre Milicia. All groups displayed linkages between gangs and left-wing leaders. They were the product of the anomie in the *barrios* expressed by the rapid growth of criminal gangs and the crisis and dispersion of the left after President Betancur's offer of reintegration (see Leal Buitrago, this volume). The immediate result was the phenomenon of 'peace camps', providing political indoctrination and military training for young people in the *barrios* after the breakdown of the peace negotiations and the closing of the camps. Also former leftist militants found employment in the protection and self-defence market, sometimes joining drug gangs. The revolutionary rhetoric helped to disguise extortion practices such as 'tax collection' and 'voluntary fees'. Other groups, such as *Los Capuchos* (the Hoods), acted as *ronderos* (patrol members), a time-honoured practice from the period of *La Violencia* (1948–53), conducting summary trials of petty criminals which gave them popular support and legitimization. The groups very quickly subdivided and many truly roguish elements took command. In 1993, Antioquia's governor estimated the number of urban militia members at something over five thousand. After 'peace talks' in that year, which later failed, most militia groups faced internal problems, splitting into new and conflicting units in open rivalry with criminal gangs and the police. After 1994, the militia groups as well as the gangs continued to exist, either growing or splitting up into smaller splinter groups.

Sources: Avilés (2001); Ceballos Melguizo (2001); Escobar (2002); Leal Buitrago (1994; 1999; 2000); Pécaut (1999); Rangel (2000).

Armed actors and violence: social and political consequences

At the beginning of the twenty-first century, how do violence and the proliferation of armed actors within Latin American societies affect social relations, citizenship and democracy? In a preliminary way, we can note consequences in the field of sociability and social relations, civil society, politics, and the state. Violence leads to fear and distrust; these two basic syndromes seem to have become endemic. Rotker (2002) and Martín-Barbero (2002) portray fear as a permanent attribute of the Latin American citizen. Since violence can come from anywhere for whatever reason, citizens become 'potential victims' (Rotker 2002: 15). As a result, no one from beyond the intimate circle of family and friends can be trusted. Public institutions meant to provide security and to protect citizens' rights are non-performing, absent or have become part of the threat. Polling institutions consistently provide data that express dissatisfaction with the performance (but mostly not the principles) of basic institutions of democracy: political parties, legislatures, state bureaucracies and legal courts.[2] Everyday life, especially in the cities, takes place in an undeclared war of low but tangible intensity. Among the poor and excluded, fear and distrust are related to permanent hazards and risks; among the middle classes, they often take the form of a moral panic fanned perpetually by the mass media.

Violence, fear and distrust contribute to the gradual disintegration of the social fabric. The long-term effects of urbanization, consumerism and individualization have not been absorbed, in Latin America, by effective mechanisms for social integration such as the law, public institutions or civic values. Instead, increasing numbers of Latin Americans live in an informal society geared up for uncertain everyday survival. Here violence finds a fertile breeding ground. Indeed, the new violence, and many of the armed actors involved in it, are clearly connected with poverty, inequality and exclusion. Violence hits the vulnerable in a disproportionate way, while many of the rank and file of the armed actors are recruited from among the poor (Pinheiro 1996; Méndez, O'Donnell and Pinheiro 1999). Until recently, the two main extra-legal armed actors in the Colombian violence, the guerrillas and the paramilitary, recruited new cadres, publicly offering twice the minimum wage. The underprivileged find themselves in a situation of permanent defencelessness. The privileged seek recourse to secluded and insulated spaces in their 'cities of walls' (Caldeira 2000), where they organize their day-to-day life in closed and guarded communities, shopping malls and social clubs.

A very pernicious effect of violence is the undermining of civil society and the emancipative strategies pursued within it. Although armed actors within uncivil society do not always have a clear or explicit political objective, since they use coercion by instinct or convenience, the effect is that they destroy the foundation of the legitimate strategies and actions of civil actors, namely the rule of law and entitlements based on politically and institutionally grounded rights. State responses to this tend to disregard these rights as well (Caldeira 1996). Violence and force are thus implicit or explicit uncivil strategies to intimidate or destroy the efforts of those seeking a legitimate public role or a peaceful and more just society (Leeds 1996; Wouters 2001).

Finally, and this is obvious, unrestrained violence means the erosion of legitimate governance. We have already discussed above the failure of the state to maintain its violence monopoly and hence to uphold the rule of law. Politicians and public agents tend to respond to this with efforts to fill the governance voids with ad hoc 'bricolage' that often serves no other purpose than to placate (middle-class) public opinion or uncertain electorates. At the same time, disenchantment with politics, and in some countries even with democracy as a value, looms around the corner. This kind of democracy-cum-violence therefore raises the question of the long-term consistency and sustainability of Latin America's democratic regimes. The paradox is that, apparently, most of them seem to have found a modus vivendi with this in-built hybridity of legitimate institutions and extra-legal violence. Will this lead to a typical model of uneasy, fragmented democracy in Latin America that permanently endures 'acceptable' levels of violence within a disputed public domain?

Notes

1 According to the statistical data presented by Briceño-León (2002: 13), violence was the principal cause of death among Latin Americans aged between fifteen and forty-four at the end of the twentieth century. Between 1985 and 1994 the number of widows in Colombia doubled, while the number of orphans rose 70 per cent. In post-war El Salvador the number of murders per 100,000 inhabitants rose from 72 to 139 between 1990 and 1995.

2 See the yearly Latinobarometro polls (<www.latinobarometro.org>).

2 | The military and their shadowy brothers-in-arms

DIRK KRUIJT AND KEES KOONINGS

Latin America's political culture is characterized by its roughness. Periodic explosions of violence are followed by periods of more diffuse and hidden, smouldering turbulence. Over the past century authoritarian rule and state-induced repression have played a central role in the reproduction of social and political antagonism in the region. With the return to democracy in the region since 1985, the significance of open state terrorism has clearly ebbed, as has the importance of the armed forces as a powerful political player in the national arena. The weight of its influence, however, especially through military intelligence coupled with paramilitary activities, can still be felt. The argument of this chapter is that, despite democratic transitions, the military, particularly military intelligence and associated paramilitary forces, continue to be pillars of veiled uncivility in society and politics. The argument is developed in three sections. First, we will consider the legacy of the so-called political armies in Latin America. Then we evaluate the realm of the intelligence community and its fault lines with respect to independent control and supervision, the dominance of the military in intelligence, the lack of technical expertise and, ultimately, of professionalism. The last section of the chapter discusses the nature of paramilitary forces and their involvement in social and political violence. In post-authoritarian Latin America, particularly in Colombia, paramilitary forces have appeared as the hidden substitute for the direct involvement of the military in extra-legal coercion and repression.

Political armies: officers and gentlemen?[1]

The true significance of the Latin American armed forces over the past century has been their political nature. Especially after the Second World War, the military constantly intervened in political matters. In this intervening capacity, generals became politicians in uniform more than the leaders of soldiers. Over the past two decades, however, the higher military echelons have come to embrace democracy and civilian rule, although they have never completely lost their established vocation of political actor. In this sense, the apparent officers and gentlemen who now direct the armed forces in the region are heirs to a long-standing tradition of political involvement, and still claim a kind of God-given right to intervene in times of crisis. Even under democracy, they advise the civilian cabinet members whenever it is thought to be convenient. The generals and the military ideologues maintain sufficient political manoeuvring space to deal with matters of national security and strategic policy.

Thus the phenomenon of 'political armies', whose officers corps is trained in both military and administrative matters and whose basic ideology was built on the notion of internal security and the stability of the state, is not completely a thing of the past.[2] In this section we will argue that a more hidden political role may be reserved for the military, now and in the near future. To understand the fragility of democracy we will point both at contextual factors and at factors that are derived from the institutional and political legacy of these political armies.

The institutional dictatorships of the 1960s–1980s created an elaborate apparatus of rule and control, and left the military with a firm commitment to their own foundational or transformation project. As a result, the retreat of the military from direct rule in the course of democratic transitions was conditional and partial. Extrication had to be negotiated by overt or covert pacts covering not only guarantees demanded by the military regarding the so-called 'permanent national objectives' but also with respect to their own past role in what the military saw as a 'just war' but what their opponents (and international opinion in general) saw as state terrorism.

During the 1990s, and the dual process of withdrawal of the military governments and the transition to civilian governments, the military now manifested itself in the form of a shadow presence, through the 'compulsory military advisers' and 'civil–military ties' between the public sector, the intelligence service and the leading generals. In retrospect, their prolonged presence can partly be explained by the armed forces' active vigilance in the negotiated institutional withdrawal. The exit strategies of the military have been the result of long and tedious negotiations with the upper echelons of the traditional economic elites of the private sector and the upper echelons of the political, and sometimes legal, system. In Guatemala (Schirmer 1998; Rosada-Granados 1999), Peru (Klarén 2000) and even in Suriname (Dew 1994) the military concluded their 'military projects' with the organization of elections for a constitutional assembly. During the protracted negotiations, the core elements of long-term military presence were translated into constitutional and/or legal terms: into 'advisory functions', into exemptions from future prosecutions, into military control of the intelligence and security system. The result of the negotiated exit pacts was a trajectory of ten to fifteen years of slowly decreasing military co-governance in some cases and accentuated military presence in other cases (Arévalo de León 2003).

The masked military presence was able to continue through the skilful use of four factors of power: the military's control over the system of intelligence, the predominance of the military over the police forces, the military task of local and regional development in remote areas, and the legal basis of military immunity and impunity. Of the four factors, the control over military intelligence has been the most important. We will discuss this issue more extensively in the next section. With respect to the police, military influence means not only direct or hidden control over police forces and the fulfilment of police tasks by the military hierarchy, but also the militaristic organization and culture present in most Latin American police forces to date (Chevigny 1995; Glebbeek 2003).

In the majority of Latin American countries, the armed forces – generally the army, but sometimes the navy as well – continue to act as the sole representative of the public sector and the state in remote and underdeveloped regions, with military doctors, nurses, dentists, veterinarians, engineers, lawyers and administrators. The connection between military and civilian functions in remote or depressed areas is reinforced by a 'traditional' military mission of local development and programmes of 'civic action' executed by the armed forces for the local population. These were originally conceived as instruments for the prevention of war and for counter-insurgency; more recently this has been incorporated into discourses of the promotion of human rights and social development by the armed forces (as in the case of Colombia and Venezuela).

The immunity and impunity problem has in part to do with the way human rights violations committed by the security forces during the dictatorships are dealt with by the successor civilian governments. While still in power the military tried to avert this problem by institutionalizing impunity through so-called amnesty and 'full-stop' legislation. This has led to a situation in which dealing with the legacy of human rights violations has continued to be problematic. Democratic governments have been unable to create (or quite slow in creating) conditions of accountability towards human rights violators. This was mostly out of fear of a military backlash, or due to the continuation of military tutelage, concern with other priorities, or lack of political interest. Special legislation and the ready delegation of judicial processes to the military justice system favour the practice of relative immunity in Brazil, Colombia, El Salvador, Guatemala, Honduras, Peru and other countries. The custom of utilizing the system of 'faceless judges' and anti-subversive legislation in

Colombia and Peru supports the fearlessness of the military (and the security forces in general) with regard to the past or present violation of human rights. The existence of military courts in matters that are purely civilian emphasizes relative military privilege in terms of current and common justice.

Despite the fact that the end of the cold war has made the use of blatant anti-communism obsolete, the formulation of military missions and roles retains strong elements of national guardianship, constitutionally sanctioned interventions of the 'moderator' type, a military view of domestic order and stability, developmentalism, and civic action (Fitch 1998). It is noteworthy that threat perceptions have been adapted to the post-cold-war context: the internal enemy of 'Marxist subversion' has been traded in for more diffuse, socially and morally defined threats to national values and objectives. 'Narco-terrorism', Maoist guerrilla warfare, ethnic tensions and poverty-induced troubles have been cited as potential threats meriting continued attention by the military.

Since 11 September 2001, however, the 'global war on terrorism' declared by the world's only superpower has given new impetus to the notion of fighting internal, invisible enemies through the doctrine of 'asymmetric warfare'. Worldwide, massive military intervention by the USA, combined with the deployment of 'special forces' (such as Delta Force, Navy SEALS, SAS) and the use of local paramilitary forces, gave new respectability to domestic armed groups that until recently were considered 'undesirable'. It has also led to the reinvention of security thinking as a rationale for grounding political regimes. It may be feared that such regimes, which are gifted with a strong hand against internal enemies by using an extensive domestic intelligence apparatus and an array of paramilitary forces, will reappear in Latin America. Therefore, it will be useful to look more closely at the current role of military intelligence and paramilitary actors.

Intelligence: secrecy, impunity and action

During the 'internal wars' against 'communist subversion' by the heavy-handed military governments of the 1960s–1980s, the instrument of power par excellence was the array of parallel services: military intelligence, the security bodies, the police and para-police bodies and the paramilitary groups. Military and civilian intelligence, almost always unified under the orders of the ministry of defence, was directed against 'internal enemies' within the national territory.

In most democracies of the North, even in the current age of tough action against terrorism and 'rogue regimes', public scrutiny and parliamentary control over the security and intelligence community are possible. Most NATO countries maintain an essential supervisory function, through their democratic representatives, over 'the management of the octopus', to use Turner's (1985) emblematic typification of the Western intelligence community. Every now and then, US Congress commissions independently evaluate the intelligence services, as do the British, the French, the Germans, the Canadians and the Scandinavians. This is the first point where, in most Latin American dictatorial and even post-dictatorial regimes, a kind of fault line emerges. At least until the late 1990s most Latin American countries were confronted with a lack of effective parliamentary control over military affairs and national security matters, and with the timidity of the people's representatives regarding such matters. Assertive and authoritative monitoring of the security sector, the intelligence community and especially its predominant military branches has been lacking. Efforts to establish a competent and efficient independent police force with its own forensic and investigative capabilities, as well as initiatives to enforce civil control of overt and covert military activities, have been generally accompanied by a certain willingness to honour the relative and undisputed autonomy of military intelligence and its superiority on issues of external security threats and internal threats to the state and public order.

A second fault line is that in Latin America the military generally predominate in intelligence matters. This phenomenon derives from the long history of Latin America's armed forces as political armies, whose characteristics are mentioned in the first section of this chapter. In line with the role extension of this 'political soldierism', national security issues, national intelligence and military intelligence tended to coincide. Under the authoritarian regimes, intelligence and security appeared to stand for 'control of the internal enemies' and 'manoeuvring space for action', implying the use of paramilitary instruments and paramilitary justice. A protective shield of preventive identification of 'communists', 'terrorists' or even 'adversaries of the regime' and 'supposed enemies of the regime' was placed around the social fabric of society, in an ambience where impunity and immunity were generally present as an additional guarantee against control from outside. These structures of military power and role expansion survived in the Latin American intelligence communities after the return to formal democratic rule. This hidden face of the Latin American political armies could continue to flourish in the intelligence community, where some generic characteristics of the intelligence sector (Herman 1996: 328–9) reinforce the above-mentioned 'organizational culture': the separation from society and the feeling of 'being different'; the sense of fulfilling a sacred mission, a cult of patriotism and 'serving the country'; and the sense of 'being special and being chosen', induced and multiplied by the secrecy and concealment in matters of numbers, organization, funding and sometimes organizational existence. The ambience of mission, of a mysterious 'calling', of being a kind of saviour of the nation, facilitates the blurring of the boundaries between overt and covert action, the mere identification of adversaries and their elimination from society, justice by law enforcement and paramilitary justice.

The predominance of the military in this covert domain can be explained by the above-mentioned lack of zest on the part of the democratic institutions in control. This lack of control, however, is only one factor. Another factor is an apparently strange phenomenon in post-dictatorial Latin America: the public's continued confidence in the military institutions as such. In most polls in the 1990s about confidence in democratic institutions and their stability, a majority of respondents express confidence in the armed forces and their leadership. This public sense of 'indebtedness to the military' is also translated into confidence in matters of security and intelligence. Even in Guatemala, where after so many military governments and so many years of civil war a kind of institutional mistrust towards the military was to be expected, the contrary resulted. In polls, in electoral campaigns, in a referendum, the public demonstrated their overall confidence in the military. Despite the creation of a secretary of civil intelligence with ministerial status – for whom military input is supposed to be one of the many sources of information and intelligence gathering – even Guatemala's cabinet members tend to bypass this new secretary. When personal matters are at stake, where problems with taxes and personal security are involved, ministers, secretaries and *delegados presidenciales* find their way to military intelligence for a judgement and a solution.

A third fault line is the relative lack of technical expertise regarding intelligence and security matters in post-cold-war Latin America, at least in comparison with NATO countries, in terms of both personal resources and equipment. The personal expertise lag is basically due to the fact that armed military intelligence was – and still is – mainly oriented towards internal threats. Worrying about internal enemies is relatively inexpensive and does not require enormous investments in advanced technological hardware. The technological lag is even more serious: of all Latin American countries, only Brazil has any kind of military equipment industry that has a competitive significance in the export market. In terms of SIGINT capabilities (radio communication, interception, crypto-analysis, computer-assisted data analysis and electronic intelligence), in fact, only the USA and maybe a few other NATO countries are serious providers of technical and analytical support in Latin America. This

---

Box 2.1 Peru's Sistema de Inteligencia Nacional (SIN) during the Montesinos years (1990–2000)

Political power in Peru was concentrated in a triumvirate represented by Fujimori (president), Montesinos (intelligence chief) and Hermoza (military commander). The regime was based upon a series of overlapping institutional control circuits (Kruijt and Tello 2002): first, control over the armed forces, through presidential appointments and political purges, sweetened by opportunities for corruption and bribery; second, control over the intelligence community, paramilitary forces and death squads; third, control over the justice system; and fourth, control over the media of mass communication. The longer the regime lasted, the more it had to rely on intimidation and corruption and the more the SIN (Sistema de Inteligencia Nacional) was transformed into an instrument of veiled terror, intimidation and corruption of politicians, religious leaders, judges and even the military establishment. Among the circles of the military officers who were removed from the armed forces' leadership at the very beginning of Fujimori's government period, the SIN, led and restructured by Montesinos, was nicknamed the *Gestapito* (little Gestapo). The link between intelligence, corruption, blackmail and paramilitary activities within Montesinos's SIN gives the comparison enough sense.

Nearly immediately after the appointment of Paniagua as transitional president and Pérez de Cuellar as minister-president, Admiral Panizo, the top navy commander retired by Fujimori in 1990, was asked to clean up the SIN. He took up residence at Montesinos's office the next day and ordered an evaluation of the budget and personnel by independent inspectors and accountants.[3] Montesinos's personal assistants showed him the contents of six office vaults with cash 'to give away to anyone and everyone sent in by the president'. His first conclusions were astonishing: 70 per cent of the SIN's budget was assigned as 'earmarked expenses' (*gastos reservados*): monthly

---

technical intelligence superiority of Western powers has created a long-lasting dependence and vulnerability among their Latin American counterparts. This vulnerability is not only limited to strictly military intelligence issues, but is also felt in the investigative capacity with respect to drug production and trafficking, terrorist threats, criminal organizations, and even in matters of forensic research. The fact that Latin America's intelligence communities are not characterized by intensive data exchange is an additional reason for over-dependency on good bilateral relations with US military and civilian intelligence providers

transfers authorized by presidential decrees (*resoluciones supremas*) whose only text was: 'This is a document that justifies whatever expenditure.' Other budget lines were rechannelled from the expenditure of the armed forces. Cars, computers and other technical equipment were registered as the property of third persons.

Panizo described the existence of two SINs: a 'real' and a 'virtual' SIN, the latter engaged in illegal activities such as protection and personal security (three hundred bodyguards for Montesinos), death squads, corruption, blackmail and extortion. Whoever received money in bundles of dollars at Montesinos's office was filmed on video. Of these approximately 1,500 *Vladivideos*, around a hundred were shown to the general public on TV. Former President Fujimori is supposed to have carried with him to Japan the most incriminating and ignominious videos. SIN staff members (*planta estable*) numbered at least four thousand complemented by a huge but unknown number of 'contracted outsiders' and voluntary advisers. The existence of a death squad within or around the SIN (the *Grupo Colina*)[4] had been the subject of public debate in the mid-1990s and its leaders had been brought to court, only to be granted amnesty by the president. There were other ad hoc groups. The illegal SIN officers had pseudo-military ranks: 'navy captain' instead of 'sociologist' or 'lawyer'. Most of the staff members of the 'virtual SIN' were immediately discharged, as were six hundred of the 'real SIN'. The director's office was a fortress-like complex, with a suite for Montesinos and a bungalow for Fujimori, equipped with a jacuzzi, a sauna and a gym.[5] Panizo, who interviewed all household personnel, was told that the president and his intelligence chief (referred to as 001 and 002) spent most of their evenings watching the 'catch of the day', videos filmed shortly before.

Source: Interview conducted by Dirk Kruijt with Admiral (retired) Alfonso Panizo, 14 August 2002.

(for instance, the reliance of Peruvian naval intelligence on the CIA) and for the regular provision of 'useful information' by US sources, be it DEA, CIA or FBI: data on drug mafias in Argentina and Brazil, forensic support in Honduras, or intelligence and paramilitary support in Colombia's 'war on drugs'.[6]

In Latin America, the security and intelligence sector still suffers the consequences of the role expansion of the armed forces in the previous decades, emphasizing its political instead of its strictly military or police significance. The proliferation of self-attributed political-administrative functions within the grey zone between the formally legal and de facto illegal power domains of the armed forces also had an impact on their security and intelligence capabilities, linked to the use of paramilitary activities. Here we can once more refer to the case of Guatemala, where a kind of private intelligence community-cum-criminal elite emerged from the armed forces' officers corps. In the year of the peace agreements, 1996, the then minister of defence had to oust several high-ranking officials – among which was one of Guatemala's twelve brigade generals – from the army for their proven connections with drug trafficking. Five of them continued their career from outside, using their connections with (former) intelligence members to unify drug and other criminal activities with military logistics to set up a powerful drug cartel.[7] The most blatant case of intelligence and paramilitary connections acting with impunity, however, is that of Peru during the 1990s.[8] After Fujimori's downfall in mid-2000, a murky conglomerate of parallel institutions and dark connections with the economic and political underworld became visible (see Box 2.1).

Up until now we have described the Latin American situation until the end of the twentieth century. At the turn of the century, however, in three very significant countries – Argentina, Brazil, and Mexico – a serious adjustment in intelligence matters materialized. The Brazilian intelligence community had expanded during the decades of military dictatorship as a powerful inter-linked system of formal and informal institutions of domestic espionage and repression (Fico 2001: 71–148). This frightening conglomerate of institutions survived the transition government of Sarney (1985–89) pretty well. In 1992, however, president Collor disbanded the Serviço Nacional de Informações (National Intelligence Service, SNI), and immediately dismissed more than two thousand officials (Antunes 2002: 112). The extinction of the SNI resulted in a kind of intelligence vacuum for several years. Not before the end of Cardoso's first term as president – he himself was a former victim of military intelligence, but also the son of a well-known general – was a new ministry of defence set up, in December 1999, bringing the military command structure under civilian political control. In the same month, a new intelligence system was formed, the Agencia Brasileira de Inteligencia (Brazilian Intelligence Agency, ABIN).[9] In May 2000 the Subsistema de Inteligencia de Segurança Pública (Subsystem of Intelligence for Public Security) was created as a kind of umbrella intelligence organization, of which ABIN is the *primus inter pares* and its director-general its president. The specific responsibilities of the various bodies – for instance, data-gathering on drug-related issues – are not clearly defined, and from its very beginning ABIN acquired the reputation of an organization with 'a genetic imprint of the SNI' (ibid.: 195). ABIN is also involved in domestic espionage and control, a former activity of the SNI.[10] The reduction in the military budget, the curtailment of military intelligence and of military influence, had strong resonance in military circles.[11]

In Argentina military and police intelligence were reshaped (Sain 2002; 2003c), as in the case of Brazil, in 2000 after a long parliamentary debate that took most of the two presidential terms of Menem (1989–99). The influence of the USA and the MERCOSUR countries resulted in a division of labour between the armed forces ('external security') and the police forces ('home security'). This division of labour did not occur without institutional rearguard fighting and attempts to invade the competitor's terrain. In 2002, the Argentine minister of defence attempted in vain to join his ministry of defence with that of home security. In recent years, police intelligence capabilities on matters of terrorism, drugs, money laundering and crime syndicates have been built up. It is, however, a slow process: until very recently, the Argentinian police forces were used to gather information on leftist politicians and trade union leaders instead of criminals and drug bosses.[12]

The case of Mexico's security and intelligence system is different (Benitez Manaut 2002; 2003a; 2003b). As the result of the creation of NAFTA in 1994, a silent, slow but stable integration of policies, procedures and training is taking place between the bureaucracies of the three member states, the USA, Canada and Mexico, in charge of migration, customs, police, criminal intelligence and security threats from terrorism, drug trafficking, money laundering and organized crime. It is irrefutable that this has repercussions on the functioning of military and police intelligence, and on the professionalizing process of Mexico's police forces. It is thus clear that the Latin American 'big three' are reducing the power and reach of military intelligence. In all other countries of the region, however, especially the Andean region and in most of the Central American countries, military intelligence–cum–paramilitary enforcement is still prevalent.

Paramilitary forces

Paramilitary forces have been as elusive as they have been tenacious within the domain of the semi-formal security forces in Latin America. By definition paramilitary forces operate in the interface of politics and violence. In fact, paramilitary forces in Latin America have specialized in the semi-covert exertion of political violence in a context of increased social polarization or low-intensity civil conflict. The paramilitary rarely engage in direct military confrontations with armed opponents of comparable strength but rather employ violence, coercion and terror to back up certain economic, social or

Box 2.2 Official and extra-legal parallel institutions and armed actors operating during the armed conflict in Guatemala (1960–96)

Directly state-related

- Policía Militar Ambulante (PMA, linked to military intelligence through G-2, and in 1958 officially recognized as being under the command of the Ministry of National Defence)
- Guardia de Hacienda (an independent police force with special tasks)
- Comisionados Militares (since 1979 incorporated into the Guatemalan army as support organization and counter-insurgency force)
- Comités Voluntarios de Defensa Civil (Patrullas de Autodefensa Civil or PACs, 900,000 forcibly recruited [indigenous] peasants in paramilitary units under local army command, by decree of the High Command of the Army of Guatemala in 1981)

Parallel state forces

- Movimiento de Acción Nacionalista Organizada (MANO, created in 1966)
- Comité de Resistencia Anticomunista de Guatemala (CRAG, created during the late 1960s)
- Consejo Anticomunista de Guatemala (CADEG, created during the late 1960s)
- Ejército Secreto Anticomunista (ESA, created in 1977)
- Fuerza de Acción Armada (FADA), Frente Anticomunista del Nororiente (FANO), Frente Estudiantil Anticomunista (FEA), Hermandad Blanca, Liga Nacional de Protección al Guatemalteco (death squads and regional counter-insurgency units, operating during the 1970s and 1980s)
- Mano Blanca (created in 1979)
- Guerrilla Acción Libertadora Guatemalteca Antisalvadoreña (GALGAS, operating during the 1970s and 1980s to liquidate insurgent Salvadorean refugees in Guatemala)

Parallel guerrilla forces

- Resistencia Rebelde Secreta
- Autodefensa Obrera
- Resistencia Armada Urbana

Source: Táger and Mérida 2002: 4–8.

political objectives. As such they faithfully emulate in the shadows their formal role models in the spotlight, that is to say the political armies of the region.

Before looking at the development and recent significance of the paramilitary phenomenon, let us first try to define the armed actor under consideration here. We must make a distinction not only with regard to the regular armed forces, public militias and police but also with regard to organized armed rebellion or revolutionary movements (guerrillas), organized criminal gangs and death squads. Paramilitary forces are defined as an organized form of coercive (military) capacity that is modelled upon a military format but does not belong to the official, hence legitimate, domain of the security forces. The first criterion separates paramilitary units from death squads that are usually of a more ad hoc, loosely organized nature, assembled to wield political violence and terror (Sluka 2000). Nevertheless, the boundaries between paramilitary forces and death squads are in practice often hazy. Like death squads, paramilitary groups tend to be conservative and seek to defend or restore established interests by applying violence to 'undesired' social categories and political opponents. This may or may not imply that they side with the state, or more precisely with the government in power. What sets the paramilitary apart from insurgent guerrillas is that they are usually linked to conservative elite sectors and that they tend to ally themselves openly or covertly with the official security forces. Likewise, these characteristics distinguish the paramilitary armed actor from the so-called corporate military outfits and private security firms (Shearer 1998).

In Latin America, paramilitary forces evolved from various sources. Pro-status quo social movements and political parties have been setting up armed groups throughout the past century. In many cases such initiatives were started or backed by economic elites for whom armed groups served to defend property, to repress social protests or to carve out space in (local) political arenas. Almost all these elements come together in the most recent, largest and most notorious force in the history of Latin American paramilitarism: the Autodefensas Unidas de Colombia (United Self-Defence Forces of Colombia, AUC) (Romero 2003; Leal Buitrago, this volume). We will briefly review the case of the AUC below. A final category to be mentioned is the so-called local defence forces that bring together the local civilian population in voluntary or mandatory patrols (see Fumerton and Remijnse, this volume; also Fumerton 2002; Remijnse 2003).

From the 1920s or 1930s onwards, various forms of paramilitarism came to the fore in countries such as Argentina, Brazil, Chile, Mexico and Uruguay, often inspired by conservative nationalism. Paramilitary forces were active

27

players in the Central American conflicts of the 1970s–1990s. These forces typically had links to the official security forces and to nationalistic and anti-communist political groups, performing auxiliary roles in the counter-insurgency strategies in El Salvador and Guatemala. The use and extension of paramilitary forces and death squads in Guatemala, of all Central American countries, has been the most sinister. In Box 2.2 we outline the architecture of the official, semi-official and rebellious armed actors during Guatemala's protracted civil war.

The most comprehensive case of paramilitary forces, however, can be observed in the context of the still ongoing Colombian conflict.[13] The roots of the phenomenon go back to the aftermath of *La Violencia* as, in the 1960s, the left-wing guerrilla forces with provisions for civil defence forces under the auspices of the military. For more than a decade, civil defence in Colombia kept a low profile within the conventional counter-insurgency and national security doctrines espoused by the Colombian military. The real expansion of the Colombian paramilitary came at the beginning of the 1980s with the installation, by powerful drug traffickers, of the MAS (Muerte a los Secuestra-dores – Death to Kidnappers). MAS set out to retaliate against guerrillas who kidnapped wealthy Colombians, among whom were members of powerful *traficante* families. Soon MAS developed a strategy of anti-guerrilla territorial control in the Medio Magdalena area. During the late 1980s and early 1990s, territorial paramilitary units proliferated, sometimes under the label of MAS. These were typically sponsored by large landowners and drug lords, but could also count on the technical and logistical support of the military. In this early stage, the military were reported to enlist paramilitary combatants into their intelligence operations and to support them with logistics, organizational ex-pertise and hardware such as uniforms and small arms. In exchange, military personnel received payments from drug money or money generated by other illicit activities such as emerald smuggling.

During the 1990s and up till the present, the paramilitary evolved as an autonomous, well-organized and well-funded armed actor with a specific role in the Colombian conflict. A core group of paramilitary leaders emerged from the ranks of the Autodefensas Campesinas de Cordoba y Urabá (ACCU), notable among whom were the Castaño brothers, as well as Salvatore Mancuso and others. The Castaño clan first gained national notoriety through their involvement in the Los Pepes death squad set up to counter the rampant violence of the Medellín cartel led by Pablo Escobar (Bowden 2001). After the death of Escobar in December 1993 (followed shortly thereafter by the death of Fidel Castaño in a confrontation with the ELP; see Romero 2003: 26) and the effective end of intra-cartel warfare, the defeat of the leftist guerrillas in the country became the key focus of the paramilitary, through the expansion of territorial control and the use of indiscriminate violence and terror against the civilian population. In 1997, most paramilitary groups (territorial 'fronts' and 'blocs') were united under the umbrella of the AUC, fashioned after the regular armed forces with an integrated politico-military leadership headed by Carlos Castaño, a joint operational staff, and regional and local field units.[14]

All defining characteristics of the paramilitary armed actor are present in the Colombian case. The AUC and other autonomous units are tightly organized and increasingly well equipped, to the extent that it is hard to distinguish the members of paramilitary forces from regular soldiers and officers. They espouse a conservative ideology and classic counter-insurgency doctrines, being at the same time linked to powerful, often illicit economic interests. Romero (2003) demonstrates that the rise and consolidation of the paramilitary have been closely linked to the strategies of local power holders (including land-owning drug traffickers) to resist the official peace and democratization initiatives undertaken since 1982 and to counter the rise of local social movements that threatened the prevailing power relations. He sees the paramilitary as 'entrepreneurs of coercion' who backed up the political interests of local elites (ibid.: 17). Paramilitary forces were welcomed in the hidden corridors of military intelligence, and benefited, directly or indirectly, from covert schemes of outside support, particularly within the US-backed *Plan Colombia* (later re-labelled the Andean Regional Initiative). Most importantly, the paramilitary have maintained throughout close relations with the official armed forces, despite the fact that consecutive Colombian governments have declared the paramilitary illegal. In a number of extensively documented reports, Human Rights Watch (1996; 2000; 2001) has shown the multiple ways in which the military and paramilitary act together in a complex web of counter-insurgency activities oiled by readily available illicit funding. These relationships range from deliberate inaction by the security forces to intelligence sharing, strategic backing and active logistical, tactical and operational cooperation. The clear implication of this state of affairs is that the combined military–paramilitary strategy within the Colombian conflict tends to rely predominantly on violence and terror against the civilian population rather than on precise military operations against equally violent guerrilla forces within the confines of legality, that is to say the observance of general human rights and the principles of the Geneva Convention.

This is the clearest example of the current Janus face of the security forces: compliance on paper with the principles of democracy and the rule of law, but violating these same principles in practice. Civilian governments appear unable or unwilling to counter this state of affairs, while the emphasis on repressive violence rather than on political solutions for peace adopted by the principal external agent, the United States, also tends to reproduce the cycle of violence. Still, clearly stating the illegal nature of paramilitary forces such as the AUC may yield effects in the longer term. After the AUC were placed on the US list of terrorist organizations (alongside the FARC and ELN guerrillas), Carlos Castaño gave up his position as military commander in 2001 and as political leader in 2002. With the installation of the Uribe government in that same year, however, Castaño returned as paramount leader of the AUC, but this time in order to 'participate in a peace process' while publicly rejecting practices such as drug trafficking and terrorism.[15]

Conclusion

In this chapter we have looked at the *primus inter pares* of contemporary armed actors in Latin America: the military. Over the past century, the region's armed forces have been central to problems of authoritarian rule, coercion and political violence. We have discussed the legacy of political armies, meaning the direct and active involvement of the Latin American military in domestic politics as an integral part and professional extension of military roles. As such, the military positioned themselves as 'quasi-parties' with a distinct ideology, programme and strategy to supervise or control the state and public policy. This legacy has contributed greatly to the persistence of political institutions and a political culture that continue to be at odds with the principle of accountable, democratic governance. Issues such as the persistence of tutelary powers and immunity from prosecution for past and present transgressions by the military are still part and parcel of public life in most Latin American countries.

In addition, the legacy of authoritarian rule and arbitrariness in public affairs have paved the way for the consolidation of violence and coercion within Latin American politics, even after the democratic transitions of the 1980s and 1990s. The agenda of democratic consolidation has caused, however, if not a paradigm shift, then at least a change in attitude and discourse within the military institutions in the region. They now publicly embrace democracy and human rights as the legitimate parameters for politics and state conduct. As a consequence, in a number of countries, the practice of coercion and state-induced violence has become more veiled. The (military) intelligence system has become the preserve of political manipulation and behind-the-scenes violence. In some cases, notably Colombia, paramilitary forces have more openly stepped in as 'aides' in military counter-insurgency and repression.

While the Colombian armed forces adhere to civil rule and human rights, the paramilitary units have been specializing in the dirty work of sowing terror against real and perceived adversaries of the established order.

It is to be feared that, especially given the international move towards more heavy-handed dealing with terrorism, authoritarianism, violence and coercion have not been completely eradicated from Latin American social and political life. It may well be that we will merely observe consecutive swings of a pendulum between the antagonistic poles of democratic governance and arbitrary violence in the years to come.

Notes

1 We have based this section on Kruijt (2001), Koonings and Kruijt (2003) and Koonings (2003).

2 We define political armies as military institutions that play an active and often decisive role in domestic politics and, in fact, see this as a legitimate extension of their professional role and of key importance for the fate of the nation. See Koonings and Kruijt (2002) for a conceptual exploration.

3 Formally, Montesinos acted as the president of the National Intelligence Committee, appointing figureheads as the SIN's director. Their office furniture consisted of a table, chairs, a telephone and a TV.

4 Interview conducted by Dirk Kruijt with General Rodolfo Robles, 21 June 2002. See also his *Crimen e impunidad* (1996). General Robles had the courage to bring to light the activities of the Grupo Colina; he was exiled to Argentina and Guatemala.

5 Fujimori also liked to spend the night at the Pentagonito, the fortified complex of buildings of the ministry of defence.

6 The apologetic *Killing Pablo* story, a detailed account of US technical involvement – with intelligence and logistical support, even for paramilitary operations – in the manhunt for Escobar reflects the difficulties with personnel, training and technical matters experienced by the Colombian security and intelligence organizations (see Bowden 2001).

7 *Siglo Veintiuno*, 9 April 2003.

8 For an overview of the Fujimori years, see Degregori (2000), De la Jara Basombrillo (2001), Diez Canseco Cisneros et al. (2002), Johamowitz (2002a, 2002b).

9 After a time-consuming parliamentary debate between 1995 and 1999 (see Antunes 2002: 151–95).

10 Interview conducted by Dirk Kruijt with Professor Henrique Fonseca, 23 July 2003. Fonseca was a professor at the Escola Superior de Guerra (Superior War School, ESG) at the end of the 1990s.

11 Interview conducted by Dirk Kruijt with Professor Nuno Linhares Velloso, member of the *junta consultativa* of the Escola Superior de Guerra, 31 July 2003. Professor Velloso stated that, at a certain moment, the military establishment even thought of closing the ESG, owing to lack of funds.

12 Interview conducted by Dirk Kruijt with Professor Marcelo Fabián Sain, former vice-minister of home security (26–27 June 2000), and with German Montenegro, his successor as vice-minister (14–15 July 2003).

13 This discussion is mainly based on Human Rights Watch (1996; 2000; 2001).

14 See the organizational structure of the AUC posted by their advocacy group, Colombia Libre, at <http:/colombialibre.net/organigrama.php>, consulted June 2003.

15 Stated in an AUC formal note directed to Kofi Annan, UN Secretary-General, to the US ambassador in Colombia, to the Peace Commissioner of the Uribe government, and to Cardinal Pedro Rubiano. *El Espectador*, 9 September 2002, cited on the website of the Colombian defence ministry at <www.mindefensa.gov.co>, consulted June 2003.

3 | Policing extensions in Latin America

PIET VAN REENEN

Introduction

In most countries police forces are responsible for maintaining order, protecting people and investigating crime. In some countries they are also in charge of providing help. They do this in a unique way: the resources available to the police, the powers they have, and the force they are allowed to exert, set them apart as instruments of power. It is the capacity and the authority to use force which identify the police (Klockars 1985: 12). For this same reason their role is politically highly relevant. Many scholars define police roles as being inevitaby political in nature.

As instruments of power they are sometimes used to enforce the rule of law, sometimes just to exercise political power, and sometimes simply to enforce their own will. In many countries the police do not carry out their tasks on their own. They have helpers: individuals, organizations or institutions that assist the police in their work. We call these helpers 'extensions'. We are interested in what police extensions there are, and how they relate to police forces. These helpers can be legal or illegal. Death squads are, of course, a clear example of illegal helpers in many countries. Latin America has a rich array of policing extensions, and we believe the Latin American pattern has some specific traits. By definition the violence used by these actors makes them violent actors. We have concentrated on these violent extensions, leaving aside the illegal extensions used for criminal investigation or for police intelligence work.

Research into illegal policing extensions is scarce. What comes closest is a study on what they call 'alternative policing styles' by Findlay and Zvekic (1994). They have concentrated on policing styles outside the realm of state institutions and have gathered together studies on forms of self-help, private and commercial policing and paramilitaries. Their focus differs somewhat from ours in that not all the forms they deal with are illegal or violent – they are all formally non-state, but some are legal – while our interest is on illegal activities that are in one way or another still connected with the state. Other studies on death squads provide data and theoretical notions on illegal extensions. Huggins (1991), in a comparable approach, takes vigilantism as a starting point for an analysis of extra-legal violence in Latin America. Some of that vigilantism is carried out by or on behalf of the state. Huggins also connects vigilantism with power: the power of elites within countries and the power of the state. The study of illegal policing extensions that we are engaged in uncovers the same potential and motive; policing by way of illegal extensions is exerting power in an illegal, uncontrolled and most of the time violent way. It is normally an indication of the weakness of a state. States, or governments, using or allowing policing via illegal extensions tend to be weak or in crisis. As such policing of this nature tends to destroy what legitimacy is left.

As a first step in understanding the dynamics of illegal extensions, we need to look at the activities: the process of illegal policing. Next we have to describe the way in which the extensions are connected with relevant groups and institutions. Invariably these groups or institutions are related to power: political power, economic power or force. This set of connections can be represented as a pattern. A third element in the description of illegal extensions is the process of exchange between the extensions and the other groups in the pattern; what is exchanged for what? We have undertaken this in a research project in progress.[1] In this chapter, I first present some preliminary insights regarding the differences between patterns of extension in Latin America and those in other regions of the world. I will then discuss the extensions present in two Latin American countries to illustrate the differences within the continent: one rather simple form from Brazil, and one complex pattern from Guatemala.

The nature of 'policing extensions'

An extension is defined primarily as an addition to the function of policing, mostly carried out by public institutions called police or militia. Extensions consist of manpower, facilities and/or authority to investigate, arrest or use force, and may be combined with added repressive instruments. It is important to stress that various forms of extensions can be identified and not all of them are illegal. On the contrary, there is a whole field of extensions of police capacity that is perfectly legal and helpful. A notorious historical example is the French *concierges*, functioning as the eyes and the ears of the criminal and political police in France. Such an extension using informers is well known in police forces all over the world, and in most of them it is legal. Auxiliary police systems, for instance, used in many countries as a reserve on occasions when extra manpower is needed, are perfectly legal extensions. Some extensions are illegal, and some legal extensions have the capacity to turn into illegal ones, and may do so. These are the type of extensions in which we are interested in this chapter.

We use the term 'policing extensions' rather than 'police extensions'. By using this term the focus is on the process of policing and not on the institution, and therefore on the use of power and the threat of force to control the behaviour of people. Police extensions are extensions related to the institution of the police; policing extensions are extensions connected to the control of behaviour by way of the threat or use of force. Although policing as a process will normally be carried out by the police in most countries, in a number of countries other institutions take part in these activities. For our purposes one of the institutions that is most relevant in this respect is the military. They are formally responsible for policing or for some aspects of it in some Latin American countries, and in other countries the military, though not responsible for regular policing, are called in for special operations involving the use of heavy weapons or to take over policing in times of emergency. So the military perform policing functions and may also be involved in the use of extensions. Extensions used by the military under consideration here are used to carry out activities related to policing, and not merely to supplement the police organization.

The simplest structure that one can envisage is, of course, the simple and straightforward relationship between the police on the one hand and the illegal extension on the other. The police use the extension and command its intervention; the extension carries out the orders: it threatens, ill-treats, kills or makes disappear. We have not been able to find this simple extension in Latin American countries. We know that simple extensions exist worldwide in the sphere of police crime control: the agent provocateur, for instance, and in the type of criminal activities carried out by extensions on behalf of the police.

Latin American policing extensions: basic pattern and diversity

Comparing types of illegal extension between parts of the world, Latin America differs from other continents in some respects. The main difference between the Latin American patterns and those in other regions of the world is that we have not found extensions that could be defined as 'mobilization' or 'movement' types of extension in Latin America. Violence carried out by illegal policing extensions in Latin America is a specialized and small-scale activity, directed at killing or maiming or the threat of them. In death squad activities only a few people are involved. A death-squad-type extension requires specific skills, organization, leadership, intelligence, continuity in manpower (recruitment) and financial resources, the capacity to operate undetected and also protection of the extension from revenge or criminal investigation. Protection can be obtained through the secret nature of the organization, as well as through internal checks and discipline or the concern of interested (or threatened) third parties. The secrecy of these groups permits the denial of their use by everybody. The looseness of the relationship with the police and other actors makes such denial of involvement easy. The 'mobilization' type of extension consists in large numbers of people supporting the police: religious, political or caste-like groups acting on the command or suggestion of the police in suppressing groups hostile to their causes. Extensions of this type are generally speaking highly visible and require little or no special skills, and mobilization is usually mediated through religious, political or caste-type leaders. Although there are exceptions, there is usually little organization in the operations of the extension.

A second noteworthy aspect of policing extensions in Latin America is their continuity.[2] This continuity suggests a form of institutionalization of policing extensions. It is an expression of the role such groups play in society. These roles differ between Latin American countries, as we will illustrate later, but a common element is that they are political tools for elites in these countries. These tools are better kept in the shade, denied and ignored. Policing extensions in Latin America are relatively autonomous. An explanation for this relative autonomy is that these groups know some of the secrets of their employers, who by virtue of this become dependent to a degree on the extension. The knowledge that a well-respected political leader has allowed or even asked and paid for the illegal killing of a competing political leader, for instance, is valuable to an illegal policing extension: the secret may protect the extension from being arrested or hunted down. It seems that in the sphere of violence and human rights violations the simple connection discussed above is absent in Latin America.

There are three deviations from the straightforward extension in the Latin American pattern, and we label the deviations 'diffusion'. First, there are always more than two parties involved: the police share the extension with one or more other agencies or interest groups. Such other parties include political parties, the government or government agencies, the army, security services, businesses and businessmen, and private security firms. Second, the relationships between police and extension and the lines of influence are not as clear cut as the simple extension suggests. The police or other agencies or parties involved normally do not 'command' the extensions; they have influence and sometimes power, but it is limited and shared. Third, in some Latin American countries both the police and the army are related to the extension. This combination of traits, this diffusion, has to be explained in terms of the properties of the extension, the relationships between extension and police and other agencies involved, and the use of the extension. Extensions have a life of their own; they have their own internal structure, sources of continuity and support in terms of information, secrecy and equipment. They are not just police extensions, but informal and secret institutions. The military involvement can partially be explained by the connection between the army and the police that exists in many countries in Latin America (see also Kruijt and Koonings, this volume). The army continues to play an important role in policing most Latin American countries, even to the extent that police forces hardly exist and the army also polices the country.

Latin America does not have mobilization-type extensions. And one does not need not to look too far for explanations for the main difference between the Latin American pattern of extensions and those in other parts of the world. The first explanation for the absence of mobilization-type extensions is the predominance of oligarchic or elitist patterns of government in Latin American politics through the nineteenth and most of the twentieth century (Kruijt and Koonings 1999: 7). This is considered to have been the case up to the present day; some argue that the introduction of democracies in Latin America in the recent past has produced an adaptation of the oligarchic and clientelist patterns into modern forms (Hagopian 1996: 64–86). Oligarchic rulers distrust masses and their dynamics and go to great lengths to prevent or repress mass movements. Mobilization-type policing extensions also presuppose a connection between politics, the police or military and larger groups among the population, which we have found to be rarely the case in Latin America. It is true that Latin American countries have known periods of populism and the rise of anti-oligarchic elites, some of which have gained power. In those countries where such a movement has succeeded, however, the results of the initiatives to include masses in politics merely resulted in corporatist regimes, and instability is considered to be one of their main traits (Kruijt and Koonings 1999: 8–10). The tensions inherent in these hierarchical populist alliances are considered to be one of the main causes of the rise to power of the dictatorships of the post-Second World War era. The connection between the military and the ruling class, and as a consequence between the police and the ruling class, helped shape policing extensions as a specialized activity. This included high levels of violence and required information about possible targets and their whereabouts: intelligence mainly provided by official institutions. Death squad activities are thus a consequence of a special way of dealing with political power relationships within society and of the subsequent relationship between the ruling elite and the armed forces and the police.

This rather general way of dealing with policing extensions in Latin America, and the construction of a Latin American pattern, may imply that these extensions are common in the whole of Latin America, or that they do not differ between countries. That is not what our research has found; they do differ, and for many countries no reports on extensions have been found (Amnesty International 2003). Some countries, such as Argentine and Chile, experienced them during the military dictatorships of the 1970s and 1980s, but their activities initially stopped after the return of democracy. The possible revival of a death squad is reported in Chile: a secret organization that operated during the military dictatorship and was called Comando Conjunto is reported as having been reactivated to counter the government's new policy of prosecuting more human rights violators during the period of military dictatorship.[3] In Argentina mixed gangs of police and criminals (*bandas mixtas*) are being reported, groups that to some extent are left alone by the provincial government of Buenos Aires (Sain 2002: 84–5). With regard to the differences between countries we have selected patterns from two countries, Brazil and Guatemala. They differ on a number of points. Brazil offers an example of a simple police extension; Guatemala is a complex case.

Brazil: simple patterns

Brazil provides an interesting example of a rather simple pattern of extensions.[4] In fact we can distinguish two patterns here: one for the cities, the other for the countryside. Both are relatively simple in terms of their relations between police, military and other groups or institutions. Part of the explanation for their existence lies in the past. The history of the police in Brazil is a history of violence. In this respect it does not deviate from the general tendency in Latin America described earlier. Up to the present day, policing has meant violence, and primarily violence directed against the masses of poor people (Pinheiro 1991: 168). The military dictatorship did not create this phenomenon; it did not introduce violent policing because it was already there. It reorganized it, professionalized it and merely pushed it to extremes. An aspect of this orientation towards force and violence is the militarization of the police, which began when the French began to assist the forces of Brazil in the early nineteenth century. It reached its apogee in 1969 with the subordination of the police throughout Brazil to the military (ibid.: 168). After the military retreated from politics in 1982, the military and the federal government lost control of the militarized police, but their repressive and violent orientation and their habit of acting illegally have remained traits up to the present day.

Huggins points at the initiatives of the chief of police in Rio, in the early 1960s, army general Kruel, who hand-picked a group of police officers, '*homens corajosos*', known for their willingness to die in pursuit of Rio bandits. He gave this motorized group of special police licence to take aggressive and violent action against bandits. They had carte blanche in pursuing and killing bandits. In the beginning the group operated within official police structures, but soon developed death-squad-like methods. It did not take long before bodies of known criminals were found in the *favelas* displaying the sign of the skull and cross-bones (Langgut 1978: 121). Kruel's death squad may mark the beginning of a new devolution of such informal groups out of the formal police apparatus. Such syncretism is clearly reflected in Kruel's labelling of his 'assassination squad' the 'EM' (Huggins 1997: 96). It did not take long for members of the original police team to start their own death-squad-like informal groups outside the police system. Although the aim of these policing extension initiatives was to fight a war, initially it had been the fight against crime. They killed suspected criminals. Death squads in São Paulo are also believed to have evolved from motorized patrols and the special night patrols of the civil police in the late fifties. These patrols were established to combat car theft and house burglaries and were violent in their approach from the beginning, but soon developed death-squad-like methods: ambushes and the killing of suspects (Huggins 1991: 138). Military dictatorship thus found an existing method and instrument to threaten and kill without official involvement and responsibility which could quite easily be used against political opponents in the police. Having no experience in fighting subversive movements, the dictatorship turned to the police and their experience. They reorganized the whole police, organized and directed the activities of the death squads and made them part of the military anti-guerrilla strategy.

During the 1964–85 military regime the public order police (*policia militar*) was brought under unified military control and organized on a state level. Some believe that today's police habits, and even the tactics of the illegal police extensions, found their justification under military rule and were partially taught by the military during the dictatorship (Pinheiro 1991: 175). This repressive and violent orientation can be considered a general condition for illegal and violent policing options and the use of extensions.

The Brazilian rural pattern comes closest to the straightforward policing extension. It involves relatively few parties and has a strong operational character. In the rural pattern the main activity is force and threat of force by hired hands of landowners. Often these are people employed by a landowner to work on his properties; sometimes they are *pistoleiros* hired for a rough and violent job. Victims of extensions are mostly landless people occupying land in order to protest against its uneven distribution in the country, and to demand land reform. Other reported victims are forced labourers on the large estates, trade unionists and human rights activists working on behalf of landless people and indentured labourers (Human Rights Watch 1992; 1993). Landowners use their

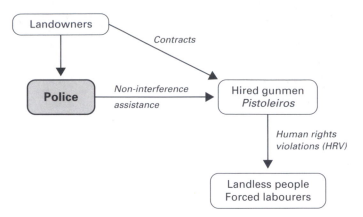

Figure 3.1 The rural pattern of policing extension in Brazil

own armed workforce and hired *pistoleiros* to remove poor people occupying their land or to punish and discipline labourers revolting against bad working and living conditions. Occupiers are threatened and removed by force or intimidated and sometimes killed.

Activists and local protest organizers are reported to have been killed by hired gunmen. The *policia militar* has different reactions towards these activities. In the case of a court order, police action to remove landless occupiers from the land is legitimate. Assistance by *pistoleiros* in these actions is not, however. If no court order is available both the activities of the police and the actions of the *pistoleiros* are considered to be illegal. Sometimes the police participate in the activities of *pistoleiros* or hired hands in a kind of combined action; sometimes their contribution is simply to stand back, allowing the crimes to occur and neglecting their duty of protecting the people against illegal violence. They are also reported as refusing to investigate crimes by *pistoleiros* (Amnesty International 1998). Apart from allowing the hired gunmen to operate or to assist the police, permitting them to act with impunity is the most common way in which the police cooperate with the landowners and their alleged assistants; coordination of action with the *pistoleiros* is also common. In these cases it is mainly the landowners or their employees who direct and the police who follow, assist or cover up the activities carried out on behalf of the landowners. In a number of cases the *policia militar* act correctly and prevent or end the activities of the *pistoleiros*. It looks as if the police do not have a defined policy or strategy, but allow and sometimes support and protect the actions of hired guns. To a certain extent, and in certain cases, one could regard the police as an extension of the landowner. It has not been established that this is the normal pattern of reaction against landless people throughout Brazil. Figure 3.1 depicts the Brazilian rural pattern.

This rural pattern is no recent invention or development. In Brazil, in the past and to a certain extent in the present, the state and private landowners have shared responsibility for policing in rural areas. This factor operates in tandem with American vigilantism (Brown 1976: 104). Another explanation lies in past oligarchical strategies by local elites trying to limit the concentration of power, especially in the field of law enforcement on a supra-local level. Power battles at federal, state and local level included the provision of a means of force – police formations – allowing such elites to be better equipped in fights (Huggins 1998: 35–7). An example of the strong position of local landowners in the field of law enforcement is the tradition of giving landowners the rank of colonel (*coronel*) in the National Guard, connecting local and primarily private law enforcement by landowners with the state and thus legitimizing the tradition (Leal 1975; Cammack 1981). On these terms landowners largely had to police their own estates due to these conditions in practice, and many still claim the right to do so based on this tradition. Until the Second World War it represented what may be called the partial sovereignty of the landowners. It has been further institutionalized or at least condoned by the mostly conservative political connections and representation of landowners.

In urban Brazil we find an extension pattern that differs from that of the countryside.[5] Here we find fewer *pistoleiros* and more death squads, and the relationship between parties within the pattern is mainly determined by supply and demand and not by the authority claims of an elite. In the urban pattern the diversion from the straightforward pattern of policing extensions, a pattern in which the police simply command an extension and the extension carries out the dirty work, is mainly in the interference of organized crime and private security companies as co-organizers of death squads and of death squad activities. A curious mix of commercial and non-commercial death squads is found. We will concentrate on the commercial ones here. These are run either by organized crime or by private security companies and are made up mostly of ex- and off-duty police officers, whose pay seems to be higher than they would receive as ordinary police officers. This is a reason for some of them to leave the police and engage in death squad activities as full-time operatives instead of as a part-time job. 'A Brazilian death squad is a team of murderers, ordinarily or mostly off duty police, usually paid as a group by local businesses or politicos for their services' (Huggins 1997: 211). The pattern can be drawn according to Figure 3.2.

The relationship with the police seems to be more functional and less hierarchical. The police sometimes carry out their own operations, and sometimes provide part of the manpower, the weapons (if these are not privately owned)

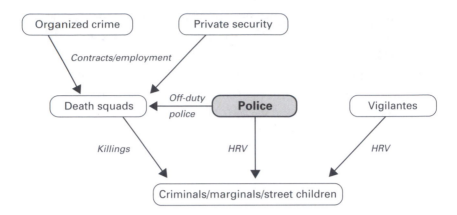

Figure 3.2 Urban patterns of policing extension in Brazil

and probably information on relevant groups and individuals, or on probable crime suspects and their whereabouts.[6] Most of the time the relationship between the death squad and the third party takes the form of a contract. Most death squads kill for money. There are some lone killers, called *justiceiros*, involved in this commercial type of relationship. They kill criminals because they are a nuisance and cannot be put in jail legally because of a lack of capacity or of evidence. Idealism or frustration can be motives for these killers. As one former police officer convicted of murder put it: 'I preferred working in the slums. I preferred the outskirts, the poorest barrios ... It's the slum dweller who needs the police. I was class conscious. I went there to protect the slum dwellers' (Fernandes 1995: 158).

An interesting trait of this urban pattern is that it is no longer connected to political power and to ruling elites, as is the case in other Latin American countries and in the Brazilian countryside. It has become disconnected from political power and commercialized. The targets have also changed. Political opponents and subversive groups are no longer the primary targets; criminals and elements of the 'dangerous class' are. Repression of political opposition has been replaced by repression of 'marginals'. One could even say that it is a form of democratization: access to death squad activities is no longer restricted to political elites but is dependent on money. In certain respects a parallel with the situation in Colombia can be drawn, though the type and level of violence differ there. But there too violence is no longer an instrument just in the hands of a government or a ruling elite, nor even only in the hands of the elite and its violent opponents. It has become a relatively free commodity, available to a number of interested parties. It is used by a number of factions and individuals for a variety of purposes (Koonings and Kruijt 1999: 11).

Guatemala: complexity

Authoritarian rule and violence have a long history in Guatemala and it can be dated back to colonial times and to the structure of post-colonial independent state formation after 1821 (Figueroa Ibarra 1991: 79). Guatemalan governments have been dictatorial and repressive for most of two centuries, and state terror, as some call it, has been a fundamental part of state domination since 1954. Although a democratic government was installed in Guatemala in 1986, it was only in 1996 that the system of state terror was ended. The system was the most violent in Latin America, and consisted of the systematic use of overt and covert violence by the military and the police against the population, resulting in 25,000 deaths between 1966 and 1980. According to conservative estimates, dating from 1983, between 1982 and 1983 an estimated 15,000 were killed and more than 1 million people displaced (GHRC 1983: 5). The armed forces commanded the actions against internal left-wing opposition and guerrilla groups. From 1954 onwards the army was restructured in order to be able to control the enemy within, and military institutions began to take over most organized parts of society. The result was a mixed military–civilian system of repression. Anti-guerrilla strategies and tactics were developed and the spread of terror was a central element in the strategy. Secret operations, the use of secret detention centres, disappearances, illegal killings and also open and brutal force were instrumental in this strategy.

In Guatemala the police became the main pillar of state terrorism under the control of and alongside the army and in the context of the latter's counter-insurgency strategy. Policing extensions, secret but not or no longer considered illegal by the government and the armed forces, became integral parts of the strategy. Covert, death-squad-like formations carrying out killings, issuing threats and making people disappear were part of it, and most of them belonged to the security apparatus. They were part of a broad range of covert operations. Most of the time there were clear lines of command between the hidden extension and what one might call the 'front' organization: the armed forces, the police or branches of the secret service. And they had a calling: the protection of the values of the country and its leaders against the evils of communism. This strategy was pursued for a great number of years and became an institutionalized routine. The police were integral to it. As Glebbeek (2003: 111) puts it: 'Subordinated to the army, all police units served one goal: fighting subversion. There was no limit to what was allowed in this fight. Illegal detention, torture, extra-judicial killings became common practice.' It became one of the bloodiest anti-guerrilla campaigns in Central America (Kruijt 1999: 47). When the peace accords were signed in Guatemala in 1996, the whole secret system and strategy,

43

including the illegal policing extensions of both the army and the police, lost their official legitimacy, their institutional bedding and their connection with the security establishment.[7] The official message was that these units would have to be disbanded. The police would be reorganized, formally disconnected from army control and demilitarized. The army would end its counter-insurgency campaign, pull back from internal policing and disband its military intelligence unit, notorious for its strategic and operational role in state terror. This process is still unfinished; many doubt its progress and some fear that it has come to a standstill. In the now post-'counter-insurgent constitutional state', the building of peace is still a very fragile process, both in the political sphere and in terms of the armed forces, as well as in society as a whole. In the armed forces, the police and right-wing political circles, the philosophy, tactics and habit of repressive policing, with secret operations using death-squad-like units and hired gunmen, persist. They live on in the minds of some police personnel and former military personnel transferred to the police. Glebbeek (2003: 172), who researched the transformation of the Guatemalan police after 1996, observed that the informal and secret networks of the police, created to carry out extra-judicial execution, to torture and detain people in secret locations in the seventies and eighties, were kept in place. The loyalties of the officers involved also remained intact. The networks were used to carry out and to hide illegal activities that partially replaced the fight against communism.

Examples of this continuation are the Patrullas de Autodefensa Civil (PAC). These civil defence patrols, the paramilitary civilian militias during the civil war, were formally disbanded under the 1996 peace accords, which ended the conflict, but in fact have continued to operate in various areas of the country and have allegedly been responsible for new abuses. Guatemalan human rights observers have suggested that this apparent official tolerance of the renewed illegal activities of the patrols reflects the links between the (in 2002) ruling party, the Frente Republicano Guatemalteco (FRG), and the patrols (Amnesty International 2002: 1–2). In addition, a number of now retired military officers with widely acknowledged ties to violent, organized crime continued to have significant influence within the army, police, judiciary and executive branch after the peace accords, according to the US government.[8] In March 2002, members of a coalition of human rights groups demanded that the government take measures to ensure the security of human rights workers, investigate the existence of clandestine groups and parallel forces linked to state institutions believed to be behind the attacks, and dismantle them. The Secretariat of Strategic Analysis produced a report on the existence of such groups, although other public officials refuted its findings.

MINUGUA, the UN organization responsible for the management of the peace process, reported that there were increased signs of the participation of clandestine groups in illegal activities linked to employees of the police, military intelligence, the justice system and the Public Ministry. These groups appeared to act with relative autonomy, and there was no evidence that they were sanctioned by government policy; however, they operated with impunity. MINUGUA found evidence of civilian and military officers linked to these groups operating both officially and unofficially within the executive and judicial branches. The US Bureau of Democracy, Human Rights, and Labor reported in 2003:

> On February 28, a shootout between members of the Criminal Investigative Service (SIC) of the PNC and military intelligence personnel killed two members of the military, and wounded three police officers. Both the then-Minister of Interior and the Director of the PNC maintained that the incident resulted from a lack of communication during a rescue operation in a kidnapping case; however, there were credible reports that the participants in the incident were, in fact, members of a clandestine criminal group attempting to steal the ransom money. According to MINUGUA and press reports, there were indications that the criminals were members of the military. There was also credible information that the police killed one of the military personnel after he had been wounded and surrendered. The crime scene was altered, and evidence was removed. In May a SIC investigator's testimony that he was ordered to modify the official reports implicated the Director of the PNC, the Minister of Interior, and others in the command structure. Further obstruction of the investigation occurred when two military officers linked to the clandestine group were sent abroad.

There were many plausible allegations of politically motivated killings by non-state actors during the year 2002, with only limited willingness on the part of prosecutors to investigate such murders. In some of these cases, evidence available to the US government was not sufficient to conclude whether the killing was politically motivated.

The conclusion is that the networks for clandestine operations are still in place. Obviously they have looked for and found new aims in organized crime but continue to pursue old aims against human rights advocates and defenders and other potential threats to the impunity of the old networks – those people considered to be the enemy of the military and police establishment.[9] Military intelligence was not disbanded until recently, and the military still operates in public order policing together with the new police. Schirmer

45

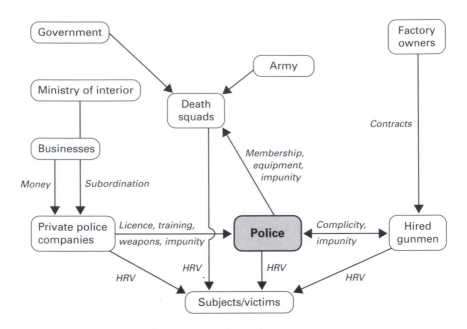

Figure 3.3 The policing extension pattern in Guatemala

(1998) observes that the intelligence sector, not disbanded, still holds undisputed sway over the armed forces, an indication of the potential political role of the army and the still-present potential for secret operations by the army or policing extensions within the country. To some extent the political connection between illegal extensions and death squad activities remained intact, and therefore the political relevance of the policing extensions is undiminished. Extensions have taken more informal and varied forms than in the past, for obvious reasons. Secrecy has also extended to the relationship between the extensions, the army and political factions.

As a result the Guatemalan policing extension pattern has evolved into quite a complex configuration (see Figure 3.3). The differences between Brazil and Guatemala are striking and include the explicit political character of the extension, its complexity and its institutionalization. In Guatemala the political character is the dominant trait in the whole pattern. Government and political parties are considered to be involved, and the extensions operate to intimidate and kill persons of political relevance. A second element is that the role of the army is more dominant and more explicit than in Brazil. Here we see the army, the police and the government involved in death squad activity, and in addition the police themselves and private police companies are known to commit gross human rights violations (GHRVs). Given the dominance of the armed forces over the police in matters of internal security and of policing in

Guatemala in the past, and to a certain extent until the present day, it remains unclear what role the police play in these extensions and how this relates to the role of the army. There is a suspicion – unproven – that secret services play a role in the operations of death squads.

A second trait is the complexity of the pattern, taking into account the great number of parties in the pattern and the number and variety of violent actors. In addition, there is an increased complexity in the pattern itself and the existence of dual or triple relationships between the actors. And we cannot even be sure that we have found all actors and all relationships.

Third, the institutional nature and relatively autonomous position of the extensions stand out. I used the term 'relatively autonomous' earlier to indicate the relationship between extensions and their influences and stressed the continuity of policing extensions earlier in this chapter. I repeat this qualification here, and formulate the hypothesis that the policing extension is a rather stable informal arrangement that has an institutionalized position in Guatemalan society. Secrecy and arrangements to keep secrecy intact are part of these arrangements. Policing extensions are part of a hidden but clearly present set of problem-solving and power-executing arrangements that fit into a wider political and administrative structure and culture. Martha Huggins's (1991: 11) characterization of Latin American states fits in nicely here and might provide us with an explanation for this relative autonomy. Describing the Latin American peripheral state, she says that state structures are the product of economic and political asymmetry, where different dominant factions or classes conflict again and again and form an unstable balance. Government then becomes dominated by a native class of civil servants and soldiers, providing some stability and leading to struggles with and between the warring elites and factions. She calls it repressive mediation. Policing extensions might be another form of repressive mediation, an extreme form one might say, fit for this type of state and developed in and for periods of extreme political instability, where less violent and more open forms of repressive mediation have become useless.

Fourth, the Guatemalan pattern makes clear once again the 'elite' character of the use of policing extensions already noted for Latin America in general. The participants are elements from vested political and economic interests in society. We assume that the private businesses and factories and the government offices mentioned will not involve themselves in extension-type activities, and provide funds for them, without the consent of their bosses. Finally, the Guatemalan pattern also brings to light the issue of 'denial capacity'. Of course, the secrecy of their existence, and operations allowing political parties, the military and the police to deny their existence and use, is a central condition for the ongoing use of illegal extensions. In this respect, however, the Guatemalans have not been very successful.

How can the continuity of this complex pattern of policing extensions in Guatemala from authoritarianism and civil war to the present situation of democratization and peace-building be explained? One explanation is the relatively short transformation period for the military and the police. They did not stop using these extensions right away. And, as we saw earlier in this chapter, they may lie dormant for a number of years, guarding old interests and old secret structures alongside ongoing political change, once they have stopped. This delay in the termination of illegal extensions is an explanation for the continuation of illegal policing extensions with a political content in Guatemala. This explanation is plausible if the peace process continues and is being strengthened.

Another explanation is of a political nature and relies on expectation of the continuity of a type of political rule that is repressive in character, which is a condition for death squad activities, and allows the use of or itself uses illegal extensions for political purposes. The peace process in Guatemala is still very fragile and unstable, and the continuity of elitist conservative political parties and factions, and the re-emergence of political leaders responsible for bloody repression in the recent past, are indications of that continuity – the continuity of a violent and repressive regime, allowing for continued secret repressive mediation via death squads.

Final observations: the threat of repoliticization

Policing extensions are illegal and therefore most of them operate in the shadows, secretly, hiding their activities and striving for impunity. Information is very scarce. Descriptions and analyses of such phenomena therefore have to be considered with reservations. Policing extensions of the Latin American variety involve acts of violence, consisting mainly of deadly violence inflicted by firearms, or the threat of it. The groups or networks responsible for this violence are small, well trained in the use of firearms and have adequate intelligence at their disposal. They operate in secret and are seldom brought to justice. Impunity is a common trait. They form relatively stable and long-lasting arrangements internally as well as with their relevant contacts and can be considered to be institutionalized. The mobilization-type policing extensions found in other parts of the world are not found in Latin America, and death-squad-type policing extensions are scarce or absent in other parts of the world.

Illegal policing extensions are not exclusively connected with the police. They have other connections allowing them to exist relatively independently of one specific institution. They are semi-autonomous and cannot be said to be commanded by one group or institution. Illegal extensions are rooted in the political past of Latin American countries. Although we do not have a complete understanding of them, some probably have their origins in the military dictatorships of the 1960s and 1970s; others, however, originated in earlier efforts to combat crime and criminal gangs in the 1950s, efforts that resulted in illegal extensions and got out of hand.

Within this general pattern, a great deal of variety can be observed. Brazil is an example of two relatively simple sets of extensions, one urban and one rural. The urban especially is interesting, as it is mainly commercial and driven by market forces. Access is not limited to long-standing political elites, but open to whoever pays. This type indicates change in Brazil. Guatemala is an example of a pattern of great complexity and with explicit political ties. It is a civil war type of extension that was official at the time, though secret, and has subsequently gone underground and become illegal. The Guatemalan extensions have so many connections, and are probably so little dependent on any one of them, that they have to be considered a semi-autonomous force within the country. They can be considered as an element of the semi-autonomous layer of civil servants and armed forces personnel mediating between political groups and factions in order to allow for some continuity in government. Extensions might be an extreme form of such a mediating process.

In a number of Latin American countries the end of military dictatorships has also been the beginning of the end of anti-guerrilla war tactics and of the involvement of the army and the police in this kind of dirty war. Although these operations have come to a halt, the capacity to organize and wage secret operations on their own behalf or to take part in illegal policing extensions is still there. It lies dormant and may be activated again. This potential for reactivation constitutes a silent threat in a number of Latin American countries. Reactivation depends, of course, on a great number of factors. A strong motive for reactivation will be a perceived serious threat to the groups involved or their members, a threat to the values the group stood for or its vital interests. This might be a new 'communist' threat. Secret wars forge secret loyalties, brotherhoods that may last a lifetime, brotherhoods that also know the tricks of the secret trade of threat and assassination.

In Brazil there are signs of such reactivation. Two witnesses for a United Nations Human Rights Commission that is enquiring into allegations of torture and illegal killings by the Brazilian police during the military dictatorship, instituted on the request of the Brazilian government, were killed in September 2003. A Brazilian human rights activist claimed this demonstrated the unassailability of death squads, notwithstanding the promise by the president to protect those who testify.[10] It is not known if these attacks are being carried out by existing death squads, be it on a commercial basis or because of old police loyalties, or if dormant networks from the past have been reactivated. The parallel with reports from Amnesty International regarding the activation or reactivation of a death squad in Chile as a reaction against the investigation of crimes committed by the military during the Pinochet dictatorship is striking. The same can be said about reports about the existence of networks of old torturers and politicians in Argentina: they are still there.[11] Some of the old commanders of units active in the Argentinian military dictatorship are reported to have amassed the belongings, property and money of people who were killed or disappeared, and some of them have made fortunes from this, creating a connection between the old hands and the commercial sector.[12] In those countries in Latin America where official death squad activities have either stopped or become illegal, commercialized and used to control crime, the possibility of their reactivation for political purposes is real.

Notes

1 For a number of countries we have described the relationship between the extension and the police, and between the extension and other institutions or interest groups. We have constructed diagrams of these relationships. We expect that the patterns that emerge in each country and the differences between countries will set us on the trail of explaining these differences. Hopefully they will also allow us to look more deeply into the relationship between extensions and the dynamics of their functioning. So the project is comparative in character, and in this first stage we hope to produce a tentative structural analysis.

We have researched who is involved – which groups/organizations are extensions:

a. How can they be characterized?
b. What methods do they use?
c. How are they related to the police and to others, and what is the pattern of relationships?
d. Who is guiding and who is being guided?
e. What is exchanged to keep the pattern operating?

2 Amnesty International and Human Rights Watch report continuity over a number of years in Brazil, Mexico, Guatemala, Haiti and Colombia.

3 The countries where extensions have been reported for 2002 are: Argentina, Brazil, Colombia, Dominican Republic, El Salvador, Haiti, Honduras, Mexico and Venezuela. Amnesty International Report (2003: 70).

4 *Sources*: US Department of State (2000), *Country Report on Human Rights Practices in Brazil*; Amnesty International (1997; 1998).

5 Regarding the occurrence of death squad activities, the US State Department

reports: 'According to public security officials, death squads in which the police are involved continued to operate. Human rights groups reported the existence of organized death squads linked to the police forces that target suspected criminals and persons considered "undesirable" – such as street children – in almost every state.' In 2000 Amnesty International reported that police death squads remained active in Mato Grosso do Sul. A 1999 report on death squads by the Human Rights Committee of the Federal Chamber of Deputies found that death squad activity with police involvement also existed in several other states, including Bahia, Rio Grande do Norte, Mato Grosso, Amazonas, Para, Paraiba, Ceara, Espirito Santo and Acre (US Bureau of Democracy, Human Rights, and Labor 2003).

6 In July 2002 the São Paulo press reported that the forty-member Group for the Repression of Crimes of Intolerance (GRADI), a military police intelligence network directly subordinate to the Secretary of Public Security, had illegally recruited prisoners to infiltrate PCC cells on three separate occasions. In the nine months between July 2001 and March 2002, the three GRADI infiltration operations reportedly resulted in seven arrests and twenty-two deaths, including that of an informant. The dead informant, twenty-two-year-old Fernando Henrique Rodrigues Batista, was allegedly killed in July 2001 by the very police who had recruited him.

Human rights activists and some within the judiciary compared GRADI to the police 'death squads' that operated in the 1970s. The police ombudsman reported that he had evidence linking twenty-one homicides to GRADI; so far no charges have been brought against GRADI officers. The São Paulo Public Prosecutor ordered an inquiry into these allegations, as did Congress's Human Rights Commission; in an official statement, however, the São Paulo Secretary of Public Security defended GRADI's actions (US Bureau of Democracy, Human Rights, and Labor, 2003).

7 For the connection between bureaucracy and violence see Huggins, Haritos-Faroutos and Zimbardo (2002: 114–16).

8 US Bureau of Democracy, Human Rights, and Labor (2003).

9 Human Rights Watch and Amnesty International report death threats and killings of human rights advocates and defenders.

10 *NRC Handelsblad*, 12 October 2003, p. 4.

11 *De Volkskrant*, 13 October 2003, p. 11.

12 Cavallo, a former Argentinian naval officer, now in custody in Spain for the killing of Spanish nationals during the dictatorship, is reported to have been placed under special protection. Spanish authorities fear an attempt on his life by former colleagues (*De Volkskrant*, 13 October 2003, p. 11).

4 | Civil defence forces: Peru's Comités de Autodefensa Civil and Guatemala's Patrullas de Autodefensa Civil in comparative perspective

MARIO FUMERTON AND SIMONE REMIJNSE

Introduction

For modern nation-states the state-building process ideally requires, among a number of requisite conditions, the establishment of a monopoly of coercive power and the ability to uphold that monopoly across a territory (Weber 1978; Giddens 1985). It thus follows that the emergence of armed actors not formally part of the legitimate armed forces apparatus of the state threatens to dilute and erode the state's monopoly of coercive power, a threat which, if left unchecked, could lead to a breakdown of governmental authority. On the other hand, a state's inability to guarantee security and protection to its own citizens may also lead to individuals employing violent self-help, or to the spontaneous emergence of vigilante groups, civilian self-defence organizations, militias, and the like. Finally, we should also bear in mind that in particular circumstances it may simply be in a state's pragmatic interests to initiate or support the formation of non-state armed actors.

In this chapter we discuss one variety of armed actor that has emerged in Latin America in the past three decades, precisely for the latter reason. Specifically, we compare the genesis, development and consequences of the 'civil defence patrols' of Peru (1980–2000) and Guatemala (1981–96)[1] in terms of two general questions. First, what has the emergence and proliferation of civil defence patrols in these two settings meant for the rule of law, civil society and citizenship, which are assumed to be prerequisites for the development and consolidation of democracy (see Diamond 1999)? Second, why, in spite of their strong similarities in terms of origin, organizational structure, counter-insurgency function and subordination to the army, did the civil defence phenomenon produce such disparate social outcomes in the comparative cases of Peru and Guatemala?

It is our contention that where such a delegation of coercive power and authority to civil defence patrols has been strictly limited and legally controlled by the state, the consequences have been generally conducive to the revival of civil society, and to the construction of citizenship and the consolidation of democracy in the post-civil-war scenario. Conversely, where the state has failed to establish or to enforce legal parameters for such groups, and has neglected to provide them with a mandate that respects the rule of law, the consequences for the civil patrols and for the population at large have tended to include a continuing climate of fear and distrust, an undemocratic and uncivil society, and the pervasiveness of the rule of force.

The genesis of civil defence patrols in Peru and Guatemala

Counter-insurgency is the fundamental rationale behind the creation of civil defence patrols in both Peru and Guatemala.

In Peru, a militant Maoist group known as the Partido Comunista del Peru–Sendero Luminoso (Communist Party of Peru–Shining Path) initiated armed struggle against the state, in the Andean department of Ayacucho, in May 1980. From 1982 onwards, the department of Ayacucho was placed under a state of emergency, resulting in military control and the suspension of numerous constitutional rights and civil liberties (see Amnesty International 1991: 16–17). Almost immediately after the military had set foot in Ayacucho they started, in the first months of 1983, to press rural peasant communities to organize civil defence committees. This initiative, however, had already been preceded some months earlier by the outbreak of violent counter-rebellion among a handful of remote highland peasant communities, who sought to defy mounting guerrilla levies and summary executions by taking up armed resistance (Fumerton 2002: 73–105). The vigilante justice these villagers exacted on suspected guerrillas and sympathizers initially met with approval and praise from various sectors of the Limeño population, including the president himself. The murder of a small group of Limeño journalists by these highland villagers, who had mistaken them for guerrillas, however, provoked a heated nationwide debate on the political violence that was rapidly spinning out of control. Even so, this did not deter other Ayacuchano peasant communities from spontaneously organizing their own self-defence groups, which they called *montoneros*.

The army's counter-insurgency strategy at this time consisted primarily of indiscriminate, brutal repression. Supplementary to this was a strategy of organizing the general rural population into civil defence committees (CDCs), in violent opposition to Sendero Luminoso. Pre-existing *montonero* groups were, in principle, brought under the nominal authority of the local army commander, when there was one. It is important to point out, however, that at this time the army's initiative in organizing civil defence did not, strictly speaking, constitute official policy. Indeed, it was pursued only sporadically, since more than a few senior officers were against the very idea of indigenous peasants being permitted to handle firearms or to exercise lethal force, even in self-defence.

In spite of the impetus provided by the army, the expansion of the civil defence groups in Ayacucho proceeded very slowly throughout the 1980s. For various reasons, the idea of communal defence encountered either extensive opposition or limited, lukewarm compliance in many parts of Ayacucho. With nothing to fight with except sticks and stones, many communities simply lacked conviction that they could actually repulse guerrilla attacks (see Coronel and Loayza 1992: 528–9). Most peasants therefore thought it better not to antagonize the guerrillas in the first place.

The initial instances of local opposition to the creation of civil defence committees did not deter the security forces from trying to coerce rural villagers into forming them, however. Occasionally accompanied by the civil defence patrols of neighbouring communities, army troops were known to pressure recalcitrant villages by resorting to tactics of violence and terror (Degregori 1987: 49; Isbell 1990: 11–12; Americas Watch 1992: 9). Neutrality was permitted neither by the military nor by Sendero, and at times not even by neighbouring peasant communities. Any reluctance to organize community self-defence was interpreted by the security forces as tacit support for Sendero Luminoso (Isbell 1990: 11–12; Americas Watch 1992). The Maoists, on the other hand, were not interested in finding a modus vivendi with the civil defence patrols, and specifically targeted organized communities for pitiless annihilation.

In Guatemala, the guerrilla and counter-insurgency campaigns of the military resulted in a continuous state of low-intensity civil war lasting thirty-six years, until a peace accord was finally signed in 1996. At the beginning of the 1980s, the fighting, and especially military repression, intensified. The indigenous population in the western highlands, where the guerrillas were most active, was hardest hit by the violence, which resulted from clashes between the two parties.[2] Between 1981 and 1983 the military used so-called 'scorched earth' tactics, resulting in more than four hundred villages being destroyed, 75,000 people killed and more than 1 million people fleeing their homes. At the same time the military institutionalized its control over the western highlands by forcing the local population to form civil defence patrols (Patrullas de Autodefensa Civil – PAC).

The newly organized civil defence patrols were a central element of the military counter-insurgency strategy of total control of the population, and were involved in perpetrating many of the reported cases of human rights abuses. Especially during the first years after their creation, civil patrols were foremost 'agents of the state', receiving orders from higher up the military hierarchy, with little room to manoeuvre at local level. They were created by the military towards the end of 1981 and set up in conflict zones in the Guatemalan countryside. The first patrols were organized in the last months of the Lucas García administration. In the spring of 1982, after dissatisfied young officers had disposed of the Lucas García regime, the head of the new junta, Ríos Montt, formalized and expanded the patrol system throughout the western highlands.

The introduction of civil patrols in any one area was conditioned for the most part by the intensity of the conflict between the army and the guerrillas and the assumed local sympathy for the guerrillas. The more conflict existed in the area, the more civil patrols were set up and the stricter the military control over the patrols. The military made a distinction between red, pink, yellow and green zones of conflict. Green zones were thought to be free of guerrillas, and were watched but generally left alone. Pink and yellow zones were visited with more military violence, because of possible ties with guerrillas. Red zones were supposedly in enemy hands from the point of view of the military. In these zones the military made no distinction between villagers and guerrillas and in many of these areas whole villages were wiped off the map. It is estimated that a total of 25,000 men were incorporated in the patrol system in Guatemala by September 1982. A year later this number had expanded to some 700,000. At the height of the civil patrol system, in 1984, about 900,000, predominantly indigenous, men were active in the patrols (Americas Watch 1986: 26).

It was not until months after the first patrols had been organized that they were formally recognized by way of Governmental Accord 222-83, which created a 'National Office for the Coordination and Control of the Civil Defence Patrols' (PDH 1994: 33). Subsequently, at the end of 1983, a 'Fund for Military Protection of the Civil Defence' was created, which was meant to provide economic assistance to the families of patrollers who were killed during combat.[3] The civil patrols were clearly an official part of military strategy. This was also apparent from their military-style chain of command. The patrols were headed by a civil patrol commander, who was often appointed by and under the control of both the local military commander and the military commissioner. Often, military commissioners themselves were appointed to act as heads of the patrols. In the towns, the patrol structure was somewhat more complicated, consisting of battalions, platoons, squadrons and rank-and-file members (Americas Watch 1986: 42). Officials from D-5 (Dirección de Asuntos Civiles – Directorate of Civil Affairs),[4] who were responsible for the political and psychological aspects of the military operations, including relations with the local civil defence patrol, organized weekly meetings at military bases for patrol commanders. Orders involving patrol duty were generated through the military chain of command.

Officially the patrols were set up to defend and 'protect the villages against guerrilla attacks'[5] and participation in them was supposedly voluntary. Unofficially, participation was obligatory for all males between the ages of eighteen and sixty, on penalty of severe punishment or even death. The patrols were used as an extension of the military's control of the Guatemalan countryside. They organized checkpoints at the village entrance, checked identity papers, set up roadblocks, searched buses and patrolled the village at night. They acted as an information network for the military, as well as taking over military tasks such as sweeping areas for guerrillas and attacking so-called subversive villages.

Thus, by the early 1980s, a tight network of repression had been put in place, encompassing not only the civil defence patrols and military forces but also police, military police, private security forces, death squads and various intelligence units (see, for example, Deli Sante 1996: 273; ODHAG 1998, Vol. II: 65–79). A society of fear arose 'in which a climate of insecurity, anxiety and suspense overshadowed all other feelings' (Kruijt and Koonings 1999: 16). People lived under constant surveillance and local society was thoroughly militarized.

State counter-insurgency and civil defence in Peru and Guatemala

Peru In the first half of the 1980s, the Peruvian security forces sought to crush the insurgency by waging a 'dirty war' in which tortures, massacres, extrajudicial executions and disappearances were simply considered 'part of the cost' of restoring peace and order. Little concern, if any, was initially paid by the 'forces of order' to respecting human rights – as evidenced by the dramatic rise in the number of civilian casualties in the first two years of armed forces intervention (DESCO 1989). As the civil war ground on, lawlessness pervaded the emergency zone as soldiers and policemen increasingly came to disregard arrest procedures, and to prefer summary executions and disappearances instead. In this anarchic climate of terror and impunity, civil defence patrols took their lead from the military and '[became] in many cases another predatory force' (Americas Watch 1992: 9). The term 'subversive' became a convenient cover for masking ordinary crimes. It also became, as in Guatemala, a convenient justification for silencing critical voices, for attacking the legal left, or for violently settling long-standing feuds and vendettas. The local civil defence apparatus, 'acting independently or in concert with military units', was at times employed in such violent acts (ibid.). In all practical senses of the words, by the mid-1980s law and order in the countryside had all but disintegrated in a spiral of violence and terror.

Although the army compelled rural communities to organize CDCs, and presumed to subordinate and control them, in actuality they made little attempt to train, provision, mobilize or utilize the CDCs in any systematic way for a larger, strategically significant counter-insurgency purpose. Rural defence groups were frequently forced to patrol with army units, poorly armed though they were with makeshift weapons (Isbell 1990: 12). In those instances they were used by the soldiers simply as a sort of *carne de cañón* – made to march a short distance ahead of the troops in order to flush out any rebels possibly waiting in ambush (del Pino 1993b). Beyond this the army did not see it worth their time and effort to develop the capabilities of the CDCs, nor to create more sophisticated mechanisms of control over them. Indeed, given that army detachments were normally garrisoned only in the larger strategically important towns and cities of Ayacucho, any 'control' they exercised over the daily lives of rural inhabitants and the CDCs of more remote parts of the countryside could have existed in name only.

Even though state repression abated markedly during the García period, security forces nevertheless continued to prosecute a more selective 'dirty war' of disappearances, torture and extra-judicial executions. In the countryside of Ayacucho, the army's refusal to continue military actions against the guerrillas for fear of incurring accusations of human rights violations left the peasants feeling totally abandoned. In addition, the increasingly open hostility shown by army political-military commanders towards the civil defence groups, with some officers even attempting to dismantle them, left peasants feeling betrayed (Fumerton 2002: 120–3). Many organized rural communities in the Ayacuchan highlands therefore decided to disband their CDCs. After reassessing the situation, most peasants concluded that the prevailing winds of power were now blowing in the direction of Shining Path, and thus reacted accordingly by opting to accept or to accommodate the insurgency into their daily lives.

Surprisingly, it was during this period of crisis that the civil defence organizations known as the DECAS (Defensa Civil Antisubversiva) rose to become the most organized, most sophisticated and militarily powerful of all the civil defence organizations in Peru. The DECAS emerged and developed in the remote Apurímac river valley, which was not only one of the most important centres of coca cultivation in South America but also a frontier area where, besides the authority exerted by localized military garrisons, state control was virtually non-existent. Through a combination of shrewd leadership and clever alliances made with local marine infantry commanders (in opposition to army detachments) and with local Colombian-linked drug traffickers, the DECAS were able to secure modern firearms and weaponry, and thereby push Shining

Path out of the Apurímac river valley completely (del Pino 1996, 1993a). In the valley, an abundance of money, arms and relative autonomy from state (even from military) authorities contributed to the rise of local jungle 'warlords', with the power to administer their own brand of justice with the backing of the local DECAS defence group, which they employed as their own 'private army' (Starn 1998: 240–2). In the final months of his administration, President García became impressed by the achievements of the DECAS, and took symbolic steps to show his support for them by personally distributing state donations of shotguns. This action provoked heated national debate on the legality and advisability of distributing firearms to the peasantry, even for the purpose of self-defence. Nevertheless, it also set a precedent that would be taken up with greater intensity by his presidential successor.

In fact the Fujimori government proceeded to incorporate the peasantry into the counter-insurgency struggle by granting statutory recognition to the civil defence groups, which were given the official title of Comités de Autodefensa y Desarrollo. For unlike García, Fujimori was quick to realize that peasant militias, if provided with adequate government backing and encouragement, had the potential to become an invaluable counter-insurgency force. His first step in this regard was to promulgate in 1991 legislation that bestowed legal recognition on all accredited civil defence organizations in the zone of emergency. In effect, this served to transform the civil defence groups collectively into the 'fourth branch of the armed forces' (Kruijt 1996: 246), entitled to wield specifically defined sorts of firearms. It was a pivotal step that would ultimately contribute to the defeat of the insurgency movements in the country.

From about the mid-1990s onwards, the army also introduced certain bureaucratic formalities and controls in the operational practices of the CADs. These included such mechanisms as obliging CADs to submit a written formal report every week; or requiring CAD patrol commanders to obtain a signed declaration from the leaders of every community they visited stating that while in the village the patrollers did not commit any abuses or crimes. In addition, whereas members of the security forces were effectively immune from criminal charges, the army and the police did not hesitate to indict civil defence patrollers accused of committing violent crimes or engaging in other illegal activities, such as drug trafficking. Such controls and protocols designed to make civil defence patrols more accountable to the military for their actions were aimed not only at preventing the rise of civil defence 'warlords', and at pre-empting criticism of human rights abuses, which were both problems frequently observed among the DECAS (Americas Watch 1992: 9; Amnesty International 1991: 21; Degregori 1989); in fact the principal purpose of such controls lay in the military's larger objective of winning the hearts and minds of that portion of the rural population which had thus far refused to organize CADs.

Guatemala After the initial years of tight military control, during which the Guatemalan military consolidated its grip both on the rural communities and on the civil patrol structure, the space to manoeuvre for local patrol commanders seemed to become somewhat greater. Civil patrols were not only the forced handymen of the military; they were also local organizations headed by local civil patrol commanders, who were often trusted army allies that kept the military informed about the community. Communities and their inhabitants were under continuous observation. People were constantly aware of their own visibility and that of their actions. Surveillance and control extended also towards the behaviour of the people who actually carried out the surveillance – that is, those participating in the patrols. Participation in the patrols forced people to control and supervise their own behaviour and that of their families. Not behaving according to the standards of the patrol commander, the military commander or the other patrollers could mean punishment or death. Sometimes patrollers were killed by other patrollers, for example when they let a prisoner escape or because they refused to continue patrolling (CEH 1999, Vol. X: 1,372, 1,366). Patrols incorporated more and more civilians into the terror apparatus, thereby also incorporating part of the target population into that same apparatus. In some instances, the agents of terror (members of the patrols) and the targets of terror became one and the same. This ambiguity made it difficult to distinguish between enemy and friend, between 'us' and 'them'. The boundaries between these groups were not always very clear.

In some communities, these changes in military–PAC relations resulted in a slackening of patrol discipline, while in other communities patrol duty intensified. Patrol commanders had created their own little kingdoms, and had grown quite independent of the military hierarchy. They were anxious not to lose this position and therefore fervently opposed the anti-civil patrol lobby that was growing in the late 1980s and early 1990s. This lobby was headed by the widow organization Conavigua and the peasant organization CERJ.

The slackening of military control over the PAC appeared to be part of a change in military strategy 'to establish a more legitimate presence in the disputed regions, with "positive actions," local development projects and protection of allied peasants' (Kruijt 1999: 50). It also heralded a slow transition towards civilian government, resulting in democratic presidential elections in 1985. The 1985 constitution also legalized most institutions that had been set up during the counter-insurgency years, including the civil patrols whose position was strengthened by incorporating them into the military reserve structure.[6] They were renamed Voluntary Civil Defence Committees (CVDCs)[7] in 1986 in an effort to improve the image of the civil patrols. They continued, however, to be popularly knows as PACs, or, more simply, civil patrols. Public space was opened up for discussion, however, and popular organizations started to address issues related to the armed conflict, such as human rights abuses and forced participation in the civil patrols.

In January 1994 the new director of the PDH, García Laguardia, recommended that decree no. 19-86, the one which ratified the civil patrols as part of the military reserves and thus in a sense provided legal cover for their existence (Solomon 1994: 54), be revoked. This recommendation was based primarily on the large number of human rights violations committed by patrols, which were brought to the attention of his office. It was not until 28 November 1996 that the decree was indeed revoked by Congress, thus officially ending all civil patrols. However, demobilization was still a long way off and the Guatemalan government and the guerrillas were still in the midst of the negotiating process. At that moment '[i]t did not attempt to solve the military or political problems posed by the PACs' (ibid.: 48, 49), but the government committed itself to not encouraging the formation or arming new civil patrols 'unless the situation calls for them' (Popkin 1996: 11). The agreement further stipulated that '[t]he parties agree that other aspects of the Voluntary Civil Defence Committees will be dealt with later'.

At the local level, many rural communities found themselves in a chaotic situation as political activism and community life slowly re-emerged, carefully navigating the available local space so as not to collide with patrol commanders, military commissioners and the military. It was a period during which struggles over local power became more pronounced and violent. Civil patrol commanders, and others who had been building and expanding their positions of power during the armed conflict, saw the democratic opening as a danger to their positions of influence and authority, which were based on violence rather than legitimacy (Remijnse 2001: 461).

It was not until September 1996 that the issue of civil patrols was back on the negotiating table, as part of the Agreement on the Strengthening of Civilian Power and the Role of the Armed Forces in a Democratic Society. The agreement contained a comprehensive package of measures to strengthen democratic government and reduce the security functions of the state. Among other things, the army would be reduced in size, a new civilian police was to be created, and civil patrol legislation would be revoked (Armon, Sieder and Wilson 1997: 85).

The civil defence patrols and the rule of law

As the above case studies show, one cannot automatically assume a direct relationship between the manner in which a particular civil defence patrol was created and its subsequent conduct in relation to the rule of law. Rather, it appears to us that the crucial factor in this respect was a civil defence group's degree of autonomy from state authority. Also influential was the example set by the security forces in terms of whether they generally respected or flaunted and abused the rule of law and human rights.

In the case of Peru, we see that the rule of law was subverted in a number of ways over the course of the past two decades. In spite of the restoration of formal democratic government in Peru in 1980, the dynamics of 'dirty' war, along with the vicissitudes of deteriorating civil–military relations and, eventually, in the 1990s, the rise of an 'authoritarian populist' government (Youngers 2000: 7), unrestrained by mutual institutional checks and a separation of balanced powers (see Mauceri 2000), created an environment in which it was the 'un-rule of law' (to borrow a term from Méndez, O'Donnell and Pinheiro 1999) which prevailed.[8]

With regard to the civil defence groups, the evidence presented reveals that their status, function, authority and legality were highly ambiguous – at least until the promulgation of CAD legislation in November 1991. As we have seen, the attitude and the behaviour of the army towards the civil defence groups vacillated between support and antagonism throughout the 1980s. Often, civil defence patrols were encouraged by the security forces to mete out vigilante justice on suspected 'terrorists'. At other times, local army commanders regarded them as illegitimate vigilante groups, treating them with nothing but capricious hostility and contempt. Yet whether supporting or opposing the civil defence patrols, the one constant in the behaviour of the military has always been an active attempt to subordinate and control them. And even though geographic remoteness provided some civil defence groups with a degree of relative autonomy *vis-à-vis* the military, the degree and extent of military control progressively intensified, rather than decreased, in the course of two decades of civil war in Peru, culminating in the ultimate embodiment of political subordination and control – the CAD legislation. Even the powerful DECAS of the Apurímac river valley were rapidly brought under the firm control of the military once Fujimori came to power. As one would therefore expect, the army's move away from 'dirty war' tactics to a 'softer' counter-insurgency approach had a profound effect on the conduct of civil defence patrollers.

Finally, we must keep in mind that the rapid proliferation of the CADs throughout the 1990s is due largely to the initiative of local civilians, rather than to the military (Fumerton 2002: 153–223). '[I]n most places this participation no longer rests as much on military intimidation as on the collective conviction among villagers that [civil defence patrols] are desirable,' writes Starn (1998: 245). 'Commanders and civil defence committee presidents are no longer named by army officials in most villages. Instead, open assemblies elect them like other village leaders' (ibid.). In fact, ever since the first half of the 1980s, the military were permitting trusted communities to elect their own civil defence commanders (Fumerton 2002: 94–6).

Hence, as a partially indigenous initiative (recall the *montoneros*), the civil defence phenomenon in the department of Ayacucho had always enjoyed a degree of popular legitimacy right from the very start. In fact, one can safely say that by the mid-1990s, the vast majority of peasants in the department had come to regard the CADs not as just another 'predatory force', but as the legitimate and effectively sole guarantor of the peasantry's peace and security.

Before turning to military–civil patrol relations in the Guatemalan case, attention has to be paid to the aspect of diversity, which is a central aspect of the Guatemalan civil defence patrols. Although they were set up by the military as part of a wider counter-insurgency strategy, and had basically the same organizational structure, the differences between civil patrols across and even within municipalities were significant. Civil patrols were not static entities, but differed in background, the type of functions they performed and their level of military activity (Remijnse 2003: 143–7). Civil patrol commanders and members also had widely different views on the patrols and what they stood for. In one area a civil patrol could be highly hierarchically organized, heavily armed and in constant close contact with the military. In another area civil patrol members might be hardly armed at all, might undertake only some shifts on night watch, might have little contact with the local military commander, and might regard civil patrol duty as a minor obligation. Between these extremes there was ample room for variation, depending on such factors as the level and history of violence or military presence and guerrilla activity in the area. This diversity of patrol activity was partially the result of introducing civil patrols in widely different settings (municipalities) with different histories: of land disputes, of Ladino rule or rule by *indigenas*. A second factor affecting their diversity was the degree of military influence in an area. This variety had a major impact on the way civil patrols acted and carried out their assigned tasks. A third factor was the role played by the individual patrol commander. He was the one in direct contact with the military and his views on how patrol duties were to be carried out were crucial. Closely related to the role of patrol commander was the post of local military commander, who was the direct superior of the patrol commander.

During the armed conflict, the Guatemalan military, as in the Peruvian case, completely disregarded basic human rights and had no respect for legal authority and procedures. This dirty war was, as in the Peruvian case, facilitated by the proclamation of a state of siege in 1982 by General Ríos Montt, followed by a state of emergency in 1983. In a way, the state of siege law 'added little to de facto army and police powers; it merely formalized powers for arrest without warrant, secret detention, and unlimited power of search and seizure. It did add a veneer of legality to established practice' (McClintock 1985: 231).

In the communities occupied by the military, elected municipal authorities were killed or forced to step down, and their own puppet municipalities were installed. People were often randomly accused of being communist or subversive, which meant they were shot or disappeared. The utter lack of respect for human rights and the rule of law on the part of the military is documented extensively in the two documents of the truth commissions. The CEH reports that 85 per cent of the human rights abuses in Guatemala between 1962 and 1996 were committed by the military (CEH 1999, vol. V: 102). In many instances, the civil patrols were forced by the military to participate in the atrocities, especially within their own communities, thereby creating enormous rifts in the social fabric of local communities. Patrollers were ordered to torture their victims, rape women, and even drink the blood and eat the brains of their victims. Such acts of extreme cruelty are described in the testimonies given to the truth commissions. The civil patrols were clearly taught by the military not to respect the rule of law and to solve matters in an extremely violent and illegal way. In the long term this resulted in widespread vigilante justice in Guatemala, such as the current phenomenon of lynching, whereby supposed criminals are doused in gasoline and burned alive in front of an entire community.

The civil defence patrols and civil society

Numerous theorists consider civil society to be a prerequisite for democracy, in addition to presenting a counter-hegemonic check to state power and militarism (see Cohen and Arato 1992; Held 1987). Dagnino recognizes the importance of civil society as a 'crucial [space] of political struggle for the building of citizenship' (1998: 51). So, what can we say about the relationship between civil society and the civil defence patrols of Peru and Guatemala?

In the case of Peru, Starn argues that '[t]oday, many critics admit the [civil defence patrols] have contributed to a surprising resurrection of civil society ... A panoply of other civil organizations ... have also been reactivated with the new security provided by the patrols, expanding the room for local participation in village organizations shattered by war' (1998: 245).

The invaluable contribution made by the civil defence patrols to the pacification of the Ayacuchan countryside cannot be denied. The restoration of peace and order has, in turn, formed the basis for social reconstruction, through the return of NGOs and displaced communities, and the spontaneous emergence of various new grass-roots organizations such as mothers' clubs and micro-credit associations. For these reasons, can it therefore be argued, as Starn and others have, that the peasant defence patrols in the late 1990s were not only helping to build up grass-roots civil structures, but have also been an integral component of a resurgent civil society?

Based on the evidence presented earlier, the answer would have to be no. Clearly, the continuing state of emergency (it was finally abrogated in 2000), which suspended rights and freedoms and instated a military officer as the principal political authority in the region, effectively obliterated the 'autonomous public space' that is the prerequisite for the existence of civil society. Apart from this, it is clear that the rapid demise of civil society in the emergency zone can squarely be blamed on the two main protagonists in the political violence: the armed forces and Shining Path. On the one hand, Shining Path targeted popular leaders, grass-roots unions and parties of the legal left, in accordance with their strategy 'to eliminate competing organizations and forces in the national arena of popular and left-wing political struggle and to polarize the political situation such that the only two political agents are the PCP-SL and a militarized Peruvian state' (Poole 1994b: 255; see Burt 1998). On the other, the security forces automatically assumed that all left-wing parties and popular organizations were Shining Path sympathizers or front organizations, and so did not hesitate to attack any group or individual they deemed 'subversive'. The result of this crossfire on civil society was the demise and virtual disappearance of hitherto powerful peasant federations, peasant-oriented political movements and traditional political parties in the department of Ayacucho – all before Fujimori assumed power and administered the *coup de grâce* (Smith 1992; Kruijt and del Pilar Tello 2002).

The apparent resurgence of civil society entities in the Peruvian emergency zone in the latter half of the 1990s can perhaps be better described as having taken place *within a liminal phase*, whereby an unruly, chaotic society at war is being left behind, and a society at peace, embracing a functioning civil society, is becoming established. We contend, therefore, that although the peasant militias appeared to exhibit certain characteristics that liken them to a social movement participating in civil society, the context of a militarized emergency zone still in a situation of conflict, and their relationship of subordination to the authority of the military and the state, merely typified what Payne (2000) would describe as an 'uncivil movement' in an 'uncivil society' (see Koonings 2001: 404–5; 2002: 66).

As in Peru, the Guatemalan civil defence patrols did not operate in the context of a functioning civil society, which was virtually wiped out during the early stages of the armed conflict. A combination of military and patrol violence caused a social and institutional breakdown in the countryside. First, the use of selective and massive terror by military and paramilitary forces caused widespread fear and uncertainty among the population. The random and often massive violence could target anybody. Blacklists, arbitrary arrests, individual killings, mutilation and exposure of bodies, disappearances and massacres were used by the military to regain control over the rural population. Second, military violence brought social life to an almost complete standstill. The Catholic Church closed its doors, schools remained empty and indigenous villages were almost completely abandoned. Local leaders were murdered or fled their communities. NGOs stopped working in the communities, and everything connected with community work was suspended. Third, economic activities broke down, local markets ceased functioning, credit and other cooperatives were closed down, and their leaders killed or disappeared. Guerrilla activity caused the permanent flight of a top echelon of wealthy Ladinos, and the temporary flight of other Ladinos during the height of the violence. Fourth, civil authority ceased to exist and a virtual power vacuum was created as the majority of the council members were killed, disappeared or fled. Only very slowly, from the beginning of the 1990s onwards, did civil society start recovering somewhat (Remijnse 2003: 169–203).

It cannot be said, however, that civil patrols were vital to the establishment of peace and order in the Guatemalan countryside. Although from a military point of view the patrols were instrumental in ending guerrilla activity in some areas, and thus establishing order based on coercion, it is clear from many testimonies that the civil defence patrols were first and foremost used as agents of terror and as such instrumental in the tearing apart of the social fabric of local communities and civil society (CEH 1999, Vol. II: 212–30). They had no part in its reweaving. Civil patrols themselves were never spaces within which people felt they could express their opinion; these spaces of protest were situated outside the civil patrol system, for example in Catholic Church initiatives, resurgent municipal politics or the activities of popular organizations. In the Guatemalan case, civil patrols did contribute to an 'uncivil society' and continued to hinder the emergence of local political or community initiatives.

This was not only the case during the armed conflict, but continued in some instances even after their official dismantling in 1996. For example, in many of the lynching cases that have occurred frequently in the rural areas ever since the peace accords were signed, it was found that former civil patrollers were involved as instigators. Thus, it is clear that the Guatemalan patrols, like their counterparts in Peru, continue to be an uncivil actor in an uncivil society: a society where the rule of law and constitutional freedoms were suspended by a state of emergency and continuing military authority.

The civil defence patrols and the construction of citizenship

Various political theorists and philosophers of democracy have made the important observation that the rights and responsibilities of citizenship have, more often than not, been fundamentally conditioned by warfare and the obligations of military service (e.g. Giddens 1985). In fact, military institutions have played a central role in the evolution of parliamentary democracy in many of the developed nations of the world; and military service has correspondingly been an integral component of citizenship. As Janowitz observes, 'From World War I onward, citizen military service has been seen as a device by which excluded segments of society could achieve political legitimacy and rights' (1975: 77–8).

Accelerated social, cultural and attitudinal change in Peru over the past two decades suggests that a profound citizenship revolution has been gradually unfolding (see Fumerton 2002; Starn 1998; Stern 1998). That the CAD patrollers have come to be portrayed in both popular literature and scholarly discourse in Peru and abroad as 'patriot-citizens who defend Peru and their community' (Stern 1998: 475, caption) is testimony to the extent to which peasant militias had come to be seen (by outsiders as much as by the peasant participants themselves) as platforms for claiming citizenship.

For most of the history of Peru as a modern nation-state, its indigenous peasant population has been denied many of the political rights of citizenship. The violence of the past two decades, however, induced peasants to first petition, and later make demands and claim rights (see Fumerton 2002). These included, in more or less chronological order, (1) guarantees of safety, which would later develop into the language of human rights (Muñoz 1998); (2) the right to defend themselves, which was first confirmed and endorsed by General Huamán, one of the early political-military commanders who himself was of indigenous background; (3) the right to the *means* to defend themselves, which President García not only articulated, but also validated in action by distributing shotguns to the DECAS; (4) claims for economic and material assistance for civil defence patrollers and their families; and more recently (5) for financial compensation. Recognizing the invaluable contributions they had made to the counter-insurgency struggle, CAD leaders from Ayacucho mobilized in April 1999 for the explicit purpose of claiming the compensation they had been promised by Fujimori and the CAD legislation, and in so doing were attempting to stake out a political claim to citizenship. For these reasons, one may borrow an idea from Dagnino (1998: 48) and conclude that, for peasants in Ayacucho and elsewhere, one of the significant consequences of the common experience of political violence and civil defence has been a perception of themselves as subjects bearing rights.

The Peruvian case is thus a clear example which shows that citizen participation in war, in defence either of themselves or the state, can play an important influential role in the development of political culture and perception. In Peru, participation in the peasant militias gave extra impetus to citizens making claims on the state. Can the same conclusion be drawn from the Guatemalan case?

Claims were certainly made by former patrollers against the Guatemalan state. Unrest did exist among the former patrollers, and they initiated their first protest in early 1997, only months after they had been dismantled. They complained that they had not received the same economic benefits as the recently demobilized guerrillas of the URNG – 'those who destroyed Guatemala'. 'We were victims of the subversive violence, we defended our families, the department and the state, and now they do not compensate us for anything, but to the former insurgents they give money, land, water, electricity,' former patrollers stated (*Siglo Veintiuno*, 9 May 1997). Such perceptions of former patrollers of ex-guerrillas receiving preferential treatment from the state were not uncommon and not perceived as an exaggeration of the situation. The government of Arzú (PAN) refused to negotiate because, it claimed, participation in the patrols had always been voluntary and no labour contract involving compensation had ever existed (*Cerigua Weekly Briefs*, no. 26, July 1997). The unrest increased when the 1999 elections drew near. Contacts between FRG politicians and former patrol leaders were viewed with renewed suspicion, and the FRG was accused of instructing former patrol leaders to vote in their favour.

Demands for financial compensation resurfaced in June–September 2002, when former civil patrollers started reorganizing themselves all over Guatemala, following the example of patrollers in the Petén. A huge debate started, with the FRG government finally agreeing to the demands made by the former patrollers, while human rights organizations accused the government of exploiting the situation in view of the coming elections in November 2003.

They also criticized possible financial compensation for patrollers because of their prominent role in many of the atrocities committed. According to Guatemalan human rights organizations, 'Intimidation, torture, disappearances and massacres cannot be considered a dignified and remunerative job' (*Prensa Libre*, 13 July 2002). Still, the first payments for services rendered during the armed conflict have already been made by the government, during the election campaign.

The case of former patrollers reorganizing to make financial claims on the government does point in the direction of patrollers making citizenship demands. The financial claims have not been followed by claims in other spheres of society, however, while the ambiguous status of civil patrollers as defenders of the fatherland, as well as human rights abusers, has not changed. At the height of the conflict they were regarded, at least by the military and part of the Ladino population, as saviours of the fatherland and defenders of law and order. In the current post-conflict situation, however, they are considered human rights abusers and their actions during the conflict have been condemned in numerous human rights reports. Until recently people were therefore very reluctant to talk about the fact that they had been active as civil patrollers, be it voluntarily or forced by the military. It was not something to be proud of, and not something that granted people a certain position in society. This situation still remains the same, even after compensation has been awarded to a certain number of patrollers. The whole exercise seems to have revolved only around money, and much less so around citizenship.

The social legacy of civil defence patrols in Peru and Guatemala

In this chapter we have shown that the civil defence patrols of Peru and Guatemala bear a number of striking similarities, yet also exhibit important distinctions that have produced disparate social outcomes, which in turn have significant implications for the development and consolidation of democracy in these two nations. Let us quickly recap and make concluding remarks about the key points of comparison.

First, whereas in Peru spontaneous community initiatives and army instigation have both played a part (sometimes simultaneously) in the emergence of the village defence organizations, the evidence suggests that in Guatemala the military took the lead in creating the PAC (Remijnse 2001: 456). This is not to say, however, that military control meant that the PAC and their commanders could not exercise any degree of agency. Rather, as Remijnse noted, 'they evolved over time into a local power player in their own right' (ibid.: 454). That the civil defence patrols of Guatemala were a result of imposition by the military explains why local people have been, and still are, so frightened of them. By comparison, in Ayacucho, Peru, local communities themselves generated many of the earliest village defence patrols. They were the manifestation of a grass-roots counter-rebellion in reaction to increasing guerrilla abuses against the peasantry, and to the state's inability to guarantee security to its rural citizens. (It is thus also important to take into account the character of the guerrilla groups in both cases in explaining the emergence of peasant self-defence groups.) As such, it is clear that self-defence groups in the department of Ayacucho were partly the product of internal, local initiatives. This explains the widespread acceptance and legitimacy they enjoyed among the local communities, not having been the result of external imposition.

In short, for the Peruvian peasant communities that organized them, the original and enduring purpose of peasant patrols has always been one of self-defence, given that the military was incapable of providing round-the-clock protection to the peasants (and also unwilling to do so). As we have seen, throughout the 1980s the civil defence patrols were treated by the Peruvian military as peripheral, or at best auxiliary, to the state's counter-insurgency strategy, and it was only in the 1990s that the government conferred upon them a central role in the counter-insurgency struggle. The civil defence patrols of Guatemala, on the other hand, were, to repeat Remijnse, 'first and foremost used as agents of terror'. Consequently, it is revealing that whereas in places such as the northern provinces of Ayacucho the civil defence patrols were widely embraced by the peasantry as its venerated institutional mechanism for self-defence,[9] in Guatemala, by contrast, people are generally frightened of 'a possible return to the violent past, through the revival of the civil patrols' (Remijnse 2001: 467–8).

In both examples self-defence organizations have been linked to human rights abuses. Yet in the Peruvian case most of these occurred in the first half of the war, and 'to a far lesser extent than those carried out by the civil patrols in Guatemala' (Degregori 1999: 256; also see Comisión de La Verdad y Reconciliación 2003: 453–9). Unlike in Peru, an ethnic dimension also seems to have played a part in fuelling local-level political violence. That is to say, in Guatemala the civil patrols operated as a component of the state's terror apparatus, tacitly encouraged by the military to kill and sow terror among the indigenous population. In Peru, by contrast, the civil war never assumed the kind of ethnic features it did in Guatemala between the Ladino and the indigenous Maya populations. Furthermore, in stark contrast to Guatemalan security forces (Schirmer 2002), Peruvian soldiers actually came to exhibit 'greater respect for human rights' over the course of the 1990s (McClintock 1999: 242). Ironic though it seems, we have even noted that the Peruvian military eventually took measures to ensure that the peasant patrols did not violate human rights.

Another interesting point of comparison concerns the creation or defence of spaces of autonomous action. In the Peruvian case, village defence initiatives were commonly directed towards corporate, collective goals. Furthermore, whereas in the early years many civil defence authorities were selected by the military from among *comuneros* it regarded as loyal, as time went on it became the norm for communities to elect their own militia leaders at a general assembly. Moreover, the goal of civil defence in Peru was not only to provide immediate security for one's community, but also for society as a whole so as to enable the return of much-sought-after aid and development institutions – such as NGOs – to the countryside. In contrast, through the lasting fear they engendered, the PAC helped to sow popular distrust towards NGOs and their initiatives. In addition, PAC commanders – many of whom were unpopular, violent men to begin with, and thus resented by the rest of the local population – were ordinarily hand-picked by military officers, instead of chosen by their fellow villagers (Remijnse 2001). This had an important influence on the degree of legitimacy with which their communities regarded such leaders, which in turn helps to explain the lingering fear of such men. Moreover, the PAC example seems to suggest that the principal concern of many patrol leaders was to create autonomous space in order to enhance their own personal power at the local level (ibid.: 461).

Indeed, many former PAC commanders have literally transformed themselves into local *caudillos* by expanding both their power base and the fear that this inspires among their neighbours (ibid.: 465–6). To be sure, the Peruvian civil defence organizations also had their share of 'bossism' (Starn 1998), yet not to the same degree as in Guatemala, it would seem. We have already noted some of the reasons that account for this. Appointment by election was one way of preventing the rise of *caudillos* among the Peruvian civil defence groups. Another was the strict controls and legislated measures taken by Fujimori's government to ensure that the CADs did not become politicized, or develop into a political movement, or give rise to local 'warlords' who could challenge state power at the local level.

These features have resulted in a significantly distinct legacy in the two country contexts. Since the widespread demobilization of the CADs at the end of the 1990s, former CADs and their members have apparently not attempted to perpetuate themselves by turning into criminal gangs, or into private 'armies' for local power holders (see Schirmer 2002). Nor does it appear that former CAD leaders have sought to become new, mafia-like violent strongmen, or leaders of criminal gangs, as has happened in El Salvador and Guatemala. As a possible reason for this, Degregori suggests: 'The former [CAD] members did not find a market for their newly acquired military skills, given the social structure in the countryside of the Peruvian Andes where no large landholders exist; land reform and the peasant movements themselves had put an end to them' (1999: 255). Yet we saw no evidence that former CAD members were even looking for a market for their lethal skills within the post-conflict context – an observation supported by the Comisión de la Verdad y Reconciliación, which concluded, 'As far as we know, there is not a single case of a paramilitary or criminal band that has arisen out of the rondas ... ' (2003: 457). Rather, while many former defence groups have in fact assumed, in the post-war scenario, the role of 'community police' against common crime (ibid.: 461), most former CAD leaders and *ronderos* have generally returned to their pressing task of subsistence farming. A talented few, however, have set their sights on pursuing political careers, or on obtaining local government and civil service positions. This fact constitutes not only incontrovertible proof of new opportunities opening up for Peru's rural citizens; it also shows that these children of the disenfranchised are themselves now becoming part of the system. Poverty has by no means been eradicated in places such as Ayacucho. Yet the extent to which Peru's enduring economic problems constitute fertile ground for future revolution is tempered by the important fact that citizenship incorporation and enlarged democratic participation mean that peasants today may have a greater stake in preserving and defending the system than ever before.

Notes

1 This article is based on PhD research carried out by Fumerton in Peru, and by Remijnse in Guatemala.

2 See for example Le Bot (1995), ODHAG (1998, vol. III: 25–89) and CEH (1999, vol. I: 123–78) for a detailed account and analysis of the Guatemalan civil war, its background and causes.

3 Decree 160-83 (PDH 1994: 33).

4 D-5 is one of five divisions which together form the Estado Mayor de la Defensa Nacional (EMDN or National Defence Staff). The other divisions are D-1 (personnel), D-2 (intelligence operations), D-3 (military operations and training) and D-4 (logistics) (ODHAG 1998, Vol. II: 81–7).

5 Interview with former General Balconi (18 October 1999).

6 Decree 19-86, which legalized civil patrols, was published in *El Diario Oficial* on 10 January 1986. See Jay 1993: 33.

7 Comités Voluntarios de Defensa Civil.

8 While some may argue 'the rule of law presupposes the effective monopoly of the means of coercion in the hands of the state' (Koonings and Kruijt, Introduction, this volume), the numerous examples of so-called Latin American democratic

regimes infringing the rights and liberties of their citizens, using the coercive power of the state, demonstrate compellingly that this tenet should actually read the other way around: *The state's monopoly of the means of legitimate coercive power ought to be conditional upon its acquiescence to the rule of law*. History testifies that coercive power concentrated in the hands of a state unrestrained by any legal checks and separation of power is just as dangerous as a weak state unable to restrict the free use of violence by its citizens.

9 In response to a recent resurgence of Shining Path activity in Ayacucho in June and July 2003, peasant communities throughout the department have begun to reactivate their self-defence groups, and to request formal assistance from the army.

5 | Violence as market strategy in drug trafficking: the Andean experience

MENNO VELLINGA

Introduction

The small-scale production of coca in the Andean countries became the 'big business' that we know today only two and a half decades ago. During the so-called lost decade in the 1980s, most Latin American economies experienced the most severe crisis they had ever known. Amid plummeting growth rates, the drug industry experienced – paradoxically enough – a most spectacular growth. This time, contrary to the boom-bust characteristics of most growth spurts in Latin American economies, the industry continued expanding without a bust being in sight. It appears that the brand of capitalism that we find in many Latin American countries, which has been operating on the basis of a 'production-speculation' mentality, with little investment in long-term capital equipment, a focus on commerce and quick turnover and high short-term profits, generated an economic 'climate' propitious to the growth of a 'great risks – high profits' sector such as the drug industry: discouraging the development of more stable economic activities and encouraging speculation. In a situation of often weak state legitimacy, lack of accountability, inability to govern with a minimum degree of efficiency and failure to provide justice and personal security to the state's subjects, this brand of capitalism made a particular impact.

The illegitimate nature of the drug industry's business has greatly affected the market structure and strategies of the parties involved: producers and sellers, as well as consumers. The illegality of the business precludes resolving conflict through legal channels, which – given the risks and profits involved – almost automatically leads to the use of violent means. There are few ways other than violence or the threat of violence which in the end will ensure compliance in business deals. Its real or potential use has become an almost 'normal' element of market competition. The enormous money interests involved in the various phases of production and trafficking have led participants to defend their market positions at all costs.

In this chapter we will explore this issue of drug-related violence. We will analyse its role in the various phases of the cocaine commodity chain,[1] and the way in which those involved in the drug business have managed to undermine the moral fabric of the countries involved in production and trafficking, and have fuelled extensive networks of corruption while generating an explosive growth of criminal and non-criminal underground economic activities. The negative effects on the incipient processes of democratization are obvious. The lack of respect for the rule of law and the contempt for peaceful means of interest representation and mediation remain conditions that are frustrating democratic consolidation.

The cocaine industry: production and trafficking[2]

Coca cultivation is a very simple undertaking that needs little investment and/or agricultural experience. The shrub is grown mostly on small family plots that seldom exceed 2 hectares. In most regions it is cultivated in combination with other market crops and with food crops as part of as diversification strategy. Coca 'plantations' covering extensive areas are rare, and only in recent years has large-scale cultivation emerged in certain regions in Colombia under the protection of the guerrilla movements FARC and ELN, or of the paramilitary AUC. Most coca cultivation takes place in areas of recent colonization and expansion of the agricultural frontier. Coca has many advantages over other crops. It is easy to cultivate, harvest, pack and transport and, in most cases, it will have an assured nearby market. The production of coca paste – from which cocaine is produced – is easy to organize, often by the peasants themselves, and the production of cocaine itself is also not a very elaborate or difficult process.

The industry is, in fact, perfectly adapted to the conditions of an underdeveloped rural economy: the manufacturing process is not capital intensive, does not have large economics of scale, does not require large amounts of skilled labour, and uses production processes that are relatively easy to organize (Thoumi 1995: 2, 133). The threshold for new entrants to the industry is low in comparison to other legal industries. This explains the influx into the industry of people who do not belong to the traditional elites and who through this illegal business achieve an unexpected upward social mobility. At the same time these are often people from previously marginalized backgrounds with low social recognition. It also explains the flexibility with which the industry has operated in response to fluctuations in demand in consumer countries, to changes in drug control policies and to repressive operations by the military and law enforcement personnel. Repression activities generate the so-called balloon effect: wiping out coca in one region leads to an expansion of cultivation in another. In this way, suppression of coca production in Bolivia and Peru has led to an explosive growth of coca cultivation in Colombia.[3]

In coca production and cocaine trafficking major differences have developed in sector organization and market strategies between the source countries concerned. Until a decade ago, a certain division of labour was functioning between them. Colombia had specialized in the production of cocaine, on the basis of coca paste produced in Peru and Bolivia, and in trafficking. The situation since then has changed; Colombia has become independent of Peruvian and Bolivian coca growers and Peru has become a cocaine producer in its own right, as has Bolivia. In the latter country coca cultivation is up again after the demise of the *opción cero* (total eradication of illegally planted coca) strategy of the *Plan Dignidad*. Bolivia is now exporting cocaine to Europe through Brazil (*La Razón*, 7 February 2003).

In all three source countries[4] there has been growing interpenetration between the clandestine drug business and the formal economy. Many of those involved in drug production and trafficking are moving back and forth between the two sectors, and the intensification of repressive drug control policies has strengthened the tendency among those operating in both sectors to integrate activities.

At the same time, repression has resulted in the break-up of the larger trafficking organizations and the segmentation of production into smaller units that are technically simple and do not need major investment. Until the mid-1990s, the business was dominated by big drug lords *à la* Pablo Escobar. At present a smaller mafia-type drug elite still exists but their control over the business is hardly as powerful (Zaitch 2002: 54–7). Drug production has become accessible to a wider sector of micro- and small entrepreneurs. Trafficking has seen scores of new actors with heterogeneous backgrounds entering the sector, among them daring risk-takers. The use of violence to settle drug business conflicts among them has increased, now that the big drug lords, who at times managed to imposed some discipline in important sectors of the business, are either dead, in prison or have been extradited to the United States.

The growth of the drug industry: major conditioning factors

When confronting the question of why the drug industry has flourished in Latin America, and in particular in the Andean region, we come across a number of major factors: a) the general characteristics of economic development in the region and prevailing business practices; b) the crisis in the traditional agricultural sector; c) the role of the state, its structure and functioning; d) the structure of society in the region, its exclusionary nature, blocking upward social mobility for important segments of the population; and e) the geography of the region.

The drug industry – as a well-organized enterprise and not as some kind of ad hoc activity – dates back to the 1970s, although its spectacular take-off began in the mid-1980s. Its boom coincided with the worst economic crisis in Latin America's history. At the time, economic stagnation and financial crises were creating havoc among Latin American economies. The policies proposed to end this nightmare, and which ultimately were implemented, meant a radical break with the model of development that had been pursued by most Latin American countries – including the Andean nations – for the last fifty years (Vellinga 2003: 34–52; Smith 1998: 51–74). The restructuring of the economies along proposed neo-liberal lines – the so-called 'Washington Consensus' – has taken place under conditions of increasing globalization – that is, the objectives of these processes had to be realized increasingly within globally defined parameters and structures. The relations between state and civil society experienced significant changes, and so did the legitimacy and effectiveness of traditional structures of interest representation of groups and classes in many countries (Gwynne 2000: 149–62). Economy and society experienced unprecedented levels of informalization in response to massive lay-offs by the government and private companies. In Peru, the informal sector of the economy has been estimated as comprising 60 per cent of the economically active population. Informalization became a process affecting a wide number of sectors in society.

The buying power of working-class and middle-class family incomes has deteriorated to levels registered almost two decades before. Globalizing processes, in combination with neo-liberal policies, have polarized the income situation (Gwynne and Kay 2000: 141–56). The most severe instances of poverty were addressed by emergency social funds. They were managed, however, as in Peru, by the Ministry of the Presidency, and became an instrument of political patronage and clientelistic practices. Their contribution to structural solutions to the problem of urban and rural poverty has been small. The policies directed towards the agricultural sector mainly served the large and medium-sized producers. The *campesino* sector was considered to be lacking growth potential and was in fact abandoned by official politics, prolonging the crisis in the sector. Many left for the agricultural frontier on the eastern slopes of the Andes and in the Amazon where – as *colonos* – they became involved in coca cultivation.

As mentioned, the unstable nature of the growth model that we find in many Latin American countries encourages investment in short-term speculative endeavours instead of in long-term capital investments. The way in which Latin America has been integrated into the international economy, and the ensuing dependencies, explains – obviously – a considerable part of the phenomenon. Equally important, however, are domestic factors, several of which we have touched on above, such as: the strong dualisms in society and its exclusionary characteristics, the general socio-economic inequalities, the weakness of core institutions in the executive and judiciary, the rickety processes of democratization, the lack of a social and political consensus regarding the long-term objectives and means of national development, and the weak legitimacy of the state and its institutions. In interaction they have created a 'climate' that is very propitious for the growth of an illegal business, such as drug production and trafficking, laying the foundations for narco-capitalism. The institutions that would 'normally' settle conflicts and mediate between citizens in cases of disagreement in any field of daily life or business transactions are weak and do not operate properly, opening the door to violence.

The state in the Andean region – and in many other Latin American countries – has not been able to enforce its monopoly over the collective means of violence and coercion. This has been an overwhelming problem in Colombia. In Peru it has been less of a problem, and limited to specific regions, certainly after the defeat of the guerrilla movement Sendero Luminoso, which had aligned itself with narco interests. In Bolivia, there was surprisingly little violence accompanying the activities of the drug industry through the 1980s and 1990s until the implementation of the Plan Dignidad with its *opción cero* in recent years met with armed opposition by the coca growers (Gamarra 2003: 24–53).

In most coca-growing regions, the state has traditionally had a weak presence. This has created regional power vacuums that were filled by guerrilla organizations: Sendero Luminoso and Tupac Amaru in Peru and FARC, ELN and the paramilitary AUC in Colombia, in addition to grass-roots community organizations, such as the organizations the ex-miners in Bolivia took with them to the colonization areas in the Bolivian Amazon. The guerrilla movements in particular set clear limits to the presence of the state in the coca-growing regions. The peasant population in these situations has been caught between a rock and a hard place. They would like to have officially sanctioned conflict resolution systems, public services and a better infrastructure provided by the state (Thoumi 1995: 140; *Miami Herald*, 9 March 2003). But any state presence, however weak, has been fought mercilessly by the guerrillas, who assassinate anyone who would aspire to a state-sanctioned representative position, creating 'ungoverned spaces'. In Peru, in several instances, organized peasantry has been able to organize its own protection, fighting off the guerrillas. The complicated geography of the Andean region has traditionally helped the growth of illicit activities and has complicated their control. This applies in particular to Colombia, with its long tradition of smuggling and contraband activities, but also – to a lesser extent – to Peru and Bolivia. The repression of coca cultivation has pushed it back to even more inaccessible places in the Amazon forest where the peasants are even more vulnerable and subject to pressure by coca paste producers and traffickers.

The industry and its entrepreneurs

The cocaine industry is an agriculture-based industry and it shares some of its characteristics with the production of and trade in legal agricultural products (Thoumi 1995: 133). Advancing through the commodity chain, we go from large numbers of coca cultivations to fewer cocaine producers and fewer wholesalers, after which the product advances in the distribution channels with the number of sellers sharply increasing. Next to these similarities with other products, however, the differences dominate. The illegality of the business in all its phases has affected the market structure and the behaviour of the participants: producers, sellers and consumers (ibid.: 139). The risks that have to be taken into account at the various phases of production and trafficking attract a certain type of entrepreneur and 'style' the way business is being conducted and the deals that are being concluded. They will also involve a high level of violence. The interests at stake – in money terms – are often enormous. It is clear that the value of cocaine increases rapidly in a way proportionally related to the risks and the degree of monopoly at each stage of the chain (Reuter 1985: 79–95). Monopolizing trends obviously have some influence, but most of the value added should be attributed to risk-taking. A profit-maximizing strategy, consequently, will seek to reduce these risks. One can imagine what would happen to this mark-up structure if the trade were free and legal: it would collapse.

Illegality has turned violence into an indispensable element of market operations. It is being used in different ways (Thoumi 1995: 134):

a) as a means of ensuring compliance in business transactions;
b) as a means used to protect one's market or market share, to prevent infringement and/or breaks in 'the code of silence', through reports to law enforcement authorities;
c) as a means to conquer and defend sources of primary materials, precursor chemicals and smuggling routes;
d) as a means used to protect property obtained through unlaundered, illegally begotten funds against theft by competitors and/or armed groups;

e) as a means to pressure authorities or eliminate those in the law enforcement branch who present an acute danger of opposition to the interests of the drug industry.

To these sources of violence we have to add the repression that is being unleashed on coca-cultivating *campesinos* and traffickers by the forces of law enforcement and the army.

The use of violence results in forms of market competition that are very different from those in the world of legal business. Illegal businesses tend to combine economic, political and military resources, with the latter in a decisive role. Violence and trust are the two important elements in pulling off illegal transactions.

In the era of the so-called 'cartels' this violence was massive. The interests were also enormous. The term 'cartel' is confusing because in the Colombian case its meaning deviates from its normal definition in economics. Here it denotes an organization that coordinates the export interests of a number of individual cocaine producers, with the objective of minimizing risk while providing insurance in the case of seizure. These producers grew into powerful organizations, corrupting, threatening and assassinating politicians and law enforcement personnel, while building intricate social and political support networks to protect their interests. The most famous were the well-known 'cartels' of Medellín, led by Pablo Escobar, and the one from Calí led by the Rodriguez Orijuela brothers. The Medellín cartel led a frontal attack on the state, using massive violence in defence of its interests in production and trafficking, as well as in opposition to the agreement reached with the USA concerning the extradition of major traffickers.[5]

Who were these drug lords, what was their background, and what were their business practices? The most famous *narcos* originated from Medellín, and developed their business in a milieu badly hit by an economic crisis that led important segments of the working class to enter informal activities of an illicit nature (Labrousse 1993: 285ff; Gugliotta and Leen 1990).

Pablo Escobar was the son of the overseer on a hacienda owned by one of the great Medellín families. He started his career as a taxi driver, but soon discovered that the real money was to be found elsewhere. Car theft and kidnapping gave him the working capital that enabled him to enter the cocaine business. From the beginning, he was known for his ruthlessness. Anybody standing in his way – police, judges, competitors, politicians, and even government ministers – was killed. He was the undisputed leader of the Medellín 'cartel', dominating the trafficking phase of the industry, leaving cocaine production to the Ochoa brothers and the 'military' element to Rodriguez Gacha, 'El Mexicano', responsible for the wave of assassinations that hit Medellín at the beginning of the 1990s. The fierceness of the attack on the Colombian state has been explained by analysts as revenge on a societal elite that in secret had often participated in a small way in the trade, but on the other hand barred the trafficker's access to elite organizations, educational institutions and political positions. In response, the drug lords organized their own social and political circles, and compensated through extreme manifestations of *narcoriqueza*: Escobar invested widely in projects of popular interest – housing, soccer teams and other endeavours aimed at Medellín's poor strata.

Carlos Lehder, son of a German engineer who came to Colombia in 1925, was an associate of Escobar. In 1979 he bought a small island in the Bahamas, had an airstrip made and started to fly cocaine into Florida. His business became involved in the Miami drug war of the 1980s. Back in Colombia he was involved in the organization of an unsuccessful national and political party. He was eventually captured and extradited to the United States. The Ochoa brothers have a distinct background. Their father founded the faculty of veterinary medicine at the University of Medellín and owned a farm where he held racehorses, which would provide the contact with Escobar later on.

The Medellín traffickers used a distinct confrontational strategy towards the state, characterized by extreme violence, which would eventually cause their demise. The Calí traffickers operated differently, using less violence, opting rather for co-option, corruption and negotiation, employing violence only as a last resort (Clawson and Lee 1996: 165ff). The Rodriguez Orijuela brothers of the Calí 'cartel', before entering the drug business, accumulated their basic fortune through car theft and kidnapping. Their trafficking activities enabled them to become active entrepreneurs, using the proceeds from the drug trade to build an economic imperium in Colombia. They built a chain of 250 pharmacies, which facilitated at the same time the import of the chemical precursors needed for cocaine production. In addition, they owned hotels, supermarkets, radio-taxi companies, laboratories, airlines, banks and credit institutions, radio stations and soccer clubs.

The activities of the 'cartels' in Medellín and Calí have led to the emergence of a whole class of new rich, but Medellín 'society', in spite of participating now and then in their business deals, has refused to accept them in their social circles, much to the traffickers' frustration. One of the main objectives of the drug entrepreneurs has been assimilation into mainstream society in order to protect and legitimize their property, legalize at least part of their wealth, obtain an economic status and social recognition comparable to those of other rich people in the legal circuit, and allow them to participate in the political process and gain access to public office. In short, they wished to become respectable citizens, possibly also with political power, which would enable them to use an alternative to violence. The fact that they were snubbed continuously by the traditional elites explains the fury with which they directed their aggression towards the state. This phenomenon has been strongest in Colombia, because of the strength of its drug elites (Thoumi 1995: 141ff). In other countries, however, we observe a similar tendency among the drug lords to aspire to respectability over the objections of traditional elites. Remember the spectacular case of Bolivian drug lord Roberto Suarez Gomez, who, as the story goes, in 1984 offered to pay off two-thirds of Bolivia's foreign debt (which at the time stood at 3 billion US dollars) in exchange for government recognition of him as a legitimate entrepreneur. Suarez had formed, with other family members and friends, the largest drug trafficking group in Bolivia (Painter 1994: 30, 32). This way of operating in close-knit, family-oriented, geographical units has been very typical of Bolivian traffickers. It has also reduced the violence. The Suarez clan started to produce cocaine in Bolivia in the mid-1980s. Until then, base and paste had been flown out to Colombia, where they were refined into cocaine. Bolivians were not involved in distribution, which required expertise in smuggling, marketing and international connections. This changed, and Bolivian *narcos* began exporting cocaine to Europe.

In the 1980s and early 1990s the Bolivian drug lords always enjoyed protection at the highest level of government. Especially under the military governments of the 1970s and 1980s, an almost symbiotic relationship developed between the state and cocaine traffickers, in contrast to the situation that existed in Colombia. From the second half of the 1990s on, the cocaine business has been very much on the defensive, with scores of traffickers arrested. This process has involved relatively little violence. The eradication of coca by force, however, which started in 1996, met with strong resistance from the coca growers, leading to violent encounters with the drug combat unit of the army, UMOPAR. Opposition to eradication has now united in a political movement, led by the president of the coca growers' association. They achieved a strong showing in the 2002 parliamentary elections. The cocaine trade is presently controlled by smaller and bolder competitors confronting more effective law enforcement. In the past corrupt military governments coordinated interests with a single large trafficking organization. The present democratic governments are facing at least fifteen organizations that have developed significant transnational connections (Gamarra 2003).

In Peru, the drug traffickers enjoyed protection in the 1990s from President

Fujimori's security chief Vladimiro Montesinos. In those years drug-fed corruption became massive and systematic. It was directed from the highest levels of government and formed a network including the electoral college, the judiciary, the legislature, the financial sector and the military. The network is estimated to have managed $264 million annually, provided by all sectors of the industry: production, trafficking, consumption, money laundering and trade in precursor chemicals (Valderrama and Cabieses 2003: 55–73). In Peru too the drug industry has restructured through the disintegration of the 'cartels' and a regrouping in smaller and more flexible organizations. These have maintained intense competition between themselves, generating the usual amount of violence, which, however, has never reached the levels that we observe in Colombia. Also, the activities of the guerrilla movements Sendero Luminoso and MRTA in the coca-growing zones in the Alta Huallaga in the 1980s were accompanied by violence that has not been since repeated.

The repressive strategies directed towards production and trafficking have often been equally violent. They include harshly repressive actions inflicted on coca-cultivating peasants by the armed forces, the jailing and extraditing of traffickers, involuntary eradication of illicit crops – including aerial spraying (which has severely affected the *campesinos'* food production in Colombia) – production and marketing controls of chemical precursors, anti-money-laundering campaigns, seizure and confiscation of assets, etc. In Colombia, repressive strategies have had a double purpose: to eradicate coca and poppy cultivation and to combat the guerrilla movements FARC and ELN, which are financing themselves with 'taxes' on production and trafficking in areas under their control. The repressive campaigns, often conducted in coordination with AUC's paramilitary forces, have led to a savagery that reminds one of the darkest days of *La Violencia*. Indiscriminate spraying of crops, in particular in regions where the government does not have a strong presence, has made the peasants approach the guerrillas for protection and has forced coca cultivation deeper and deeper into the Amazon forest, with disastrous environmental consequences (Lee 2003).

Business practices in the drug industry

Business practices in trafficking have changed over the years, and so has the use of massive violence in confronting law enforcement and the state. The old generation of cocaine entrepreneurs that dominated the trade in the 1980s and early 1990s, and headed the so-called cartels, are not in business any more. They are either dead, in prison – in the USA or in the source country – or retired, their assets seized, invested or deposited in foreign bank accounts (Zaitch 2002:

54-7). In the course of the 1990s, general changes in international trade also affected the way the cocaine market was being organized. Flexibility, the development of a capacity for immediate response to changes in demand, transportation, distribution and law enforcement activity became the basic criteria in organizing the trade. The liberalization of international trade has facilitated the penetration of new markets while reducing risk, achieving economies of scale and modernizing the logistics of supply. It has also permitted easier coordination with the underground economy in countries overseas. The new entrepreneurs are more low profile, with a restrained lifestyle, and no criminal records. They operate in total anonymity, refrain from using bank accounts that run the risk of being traced and investigated,[6] don't use telephones or cell phones for business and prefer personal messengers to modern means of communication. Their new organizations are small and cell-like. Personnel are often recruited ad hoc as part of complex contracting and subcontracting schemes. Coordination with other organizations takes place on the basis of the special knowledge of logistics, communications, security, money laundering, investments, etc., that each may possess. Large-scale stable organizations are avoided in order to reduce vulnerability in the face of repression and active law enforcement. This does not preclude the possibility of cooperation among traffickers in order to co-insure shipments, exchange loads or share intelligence.[7] The breaking up of the 'cartels' put an end to a small number of businesses whose economic power could give them access to the highest level of government organizations (still the case in Mexico) and with a capacity to use violence on such a massive scale that the state would be undermined (as in Colombia). On the other hand, this policy has created in Colombia an estimated three hundred small refining and trafficking organizations whose activities are much more difficult to trace. Among them some fifty organizations stand out.[8] They control the export of cocaine to northern markets and function in practice as an oligopolist sector with often savage internal competition. In the USA, the development of cocaine or heroin distribution networks was helped by the presence of large Colombian immigrant communities in the big cities. The formation of these networks and their exclusive claim to markets and market share was facilitated by the proclivity of Colombians to use extreme violence against competing trafficking organizations, often killing wives and children as well as principals. The 'drug wars' of the 1980s in southern Florida give a good example of how far some would go to protect their own 'turf'. These operations were in contrast to those of the American mafiosi, 'who performed their assassinations with decency, never injuring the family of the victim and sent flowers to the funeral' (Gugliotta and Leen 1990: 106-29; Zaitch 2002: 34).

With the new, flexible ways of conducting business under the conditions imposed by illegality, which call for a loose organization minimizing risk of detection, many different types of small enterprise may be interconnected in trying to conclude a deal. Some of these enterprises will be short-lived, single operations; others may endure for a longer period of time. In many cases, perfectly legal services (for example, in transport, money laundering and investment, legal assistance, etc.) will be contracted. At the same time, the business may be extended into society by offering people outside the organization – often friends, politicians or civil servants – the opportunity to participate in an export venture as a favour. These new cocaine enterprises are heterogeneous in their structure and operation, and consist of constantly changing networks bound together through precarious and variable transactions and functioning on the basis of trust (*confianza*) and the threat of violence. There is little that makes the term 'cartel', with its suggestion of large, stable, bureaucratic structures, a plausible way of describing these business operations.

The old-style drug lords, with their elaborate trafficking organizations, are still running the business in Mexico. They depend extensively on political and police protection. In fact, in many cases leading politicians have been directly involved in the illegal trade, often even controlling it. For decades, drug trafficking was viewed as just another profitable business that could be run by politicians belonging to the PRI, taking advantage of the political position they held (Astorga 2003: 110–28). Leaders of important trafficking groups had no interest at all in organizing themselves in politics or in confronting the state. Most traffickers headed stable organizations that had been in existence for decades. This picture has changed as a result of the defeat of the PRI at the polls in 2000. Drug trafficking has since gained some autonomy from politics. At the same time however, this has made it more vulnerable to law enforcement, while the use of violence has increased to the point where the structural mediations between the political sector and drug trafficking have become blurred (ibid.: 110–28).

Conclusions

Violence, next to trust, is a 'normal' element of market strategies in illegal business transactions. This applies not only to the drug business but to any kind of illicit transaction. These elements have taken on major dimensions because of the interests involved, however. The size of the profits in the drug trade is often almost beyond imagination, and the pressure to enforce compliance in business transactions is considerable. Colombia presents an extreme example of such a development. The country has a tradition of more than a hundred years of endemic violence. Over the years, the state has not been able to establish legitimacy as an institution that indicates to the wider population what is right and what is wrong. A wide gap has grown between legally proscribed and socially accepted behaviour. For long periods the state has in fact functioned as an executive committee of the bourgeoisie, and, in these terms, Colombia has probably moved closest to Marx's definition of the role of the state under capitalism. The generalized lawlessness has included extremely high levels of violence, a phenomenon that has worsened as a result of the mushrooming growth of the drug industry. Production areas have often been out of the state's reach. Basic public services at the local level – the fulfilment of which under normal conditions would fall to the state – have been taken care of by the guerrillas and/or community movements.

The long-standing institutional weakness of most Latin American states, the strength of personalist and clientelist practices coupled with institutionalized corruption and ineffective judicial systems have made them largely defenceless against the power of the drug traffickers. The gaps in the reach of the state's governance – which increased in size and number as a result of state withdrawal in the 1980s and early 1990s – were filled by NGOs, grass-roots organizations and other types of social movement, but also by organized criminal activity. The latter may link up with international criminal organizations that give them access to international markets, offer ways to launder the proceeds of their illicit activities and give them access to arms. This has been the case in Colombia, where the Russian mafia has been suspected of linking up with the guerrillas of the FARC in an arms-for-drugs trade. In other countries (Brazil, Mexico, Paraguay, and Caribbean states) Russian transnational organized crime has been shown to be present, in all cases in connection with the drugs trade (Bagley 2003: 280–306). These crime syndicates are very powerful and aggressive. They are well versed in modern technology and business practices that allow them to operate efficiently across international borders. The strong growth in their activities may announce a new phase in the development of the drug industry, with a resurgence of powerful drug 'cartels', this time, however, managed by transnational organized crime syndicates of eastern European and Italian origin, feeding new cycles of the violence that for long has been an inseparable part of market strategies in the drug business.

Notes

1 For the concept of the commodity chain, see Gereffi, Korzeniewicz and Korzeniewicz (1994: 1–14). For its application to the cocaine trade, see Wilson and Zambrano 1994: 297–316.

2 For general information on the cocaine industry, see: Smith (1992); Bagley and Walker (1994); Painter (1994); La Mond Tullis (1995); Toro (1995); Thoumi (1995); Clawson and Lee (1996); Joyce and Malamud (1998); Leons and Sanabría (1997); Lloyd Griffith (1997); Lloyd Griffith (2002); Menzel (1996 and 1997); Labrousse (2000); Vellinga (2004).

3 Coca cultivation in Bolivia after the eradication campaign under Plan Dignidad has been picking up steam again and covered approximately 20,000 hectares again in 2002; according to CIA estimates Colombia had, at the end of 2002, 169,800 hectares under coca, Peru 90,400 hectares. *Sources*: *La Razón* (La Paz), 26 February 2003; *Guardian* (UK), 22 February 2003, *Washington Post*, 28 February 2003.

4 For Bolivia, see Painter (1994), for Peru Cotler (1999) and Morales (1989), for Colombia Thoumi (1995).

5 An excellent discussion on the use of the term 'cartel' can be found in Thoumi (1995: 143) and in Zaitch (2002: 49–50).

6 In August 2001, Colombian police discovered US$35 million in cash stashed in the walls of two Bogotá apartments waiting to be laundered and invested (*El Tiempo*, 25 August 2001). Increasingly the proceeds of the drugs trade are kept in cash transported in suitcases or strapped to the body of the traveller. In April 2002 a passenger was detained at Calí airport transporting US$1.3 million in this way (*El Tiempo*, 11 April 2002).

7 Zaitch offers a convincing account of these new business practices based on field research in Colombia and the Netherlands; the Netherlands and Spain are the most important gateways to the European cocaine market.

8 'La nueva generación de la Mafia', *El Tiempo*, 9 September 2001.

6 | Armed actors in the Colombian conflict

FRANCISCO LEAL BUITRAGO

This chapter discusses the formation and development of the armed actors involved in the Colombian conflict. It is divided into three parts. First, I deal with the period of distorted capitalist modernization (1958–90). The second part addresses the stage at which these distortions became explicit (1990–98), and the final part the outcomes, which may be described as a general social crisis (1998–2003).

Deficient political administration, guerrilla consolidation, and the rise of the paramilitaries, 1958–90

The bipartisan coalition regime of the National Front (1958–74) enabled the armed forces to subordinate the liberal-democratic institutions shaped by the process of modern state formation. The downplaying of political ideology within society, stimulated by the distribution of the state bureaucracy between the Liberal and Conservative parties, permitted the military to acquire political autonomy in the handling of public order. This handling became strategic as the armed confrontation between the emerging guerrillas and the armed forces advanced, widened and diversified.

The timid political guidelines for the military's role in society, formulated at the beginning of the National Front, were neither reviewed nor updated by the civil authorities. For that reason, the military high command adopted them in improvised fashion, in accordance with their perception of the state of public order, influenced by an anti-communist disposition, as well as by the North American political-military conception and the South American doctrine of national security.

During the National Front, the political leadership occupied itself mainly with the electoral consolidation of the bipartisan coalition. In contrast, social protests did not have much institutional impact within the political class, especially because the new regime did not allow new arenas for opposition. This protest became a matter of public order, handled exclusively by the military and the police. In addition to the guerrillas, those who merely tried to raise opposition by peaceful means were depicted as potential or real enemies by the system.

The insurgent movement was made up of various groups. The pro-Soviet

Fuerzas Armadas Revolucionarias de Colombia (FARC) was created in 1964 with help from the Communist Party, as a result of harassment suffered by peasant self-defence groups at the hands of the army. The pro-Cuban Ejército de Liberación Nacional (ELN) was born in 1965 out of the student movement and the union of oil workers. The pro-Chinese Ejército Popular de Liberación (EPL) was created in 1969 owing to a split within the FARC. The nationalist Movimiento 19 de Abril (M-19) was formed in 1974 by the radical wing of the ANAPO party, motivated by the electoral fraud perpetrated on 19 April 1970 on its presidential candidate, the former dictator Gustavo Rojas (1953–57) (Pizarro and Peñaranda 1991; Pizarro 1991).

As the ideological differences between the two National Front parties withered away and the anti-communist ideology spread throughout the military, the concept of national security began replacing that of national defence. The national security concept presumed a threat from national and international forces connected to communism, unlike that of national defence, whose motive was to safeguard the sovereignty of the state, principally against neighbouring countries. National defence became the means with which to guarantee security, and in this way was also involved in the anti-communist struggle.

In spite of the continuity of the military objectives of pacifying and defeating the guerrillas and communism, and of the persistence of certain patterns of military institutional behaviour, the military were subjected to improvisation. Each military minister had the chance to define his own policy. Yet there was a normative pattern: the exceptional constitutional measure facilitated by the constitution of 1886, commonly known as a 'state of siege', was the principal resource with which public disorder was handled. Its indiscriminate usage became prevalent in the mid-1960s, when it began to be employed more to repress the popular movements than to combat armed violence. The consequence was the de facto abolition of the rule of law. Until the promulgation of the 1991 constitution, Colombia lived entirely under this regime (Gallón Giraldo 1979; Orozco Abad 1992).

Another normative pattern was the National Defence Statute, passed in 1965 (Ministerio de Defensa Nacional 1970). It was important because no other strategic military directive was implemented during the remainder of the twentieth century, and it was elaborated under the inspiration of North American security thinking and the Latin American doctrine of national security. One of its articles defined and classified the bearing of arms. By granting to civil defence organizations the same permission to bear arms for private use as that held by the institutions of the state, a way was opened to a problem that has grown since the 1980s with the proliferation of paramilitary organizations and of self-defence groups under the control of narco-traffickers. Law 48 of 1968 opened the path to this phenomenon, and then turned the national defence decree of 1965 and its regulation into a permanent norm.

During the National Front, the political leadership of the country established in practice a dissociation of state functions, in accordance with its interests and a limited perspective. State policy remained segmented: the technocrats remained in charge of managing macroeconomics, the government coalitions handled partisan politics in a clientelist fashion, and the military command managed military issues. From its beginning, the military was convinced that the guerrilla conflict had to be dealt with only by armed force, since any other consideration implied interfering in politics. Ideological bipolarity in international politics was not considered appropriate, since confronting communism was regarded as a patriotic duty.

The installation of the government of Alfonso López (1974–78) coincided with the final phase of the army's Operation Anorí, which succeeded in destroying the greater part of the ELN. This organization would not recover until many years later (Broderick 2000). The López government did not make any great efforts to alter the bureaucratization and bipartisan clientelism that characterized state administration, nor did it make good on its electoral platform of opening up democracy in the country. These circumstances, together with the precarious economic situation, contributed to creating popular discontent which, through extensive mobilization, culminated in the national strike of September 1977, paralysing most activities in the country. At the end of that year, the generals and admirals of the Bogotá garrison publicly demanded from the president emergency measures with which to tackle public disorder. The president never had to deal with the issue, for his mandate ended (Leal Buitrago 1995).

The government of Julio C. Turbay (1978–82) began with the promulgation of the legislative decree known as the Security Statute. With this norm, which imposed a state of siege, and with the endorsement of the president, the military institutions extended their autonomy in the management of public order to unprecedented levels, leading to the thorough implementation of the national security doctrine. The repression exerted by the armed institutions of the state was expanded to the cities, without letting up on the long-term pressure in the countryside. Besides the guerrilla organization M-19, these policies also affected the middle classes, particularly intellectuals, who were suspected of being the architects and transmitters of communist ideology (Leal Buitrago 1994).

The M-19 was the only guerrilla organization whose activities were primarily urban, which contributed to their becoming the principal target for the army. The confrontation with the army led to guerrilla actions that achieved enormous publicity impact, such as the robbery of arms from a military armoury in Bogotá on New Year's Eve 1979, and the taking of the embassy of the Dominican Republic at the start of 1980, in which sixteen diplomats were held hostage for two months. The military operation undertaken after the first of these actions led to the capture of the M-19 leadership, who were subsequently put on trial in a much-publicized court-martial at the end of the Turbay government (ibid.).

The government of Belisario Betancur (1982–86) inaugurated a peace process, beginning with recognition of the political character of the guerrilla groups by means of an amnesty law. The immediate beneficiaries were members of the M-19 leadership, who had previously been condemned by a military court (Ramírez and Restrepo 1989). For that reason the military blamed the president for having frustrated their success, and for having sown the seeds of a strengthening of the guerrilla movement.

With the murder of the minister of justice, Rodrigo Lara Bonilla, in April 1984, there began a campaign of terrorism with which the narco-traffickers tried to end the actions of the state, which, although timid, had until that moment had gone against them. But government action against the narco-traffickers and their terrorism was not consistent. The erratic official conduct continued until the subsequent government, and culminated in 1989 with the 'declaration of war' against this illicit business and its violence in the aftermath of the assassination of Senator Luis C. Galán.[1]

The army's actions against the guerrillas, buried in a sort of truce ever since the start of the peace process, together with the political and military ambiguities of M-19, led to the breaking of the truce by this guerrilla group in the middle of 1985. This did not happen with the FARC because this organization based its peace strategy on the formation of the Unión Patrótica (UP), a political party connected with the Communist Party. Nevertheless, the UP could not separate itself from the influence of the armed movement, which contributed to its subsequent failure and annihilation by the paramilitaries. The ELN and the EPL, however, rejected the government's politics of peace from the very start.

Towards the end of 1985, the M-19 committed its greatest political error: it seized the Palace of Justice in Bogotá. This episode had a bloody outcome in which more than a hundred people, including magistrates, guerrillas and visitors, were burnt to death. This was the result of the guerrillas' error of judgement – they had expected a moderate reaction from the military owing to the importance of the hostages. In fact, it was the political background of the battle which carried more weight in the military offensive – so the army was given a unique opportunity to underscore its political autonomy *vis-à-vis* the president and the M-19 at the same time. In this way the military recovered the initiative in handling matters relating to public order. During Betancur's last months as president, the peace process faced setbacks as the level of anti-guerrilla military actions escalated.

The peace policy was suspended for much of the time during the government of Virgilio Barco (1986–90). The ceasefire that the previous government had granted to the FARC was formally maintained, until an ambush against the army brought it to an end in 1987. The guerrillas succeeded in extending their actions by multiplying the fronts on which they operated, and through the formation of an alliance under the umbrella of the Coordinadora Guerrillera Simón Bolívar.[2] The failure of the government's attempts to contain the guerrillas added to the mass mobilizations and strikes that Barco faced from the very start of his term in office. At the end of 1988, however, the army opted to take advantage of M-19's position in order to advance negotiations aimed at convincing the guerrilla organization to demobilize, owing to the heavy political and military attrition that it had suffered. This situation was in contrast to the intransigent attitude of the ELN and the FARC. This process with the M-19 reached a favourable conclusion at the start of 1990 (Pardo Rueda 1996).

The Barco government had to confront a mounting dirty war – above all the extermination of the UP – which was the result of the expansion of narco-trafficking, and the support it provided to the formation of paramilitary groups. In 1988 the level of paramilitary actions increased, and took the form of massacring farmers and murdering judges, magistrates, journalists, police and public figures, of which among the most prominent was the general prosecutor of the nation. Towards the end of this period, Senator Galán, a strong presidential candidate, was assassinated in the midst of the declared war on narco-trafficking. Also assassinated during the presidential campaigns were candidates of the left, such as Bernardo Jaramillo of the UP and Carlos Pizarro of the M-19.[3] Thus the defenders of privilege in Colombian society erased from the political scene representatives of the non-violent left, and reinforced the intransigence of those committed to armed struggle.

The diversification and expansion of the violence placed the issue of the military's inefficiency in managing public order on the agenda. Added to this was the matter of links between military officers and paramilitary groups. These circumstances enhanced the political capacity of the executive and other branches of public power *vis-à-vis* the military, and contributed to the process by which peace with the M-19 could be made. In 1987, a Supreme Court ruling put to an end the authority of military courts to try civilians; and a civilian was named as the attorney delegated to the armed forces. In 1989, the general prosecutor of the nation overturned the impediments against the public ministry's ability to investigate and sanction members of the armed forces in active service; and a judgment by the court obliged soldiers who had committed crimes while off duty to be tried by civilian judges.[4]

The greatest political challenge of the Barco government was the so-called 'war of the president' against narco-trafficking, which was pursued in the final year of his mandate. More than simply a war against the business of drug trafficking, Barco's campaign focused on one of its manifestations: the violence that came to be known as 'narco-terrorism'. The president sought to involve in his war as many social forces as possible, but few responded to his call. Even within the military there was reluctance, owing to the fact that a great many were already linked to the narco-traffickers. Even so, the armed forces entered the 'war'.

Although the USA considers drug trafficking to be a threat to its security, in Colombia this preoccupation does not exist: it was 'narco-terrorism' and not narco-trafficking per se which was considered to be dangerous. Even so, Colombian governments instigated measures against other aspects of drug trafficking, to a great extent as a result of American pressures (Tokatlian 2000). The conflict with narco-trafficking during the government of Barco contributed to the final incorporation of the M-19 into civil life, in addition to making it possible to initiate dialogue with the EPL.

The failure of the civil control of military policy and the strengthening of armed actors, 1990–98

Although the drafting of a new constitution failed to take advantage of the opportunity to make changes in military matters, the government of César Gaviria (1990–94) nevertheless advanced important reforms in matters of defence and security, which transformed the traditions laid down since 1958. This government sought to change the relationship between the military and the civil institutions of the state, and to develop a new strategy of security. With the creation of the role of presidential secretary for defence and security, the presidency assumed the political role that previously had always been granted to the ministry of national defence.

In the first year of his government, the president appointed the secretary of the Council for Defence and Security as the new minister of national defence. For the first time since 1953, a civilian assumed a ministerial office that had previously been reserved for generals in active service. In this way, the problems of defence and security were explicitly recognized as problems of a political rather than a military nature, despite the fact that the handling of these matters leaned heavily on the armed institutions of the state.

The work of the presidential secretary was oriented towards the pursuit of the principal actors in the violence: guerrillas, narco-traffickers and paramilitaries. It helped elaborate the policy of handing over to the appropriate judicial authorities drug dealers who gave themselves up, but its main achievement was the formulation of the 'National Strategy against the Violence', which was promulgated in May 1991.[5]

The policy of combating the armed actors consisted of the creation of legal incentives and guarantees that made it possible to bring them to justice as delinquents so that they might be tried and punished. Its implementation fell to the district attorney – one of the institutions created by the 1991 constitution – which gave this policy the character of permanence. The strategy was based on the recognition of different forms of violence, and the need to treat them in different yet coordinated ways.

From the very start the new government began dialogues with the guerrilla groups of the Ejército Popular de Liberación (EPL), Partido Revolucionario de los Trabajadores (PRT), and the indigenous Quintín Lame group. In spite of these steps aimed at a political solution, in December 1990, on the day of the elections for the Constituent Assembly, the army captured Casaverde, the headquarters of the FARC. With the taking of Casaverde, the government had subordinated its political vision to its short-term military interests. The operation achieved only a territorial occupation, and the military satisfaction of having regained internal sovereignty after seven years of being denied control of this location as a result of the inertia of the 1984 ceasefire. In the medium term any advantage obtained was lost owing to the offensive launched by the Coordinadora Guerrillera in January 1991. After the failure of the supposed military objective of exterminating the secretariat of the FARC, the army was perceived to be harassing the guerrillas in search of short-term successes so as to make up for its loss of image. All the media were critical of the military's inability to restrain the guerrilla assaults. Under these circumstances, the government announced its decision to begin an unconditional dialogue, and consequently the guerrilla offensive eased.[6]

In 1991, in the middle of the promulgation of the new constitution, the dialogue suffered difficulties. In 1992 the difficulties were prolonged, with intermittent escalations in guerrilla actions, and the transfer of the negotiations from Venezuela to Mexico. The military competition between the army and the guerrillas, and the dismay felt by participants in resuming talks, culminated in the stagnation of the dialogue.

During most of this process the policy of bringing criminals to justice had little to do with the peace process. The first to benefit from the policy were the delinquents from the Medellín cartel, who gave themselves up between 1990 and 1991. But the subjugation of the drug baron Pablo Escobar was the main objective of the government, and fulfilling it would be proof of the success of the new measures (Leal Buitrago 2001).

After the surrender of Escobar, the government responded to those who questioned the policy of bringing criminals to justice that narco-terrorism had been controlled, and the most important drug baron was behind bars. But in July 1992 an event took place which had great political impact during the government of Gaviria: the escape of Pablo Escobar from his 'maximum security' prison. As information became available, the country came to know in detail the bureaucratic inconsistencies and faults that facilitated the escape.

The seriousness of the escape lay in the failure of the submission policy, intended to persuade drug barons to give themselves up in exchange for a guarantee that they would serve their prison terms in Colombia rather than face extradition to the USA. The president insisted on its validity, but he also put a price on the heads of the fugitives and demanded their unconditional recapture. The so-called Bloque de Búsqueda (Search Bloc) was formed, a unit consisting of military and police, many of them trained in the USA, and with the support of the security institutions of that country. Repressive enthusiasm mingled with talk of 'war' with the guerrillas, already stirred up by the difficulty of taking measures different from those employed by the military. Guerrillas and narco-traffickers (at least the Medellín cartel) were therefore given the same official indiscriminate treatment (Sánchez Gómez 1990).

For the government, the major problem in the matter of security during 1993 was the hunt for Pablo Escobar. In October, after nearly fourteen months of activity, the expenses of the Bloque de Búsqueda rose to over 10 billion pesos. It was undeniable that the defensive apparatus of the drug baron had suffered serious damage. In an unexpected action, Pablo Escobar was killed in Medellín by a group of the Bloque de Búsqueda in December 1993. This event served to compensate somewhat for the prolonged inefficiency and the high costs in economic terms and in lives of what was the most publicized armed operation in the modern history of the country.[7]

At the beginning of 1993, the Corriente de Renovación Socialista (CRS), a dissident group from the ELN, reiterated its desire to enter into negotiations with the government. This situation reawakened the hope that the government might revive the political initiative with which it had initiated its security policy. But the declaration by the minister of defence promising a quick military defeat for the guerrillas pointed in an altogether different direction.[8] It was evident that the official martial vision that had been provoked fourteen months earlier, with the declaration of 'total war', persisted. The CRS agreed to demobilize, but the government did not show much willingness to negotiate, as indicated by its lack of interest in the use of political means to achieve peace.

Although it is undeniable that the decision to treat guerrillas in the same way as narco-traffickers and common criminals can be explained in part by their political degradation, the new strategy showed that the government had not understood the changes that had occurred in the so-called subversion. For example, the rise in extortion and kidnappings demonstrated the eagerness with which the guerrillas sought to obtain resources to compete against the state with military means. Likewise, the FARC and the ELN had initiated an exceptional campaign of repoliticization and legitimation through the control of local 'politics and administrative entities'. The political class became aware of the problem of 'subversive political infiltration' in the popular election of mayors, combined with the absence of state social action in many municipalities.[9]

In spite of the errors committed by the Gaviria government in security matters, there were some successes in the final months of his term in office. In April 1994, the final agreement for the demobilization of the CRS was signed. Likewise, the following month a peace and demobilization agreement was signed with the Popular Metropolitan Militias of the Aburrá valley [the valley in which the city of Medellín is located – eds].[10]

From 1993, the government of the USA pressed the Colombian state to expand its fight against drug trafficking, in particular against the Calí cartel. The government therefore had to abandon the established differentiation between terrorism and narco-trafficking – a continuation of the policy that was implemented at the end of the previous four-year presidential term – and had to target the remaining manifestations of that illicit activity, which until then had received secondary attention.

In 1994, the presidential campaign of Ernesto Samper took place in a period in which the ongoing interference of the narco-traffickers in national politics was criticized. But the fact was that the connections between narco-traffickers and politicians continued through clientelism and corruption. The five or more million dollars that the Calí cartel contributed to the presidential campaign of Samper, with the aim of buying support to prevent extradition, and to maintain a sense of complacency towards its activities, served to detonate a new crisis. From the beginning, this scandalous situation stamped a seal of weakness upon the government of Samper (1994–98). The crisis became more acute in April 1995, when the district attorney reopened a case (archived under the number 8,000) because of numerous indications that businesses owned by the Calí cartel had paid the campaign costs of a number of congressional members belonging to Samper's party (Leal Buitrago 1996).

The central executive, with the exception of the armed forces, served as a shield in defence of the president. After the unsuccessful attempt of the Gaviria government to enable civilian authorities to direct military policy, the military had recovered the initiative in the handling of public order. The 'total war' against the Medellín cartel and the guerrillas, unleashed in the final years of Gaviria's term in office, facilitated such a recovery. The first two civilian ministers of defence (the second under Samper) assumed responsibility for military decisions, but they were unable to counteract the autonomy of the armed forces in charge of executing them.

The guerrilla offensive that was unleashed with the outbreak of the political crisis confirmed the inefficiency of the military and the degree of improvisation in the handling of public order. This situation persisted owing to the setbacks suffered against the guerrillas during the final two years of the Samper government. A presidency in crisis eventually came to be the normal state of things from May 1997 onwards, after the resignation of the attorney general who had initiated the reopening of case number 8,000 with the tacit support of the USA. With this further intensification of the crisis, the nation's idea of forcing the fall of President Samper was finally abandoned.

The political crisis and the consequent absence of a peace policy also affected military control of public order, in addition to stimulating guerrilla groups to increase their actions and expand their sphere of influence. The public order situation worsened with the expansion of the paramilitary groups, and the unification of their objectives at national level through the creation of the Autodefensas Unidas de Colombia (United Self-Defence Groups of Colombia, AUC) in April 1997. The AUC was born out of the operational fusion of various groups located in distinct parts of the country. The government's preoccupation with riding out its own crisis led to a lack of attention to security requirements, resulting in its losing legitimacy in the eyes of the military, which consequently ignored the government's decision to confront the paramilitaries (Melo 1990; Medina 1990).

The most important effect of the political crisis on the military, although indirect, was its successive misfortunes in the war against the guerrillas from 1996 onwards. The end of the Samper government in 1998 left behind hundreds of dead, and around three hundred members of the armed forces captured, in addition to the meagre results obtained from large but extremely expensive military operations.[11]

Owing to these setbacks, the military began to lose the autonomy they had obtained in the first twenty months of the Samper government. Faced with this, the senior commanders thought little about reviewing their institutional structure with the aim of identifying and changing the factors that ran counter to organizational order, tactics, strategy and ideology. This chaotic situation led to numerous public calls for the government to recognize the urgency of restructuring the military institutions.[12]

Unlike its predecessor, the Samper government did not change military organization in qualitative terms. Under Gaviria, the experiment of creating units of professional soldiers was institutionalized. These grew from around 2,000 in 1990 to more than 23,000 in 1994. During Samper's term in office, the number of professional soldiers did not increase, nor was any significant variation attempted in the operational methods of confronting subversives and paramilitaries. The proportion of servicemen available for operations was also not changed, remaining around a third of the total number of servicemen in the armed forces as a whole.[13]

With regard to the problem of drugs, the Samper administration attained the highest level of 'North Americanization' of the war on drugs. Owing to this president's eagerness to respond to external pressure, the illicit drug trade became the preponderant factor in national security during the term of this government. The result of this focus on the war against drugs was that subversion and the problem of the paramilitaries did not receive the attention they deserved, which facilitated the unusual expansion of the guerrillas and paramilitaries.

Government action was also directed against the drug traffickers themselves. The pressure exerted by a carbon copy of the Search Bloc operation that eliminated Pablo Escobar, and the policy of surrender and negotiation promulgated by the office of the attorney general, resulted in the capture and surrender of the leadership of the Calí cartel in 1995. But the Samper government's achievements in the war on drugs were discouraging, despite the increasing support of the government of the USA, which was the instigator of the policy. The area devoted to illicit crops in Colombia grew from 40,100 hectares in 1990 to 50,900 in 1995; and from 79,500 in 1997 to around 100,000 in 1998. In the latter year, the country was the world's largest producer of coca, with more than 40 per cent of its total area cultivated for coca. Between 1990 and 1998 the government sprayed more than 120,000 hectares, a surface area similar to that being cultivated in 1999.[14]

The guerrillas underwent obvious changes during the years of the Samper administration: they consolidated their financial autonomy and expanded their control of territory and populations. The capture of resources afforded by drug trafficking, especially by the FARC, and brigandage activities such as kidnapping and extortion, strengthened them. Between 1991 and 1995, 42 per cent of the guerrillas' income came from illicit crops (production, security and the so-called *gramaje* levy on coca farmers and cocaine producers and traffickers), 22 per cent from kidnappings, 17 per cent from extortion in the mining sector (petroleum, gold and coal), 15 per cent from extortion from cattle traders, agriculturalists, merchants and others, and the rest from the diversion of official funds and royalties (Echandía 1999; Rangel 1999).[15] The augmentation of their sources of income permitted the guerrillas to move the search for the political backing of the social sectors into the background, and suggested the success of the militarization of their politics. They spread to regions with dynamic economic activities and notorious social inequalities, as suitable places for the exploitation of natural resources. The violent operations, not necessarily military in nature, became the fundamental means by which to win new political opportunities through inflicting terror on the civilian population (Rangel 1999; Peñate 1999).

In 1978 the FARC operated on eight fronts. By 1986 they were fighting on thirty-two fronts, and by 1995 on sixty-five. On the other hand, the ELN had three fronts in 1978, eleven in 1986, and thirty-two in 1995. The case of the EPL was different. Whereas it had four active fronts in 1995, five years later most of the group had demobilized. The rise in the number of guerrilla fronts can be seen as a reflection of the rise in the number of guerrilla combatants. In 1986 the FARC had around 3,600 fighters, which by 1995 had grown to around 7,000. The ELN had 800 combatants in 1986, and 3,000 by 1995. The new guerrilla fighters, organized along new fronts, occupied areas where previously such groups were absent. Whereas in 1985 the guerrillas had a presence in approximately 170 municipalities, three years later they had managed to establish themselves in nearly 600 (Rangel 1999).

Its military might thus fortified, at the start of 1998 the FARC ordered the government to demilitarize or to clear out of five municipalities in the northeast of the Amazon region before it would begin a tentative dialogue aimed at a possible peace process. A meeting in July 1998 between President-elect Pastrana and Manuel Marulanda 'Tirofijo', leader of the FARC, opened up a number of possibilities. The leaders of the ELN resorted to another strategy:

in Mainz, Germany, they signed an agreement with members of the National Peace Committee to begin a dialogue with distinct social sectors.[16]

In the midst of a worsening security situation, an economic recession unfolded. Adverse external economic factors combined with the increasing fiscal deficit and unemployment, the decline in industry and the low capacity for saving in the country. In addition, the government's handling of macroeconomic and fiscal policies turned out to be very inefficient (Clavijo 1998).

Plan Colombia and the escalation of the war, 1998–2003

President Pastrana (1998–2002) garnered sufficient legitimacy to initiate a new peace effort. The depth of the political crisis and the fragility of the economy obliged the government once again to administer its political capital with skill and responsibility; but the rise in violence, the stagnation of the peace process and the economic crisis that exploded in 1999 all contributed to the rapid deterioration of the government's image.

The government's eagerness to secure peace quickly, which it believed in the beginning would be easy, enhanced the advantageous situation the guerrillas had inherited from the government of Samper. This left the FARC in total control of the area they had conquered, granted to them as a 'demilitarized zone'. The president's closed circle favoured a scheme in which the 'strategy' was to adapt to the circumstances of the moment. There was no participation from the communities within the conflict zone; no attempt to consolidate the permanence of the civilian authorities and the rule of law in the area; no kind of supervision was set in place; the temporary nature of the process was not discussed, nor were the contents of a possible agreement; and there was no policy document whatsoever spelling out the rules of the game. In addition, the decisions of the government were made in reactive fashion, almost always responding to the initiatives of the FARC. The sequence of problems, combined with the aggressiveness of the guerrillas in the regions in which they operated, and the use of the demilitarized zone as a place to keep those who had been kidnapped and from which to negotiate their ransoms, undertake extortion, train their combatants and maintain a logistical rearguard, led to the increasing unpopularity of the demilitarized zone and to rising scepticism in public opinion concerning the peace process.[17]

Meanwhile, the process of dealing with the ELN was long and complex. During the year and a half that it took the government to decide whether it would speak with the ELN, the paramilitaries took the opportunity to increase their control and to mobilize authorities and the population to reject the official decision to create a 'zone of coexistence' within which negotiations could take place. Over the years the ELN's behaviour towards the civilian population of this area facilitated the political and military work of the 'self-defence' organizations. The military relapse of the ELN and its need to be heard had encouraged their terrorist actions. The government changed its mind very late. By the end of 1999, it had wasted the opportunity to pursue two parallel processes, and to promote a political approach that would have yielded good dividends. The government's tough attitude towards the ELN was not consistent with the policy of appeasement it pursued with the FARC.[18]

The peace process culminated in February 2002, after successive outrages committed by the FARC. The events of 11 September 2001 in the USA were influential in the president's decision to end the process. From the start of the process, the FARC took the initiative and kept it throughout. Its military successes, accumulated over the years, as well as the political dividends derived immediately from its military actions, led it to believe that the peace process was advantageous in so far as it was politically complementary to its military expansion.

But neither could the government change, by military means, the FARC's belief in the political utility of the peace process for military ends. The change in military organization required by unconventional warfare that was brought about by Plan Colombia during the Pastrana administration, with support from the USA, was insufficient.[19] The disturbing growth of paramilitarism was the clearest proof of the failure of the state's military policy aimed at curbing the FARC's determination to fight, ending the presumed role of the paramilitaries in the strategy of the armed forces. The case of the ELN was different. Rather than the armed forces, it was the paramilitaries who reduced its military capacity, although not its will to fight.

In the first half of 2001, the paramilitary groups totally surpassed the atrocities committed in previous years. This generated the repudiation of national and international institutions, and resulted in the inclusion of these groups in the United States's list of foreign terrorist organizations. This response contrasted with the complacency of important sectors of Colombian society, which saw in the actions of the paramilitaries a possible solution to guerrilla excesses.[20]

The process of receiving military aid from the USA was put in motion as part of restructuring the military. The $30 million received by Colombia in 1995 for the war against drugs was enlarged to $83 million in 1998, and then to $294 million in 1999, this last amount being larger than that received by the rest of Latin America and the Caribbean in that year. Under the State Department's International Program for the Control of Narcotics, Colombia received $13.5

million in 1996, $57 million in 1998 and $203 million in 1999, most of which was destined for the national police. From 1999, financial support for the armed forces was increased. Before financial aid from the USA was increased, the Budget Committee (Comisión de Racionalización del Gasto Público) calculated that in 1997 the cost of the war had reached $3.7 billion, equivalent to 4 per cent of gross domestic product.[21]

At the start of 2000, the Clinton administration presented Congress with a request for aid for Colombia worth nearly $1.6 billion, in support of Plan Colombia. The project was approved in July 2000, to last two years. From a total of $1,319,100,000, $860,300,000 (65.2 per cent) was earmarked for Colombia, $110 million (8.3 per cent) for Bolivia, $32 million (2.4 per cent) for Peru, and $20 million (1.5 per cent) for Ecuador. Eighteen million dollars of anti-drug aid was to be shared by Brazil, Panama and Venezuela. The rest was granted to US anti-drug agencies, and to its Classified Intelligence Program. Of the funds destined for Colombia, $519,200,000 (60.4 per cent) was used for military assistance, and $123,100,000 (14.3 per cent) to assist the national police. The donations from other countries were small owing to the perceived identification between the US War on Drugs and Plan Colombia (United States General Accounting Office 2000; Departamento de Estado de EU 2001; Roy 2001).

US spokesmen had pointed out the convenience of extending and regionalizing the plan so as to make it more effective. At the presidential summit in Quebec, this idea took shape in the so-called Andean Regional Initiative (Storrs and Serafino 2001). In May, President Bush presented to the Senate an aid proposal for fiscal year 2002 worth $882 million. This initiative contemplated promoting alternative crops, combating corruption and strengthening the democratic institutions of the region, including Brazil and Panama. This project was ratified in December 2001, with a budget of $625 million, thereby regionalizing the component of Plan Colombia that was being financed by the United States.

Owing to the conflictive atmosphere in Colombia, the public became increasingly aware of the security issue, until, towards the end of the Pastrana administration, it was most widely felt to be the country's greatest problem. This situation helped Alvaro Uribe to win the 2002 presidential elections, under the banner of his policy of 'democratic security'. Subversion had grown, nurtured by the financial autonomy gained through narco-trafficking and activities such as kidnapping and extortion. On the other hand, the expansion of the paramilitaries was facilitated by the reluctance of the military and the police to contain them, by the aggressiveness of the guerrillas to which they responded, and their own participation in narco-trafficking. The worsening of the situation of the country legitimized, in public opinion, solutions based on force, at the same time discrediting a political solution, which was identified with the dialogue between the government and the FARC, and above all with the excesses in the demilitarized zone.

In the middle of 2002, on the eve of the change of government, a shift occurred in the strategy of the FARC. Since the 1980s this guerrilla organization had sought to gain control of territories, inhabitants, resources and local power bases. But now the FARC attempted to put in jeopardy the governance of the country by means of threatening and terrorizing municipal authorities, this in spite of the benefits they had gained through their influence over local authorities, mining companies and illegal crops. This policy shift boosted their earlier threats to transfer the war from the countryside to the cities. The clearest indication of the urbanization of the war was an attack with homemade mortars on the seat of government at the very moment that Uribe assumed the presidency. It was therefore clear that the FARC had taken up the challenge of designing an alternative strategy when there appeared to be no possibility of reopening a peace process, with a new government prepared to assume the risks of open warfare.[22]

Uribe sought to widen the involvement of the international community in the problem of drugs that sustained the armed conflict, and in so doing to obtain active support to solve it. To this end, the president backed the creation of a multinational force to support military actions against narco-trafficking and subversion. The president's eagerness, arising from his attempt to incorporate the internal armed conflict in the global war against terrorism, and the need to enlarge the amount of military support provided by the United States, even led him to declare Colombian backing for the unilateral declaration of war by the United States on Iraq, in the face of the vast global mobilization of opposition to this decision.[23]

Until August 2003, the deepest national concern with respect to the possibilities of peace revolved around the numerous kidnappings being committed, by the FARC in particular. This guerrilla group had accumulated numerous war trophies through the kidnapping of well-known political figures, in addition to abducted military and police personnel, some of whom were kept captive for several years. With these trophies they attempted to obtain, through exchanges, the release of numerous guerrillas imprisoned in jails throughout the country. Ever since the collapse of the so-called peace process, humanitarian exchange has been promoted by those who have been concerned about human rights and for the families of the abducted. In early May 2003, this situation led to a failed attempt by the army to rescue a governor and a former minister, resulting in the FARC executing their prisoners, along with eight captured soldiers.[24]

The government touted the possibility of negotiating with the paramilitary groups, after which problems arose with respect to the paramilitary unity that was attained with the creation of the AUC during the Samper presidency. When, in 2001 and May 2002 respectively, the United States and the European Union included the paramilitaries, along with the FARC and the ELN, on their list of terrorist groups, it created for the AUC a contradictory situation that affected their fragile unity in the final months of the Pastrana government. Before this problem arose, they had assumed that their stated goal of 'defending' the state from subversion made them invulnerable to American anti-terrorist politics. In addition, the so-called self-defence groups felt sure of themselves, particularly after encountering within the armed forces little appetite for fighting them. The military tended to see them as allies, despite the atrocities they committed against the civilian population. But what the paramilitaries did not count on was the connection made by Washington between organized crime and the drugs problem, a situation enhanced by their obsession with confronting terrorism.[25]

Upon completion of his first year of government, and in spite of his failure to achieve clear results with a policy of democratic security and in dealing with the terrorist actions of armed actors, the prestige of President Uribe, together with public support for his policy, remained high.[26] The persistence of Uribe in pursuing his hard-line approach and the great care he takes in handling his public image have perhaps been the main factors behind the maintenance of this support.

Conclusion

The most obvious problem that confronts Colombia is the lack of political clarity in the handling of security. The real difficulty in elaborating a coherent and broad policy in a country with the present characteristics of Colombia lies in reconciling the reality of war with the search for peace. A political regime with great shortcomings in its exercise of democracy, yet one that has not become a dictatorship, affected by an armed internal conflict involving subversives and paramilitaries, needs to confront this conflict without undermining its limited achievements in matters of civil rights. The objective is to create the minimum conditions in which to obtain a peace that permits the necessary steps to be taken in the development of democracy, and in this way secure a lasting peace.

Notes

1 Some of the ideas for the rest of this chapter were taken from Leal Buitrago (1994).

2 The Coordinadora Nacional Guerrillera (CNG) was created in 1985 after the termination of the ceasefire with the M-19 and the EPL. These groups brought together the ELN and the Ricardo Franco, a splinter group of the FARC. In 1987, the Coordinadora Guerrillera Simón Bolívar (CGSB) was created after a meeting of the leaders of the FARC, the M-19, the EPL, the ELN and other minor groups (Pardo Rueda 1996).

3 Between 1988 and 1990, a total of 1,940 persons fell victim to political killings in diverse regions of the country (ibid.).

4 *El Espectador,* 27 May 1987; *Diario Oficial* 38649, 10 January 1989, 38651, 11 January 1989, and 38669, 29 January 1989.

5 'Estrategia Nacional contra la Violencia', *El Tiempo*, May 1991.

6 'Casa Verde: el contragolpe', *El Tiempo*, 13 January 1991; 'Viraje en la política de paz del gobierno', *El Tiempo*, 10 February 1991.

7 In large part the success of the Bloque de Búsqueda can be attributed to the criminal and clandestine collaboration provided by its competitor the Calí cartel, and by the group known as 'Los Pepes' (persecuted by Pablo Escobar), made up of competing narco-traffickers. At the same time, support was also clearly provided by the US government through the DEA, the CIA and Delta Force. See 'Killing Pablo', *Semana*, 967, 13–20 November 2000.

8 'Diálogo con la CNG, pero sometida: Min-Defensa asume la responsabilidad de que en año y medio se negociará de nuevo', *El Espectador*, 14 March 1993.

9 'Ási eligen los élenos sus alcaldes', *El Tiempo*, 22 August 1993.

10 These decrees permitted the incorporation of the demobilized guerrillas into Congress, and offered other benefits. *Diario Oficial*, 41420, 5 July 1994.

11 'Golpe tras golpe', *Semana*, 827, 9–16 March 1998; 'Guerra es guerra', *Cambio16*, 269, 10–17 August 1998.

12 The Defence Intelligence Agency and the International Institute of Strategic Studies, in the USA, confirmed that the armed forces were losing the war against subversion, whereas the army should in fact be able to defeat the guerrillas in five years. 'El Ejército colombiano es inepto: New York Times', *El Tiempo*, 23 June 1998.

13 In 1994, the army had 125,454 combatants, of which 20,898 were professional soldiers. The navy had 17,681 effective servicemen, and the air force 8,921. Ministerio de Defensa, *Memoria al Congreso Nacional 1993–1994,* Bogotá: Imprenta y Publicaciones de las Fuerzas Militares, 1995, p. 171. In 1997, the figure for the army was a little lower than in 1994: 122,659 servicemen in total, of which 18,529 were professional soldiers. Ministerio de Defensa, *Memoria al Congreso Nacional 1996–1997*, Bogotá: Imprenta y Publicaciones de las Fuerzas Militares, 1998.

14 *El Espectador*, 30 January 1998.

15 The Consejería para la Paz de la Presidencia de la República estimated that in 1994 the FARC were operating on fifty-eight fronts and commanded 6,200 guerrillas, and the ELN on thirty fronts with 2,700 guerrillas. By 1998 the FARC were fighting on sixty-three fronts with 6,700 combatants, and the ELN on thirty-three fronts with 4,500 fighters. See also M. A. Vélez (2000), 'Farc-Eln. Evolución y expansión territorial', Bogotá: Universidad de los Andes.

16 'Se abrió diálogo con las Farc', *El Tiempo*, 10 July 1998; 'Contacto en Mainz', *Semana,* 844, 6–13 July 1998.

17 An inventory of newspaper clippings on the peace process, from June 1998 to December 1999, is to be found in Depaz (2000a).

18 An inventory of newspaper clippings on the peace process with the ELN, from June 1998 to December 1999, is to be found in Depaz (2000b).

19 At the end of 2000, the minister of defence announced that the army consisted of 43,000 professional soldiers, and that by the end of the government's term in office this number would have reached 55,000. The army grew from 101,000 servicemen in 1990 to 121,000 in 1994, and from 135,000 in 1998 to 135,000 in 1999. With the addition of the navy and the air force, the armed forces numbered in total 169,000 servicemen in 1999. See 'Las relaciones algebraicas en la guerra irregular', in Ministerio de Defensa (1999), *Colombia. Defensa Nacional.*

20 In 2000 there were eighty-three political killings attributed to the paramilitary groups, which have claimed a total of around six hundred victims. It is estimated that there are around eight thousand members of those called 'self-defence' groups. *Sources*: 'El desmadre de los paras', *Semana*, 986, 26 March–2 April 2001; 'Sanciones a "paras" a partir de junio: EU', *El Tiempo*, 1 May 2001.

21 'Presencia militar de Estados Unidos en Colombia', in Latin America Working Group & Center for International Policy, <http: www.ciponline.org/facts>; 'La pelea más cara del mundo', *El Tiempo*, 6 January 1999.

22 'Alcaldes en la mira', *Cambio 16*, 468, 10–17 June 2002; 'Terrorismo desafía a Uribe', *El Tiempo*, 8 August 2002.

23 Phil Stewart, 'Colombia asks Neighbors to Join Drug War', 15 October 2002 (<www.ciponline.org/demilit.htm>); 'Uribe, el Blair de A. Latina', *El Tiempo*, 19 March 2003.

24 'En el limbo', *Semana*, 1,085, 17–24 February 2003; 'Farc asesinaron a rehenes', *El Tiempo*, 6 May 2003.

25 'Pedido de extradición hizo estallar a las AUC', *El Tiempo*, 20 March 2003; 'Abren puerta para diálogo', *El Tiempo*, 13 December 2002; 'Indulto cobijará a "paras"', *El Tiempo*, 28 January 2003.

26 'Qué se espera de Álvaro Uribe', *El Tiempo*, 7 August 2003.

7 | Venezuela: the remilitarization of politics

HAROLD A. TRINKUNAS

On the evening of 11 April 2002, the third day of a general strike, elements of the Venezuelan armed forces rebelled against their commander-in-chief, President Hugo Chávez Frias.[1] Reacting to the bloody outcome of clashes between pro- and anti- government demonstrators near the presidential palace, the commander of the army, General Efraim Vásquez Velasco, announced in a nationally televised address that he would no longer obey presidential orders. General Vásquez accused Hugo Chávez of preparing widespread repression of anti-government strikers and demonstrators, and he ordered military units under his command to disregard further government orders and remain confined to base. High-ranking generals and admirals soon followed Vásquez on to the airwaves, expressing their solidarity with his position and their refusal to support President Chávez. In the early hours of 12 April 2002, the senior military officer in the Venezuelan armed forces, General Lucas Rincón Romero, announced the resignation of President Chávez, and the formation of a transitional government under the leadership of Pedro Carmona Estanga, president of the national federation of chambers of commerce (FEDECAMARAS) (Hernandez 2002).

Less than twenty-four hours after becoming the head of a transitional government, Pedro Carmona was forced to flee the presidential palace to make way for pro-Chávez civilian and military forces. These swiftly engineered Hugo Chávez's return to power, and the generals and admirals who had so recently refused to support his government reversed their positions, many scrambling to provide explanations for their behaviour during the rebellion. Amid the celebrations of his supporters, Chávez advocated a new policy of national reconciliation, but also ordered the detention of high-profile military officers associated with the events of 11 April 2002 (Olivares 2002a).

At first glance, what may seem most surprising about these events in Venezuela is the failure of the coup against President Chávez, particularly given the continuous political turmoil that characterized his administration, the mass demonstrations against his regime, and his growing unpopularity during 2002 as evidenced in local political polls. The military rebellion against the democratically elected government, the first since 1992 and only the third since 1963, is of great significance, however, since it confirms that the armed forces, the institution best equipped to employ organized violence in Venezuela, have re-emerged as a political actor (Trinkunas 2002a). The breakdown of civilian control in what was once the most stable democratic regime in Latin America has serious implications for democratic consolidation in Venezuela.

Despite the deinstitutionalization of civilian control in Venezuela, constant rumours of military unrest, and more or less continuous civilian protest since the events of April 2002, however, the Chávez administration has managed to survive and, to a certain extent, defeat its domestic opponents. After a number of purges in the wake of the April 2002 coup attempt, the armed forces have become the last bastion of the regime. Their internal role in supporting the regime, once confined to events best characterized as military support to civilian authorities and domestic humanitarian operations, has become increasingly repressive in nature. This became evident during the prolonged general strike of December 2002 to February 2003, when National Guard and army military police units were repeatedly used to confront civilian protesters, and the Ministry of Defence Military Intelligence Directorate played an increasingly brazen role in the administration's surveillance of its domestic opposition. The growing use of the military in internal security roles has been paralleled by an increase in organized violence by civilians.

This chapter explores the linkages between the growing role of the military in Venezuelan politics and the swelling tide of political violence in the country. It argues that the expanded domestic role of the armed forces has been accompanied by a breakdown in the institutions designed to control and oversee military activities. Moreover, disputes about the control of civilian security forces and the emergence of armed civilian political groups have eroded the state's monopoly on organized violence. These events have taken place in a regime that increasingly lacks institutionalized mechanisms for political dispute resolution among pro- and anti-Chávez forces. In combination, these factors suggest that violence will become an increasingly prominent feature of Venezuelan politics, and they call into question whether democracy will persist.

I will also argue that, in the case of Venezuela's current political crisis, the use of the armed forces in domestic operations, the deterioration of civil–military relations and the growth in civilian political violence are not directly linked in a causal fashion, but are rather all the product of the transformational political project of President Hugo Chávez. The expanded political role of the armed forces is only a reflection of the elected leadership's efforts to secure military support for its political agenda, rather than the result of an internal desire for role expansion by the officer corps. The reaction that the government's use of the military in domestic operations has provoked, both within the military and in civil society, indicates that the armed forces are not a reliable ally of either the Chávez administration or its political opposition. This suggests that the violence that accompanies this political confrontation is increasingly likely to be organized by civilians, further eroding the state's monopoly of the use of force in society.

The role of the military in the Punto Fijo democracy

Until the 1990s, Venezuela was often seen as a democratic exception in a region characterized by political unrest, military coups and revolution. Venezuela's democratic success rested partly on the ability of its political leaders to institutionalize civilian control over the armed forces. Unlike in many Western democracies, government control of the military in Venezuela did not depend on legislative oversight of roles and budgets or a civilian-led ministry of defence. Rather, since the 1960s, Venezuelan political leaders followed a strategy of 'divide and conquer' *vis-à-vis* the armed forces, which later became embedded in the very institutions of civil–military relations. These institutional arrangements were designed to inhibit cooperation or 'jointness' among the army, navy and air force. They also drove a wedge between senior officers, whose promotions were controlled by the Congress and the president, and junior officers whose careers depended strictly on merit. Moreover, even though political leaders paid lip-service to the armed forces' national security doctrine, which called for military participation in economic and social development, successive civilian governments carefully restricted the role of officers and soldiers in any activity that was not directly related to national defence. The result was armed forces that found it difficult to cooperate, especially in anything as risky and ambitious as a coup d'état, and were tightly focused on professional and defence-related issues (Trinkunas 2000: 101–3).

By the 1980s, the crisis in Venezuela's state-led development model sparked political and social consequences that began to affect the armed forces. Junior officers were increasingly disgusted by the corruption that they believed pervaded military and political elites and began to conceive of political alternatives that better reflected their concern for the underprivileged. As products of a military educational system that emphasized leadership, self-sacrifice and nationalism over political and economic reality, the most successful of the conspiratorial groups, Movimiento Bolivariano 200, rejected the possibility of change within Venezuela's democratic framework and began to organize a coup d'état. Lulled into complacency by the prolonged political quiescence of the armed forces, civilian and military elites ignored the growing evidence of military conspiracy under the leadership of a highly regarded army officer, Hugo Chávez Frias.

In part, the neo-liberal economic policies of the second government of Carlos Andrés Pérez provided a pretext for the 1992 coups. Shortly after his inauguration in 1989, widespread rioting and looting shook many Venezuelan cities. Military units were called in to restore order, resulting in hundreds of civilian casualties, and many of the junior officers who led these troops were appalled by the blood-letting. The highly negative impact of the Pérez administration's economic policies on military salaries and benefits was keenly felt by many officers, further sowing unrest within the armed forces. In this fertile ground, Lieutenant Colonel Hugo Chávez was able to organize a coup against the government in February 1992. Mounted entirely by army units, the coup failed in the face of resistance by the other branches of the armed forces. Similarly, an air force coup in November 1992, led by officers sympathetic to Chávez's message, failed owing to a lack of support within the army. The institutions of civilian control of the armed forces remained strong enough in the 1990s to make a successful coup d'état very difficult, but even an unsuccessful military rebellion tipped Venezuela's democracy into crisis (Trinkunas 2002a: 53–64).

Although President Carlos Andrés Pérez survived the events of 1992, the coups sparked increasing political and social protest against his administration and his policies, and the Congress eventually impeached him for misuse of government funds. The 1992 coups also set off a wave of conspiracy and unrest within the armed forces as some officers took sides for and against Hugo Chávez, even though the great majority maintained a professional detachment from politics. President Rafael Caldera, elected in 1993, restored a measure of unity within the armed forces by purging both Chávez's supporters and his right-wing opponents from the officer corps. The ghosts of these divisions remained in the officer corps, however, and would regain their vigour in the future (Romero 1997: 7–36).

The events of 1989 and 1992 revealed an internal contradiction in the Venezuelan armed forces: on the one hand, a deep concern on the part of a minority of officers over political and social issues, which Chávez capitalized on; on the other, a majority that was not interested in a domestic role, much less a political role. In fact, the poor performance of the Venezuelan armed forces in the 1989 domestic order mission and the high number of resulting civilian casualties are a reflection of their inadequate preparation for such a mission and their lack of interest in such a role. By the early 1990s, the Venezuelan armed forces had spent two decades preparing for external defence missions, mostly against neighbouring Colombia, rather than participating in domestic roles and missions. The failure of the 1992 coup attempts is another example of the lack of interest among the majority of the officer corps in assuming a more prominent role in domestic affairs. The bottom line is that between the end of counter-insurgency efforts in 1969 and the 'Caracazo' of 1989 there had been little call on the military to employ organized violence in defence of the regime. Moreover, President Rafael Caldera (1994–99) was largely successful in restoring the status quo that existed prior to 1992.

The erosion of civilian control of the armed forces in Venezuela

Having failed to achieve power by military means, Hugo Chávez succeeded brilliantly in the political realm. Despite beginning his campaign with single-digit poll ratings at the beginning of 1998, he swept the December presidential vote with one of the highest approval ratings in Venezuela's democratic history. One of the planks of his left-of-centre political platform was the reform of civil–military relations to correct what he perceived as the perverse aspects of the system created by his predecessors. When his reform programme was implemented, rather than modernizing civilian control of the military, President Chávez's reforms dismantled it, substituting personalized control of the armed forces for the previous institutional arrangements.

The Chávez military reforms initially focused on three aspects: loosening the constitutional and legal constraints on political activities by the armed forces; expanding their role in social and economic development activities; and removing legislative influence over military promotions. As part of the reform of Venezuela's constitution, the Constituent Assembly deleted articles barring military deliberation on political issues and granted active-duty members of the armed forces the right to vote, which had been withheld under the 1961 constitution. The armed forces' role in development activities also greatly expanded under the president's Plan Bolívar 2000, which channelled large amounts of social welfare funding away from civilian agencies and towards the military garrisons in each Venezuelan state. As a result, the armed forces became involved in infrastructure construction, repairing schools and hospitals, and even the sale of consumer goods at cut-rate prices in popular markets in an attempt to hold down inflation. President Chávez also relied on hundreds of military officers seconded to positions in the public administration to enforce his authority over the state bureaucracy, which he perceived as having been colonized by his political opponents during the previous four decades of civilian rule. Finally, Chávez took control of military promotions, alleging that the legislature's role in this process during the previous four decades had politicized it. Instead, all military promotions were to be approved directly by the president and his minister of defence (Trinkunas 2002a: 65–72).

Although some aspects of these reforms proved popular with the officer corps, the overall impact on civilian control of the armed forces was negative. The extension of suffrage to the armed forces was appreciated by the officer corps and helped to solidify initial support for Chávez in the military. Similarly, some officers, particularly in the army, genuinely appreciated the new opportunities to contribute to Venezuela's development through participation in the Plan Bolívar 2000 and public administration. On the other hand, expanded social welfare roles for the armed forces also created new opportunities for corruption by some in the military. To the chagrin of more honest officers, charges of corruption involving the armed forces became daily fare for the media (Cardona Marrero 2001a). In addition, military officers in the public administration had important roles in shaping public policy, and as a result they became de facto political actors.

Most critically, President Chávez used his control of promotions to reshape the officer corps, favouring officers who supported his political agenda with plum commands and assignments. Numerous generals and admirals, many of whom had opposed the 1992 coup attempts, were shunted into administrative duties, retired or were placed on leave. Naturally, this generated discontent and opposition among military officers excluded from the president's favour and increased the politicization of military promotions. As we will see in a moment, it actually led some military officers to hold press conferences publicly criticizing the president. Taken in their totality, the Chávez reforms of the armed forces undermined a number of the traditional elements of civilian control in Venezuela. In the absence of institutionalized control of the armed forces, President Chávez could rely only on personalized mechanisms to maintain the loyalty of the officer corps. As the events of 11–14 April 2002 demonstrated, this is a weak reed on which to rest the stability of a democratic government.

The growth in the military's domestic role in the first two years of the Chávez administration had a mixed impact on the armed forces. The greatest negative impact came in the area of readiness, with persistent reports of inoperability of military equipment owing to the stagnation in the portions of the defence budget allotted to operations and acquisitions. In the army, it is reported that enlisted troop strength has dropped 40 per cent and, depending on the unit, 25 to 30 per cent of armoured assets are not operable. The air force and the navy are reportedly worse off in terms of readiness (Romero and Romero 2002a, 2002b, 2002c). Also, some retired officers alleged that military preparedness had been affected by the diversion of personnel to support activities of the Plan Bolívar 2000.[2] The ministry of defence has spent more on salaries for personnel and made large budgets available to garrison commanders to execute activities related to the Plan Bolívar 2000 (approximately 200 billion bolívares in 1999–2002), but the overall budget has declined in 2001 and 2002, which means that operational and acquisition budgets have been squeezed (Armas 2003; Cardona Marrero 2001b).

Until 2002, the role of the armed forces in domestic 'law and order' missions was relatively restricted, although there have been allegations by local human rights organizations that the military used excessive force during its operations to support civilian authorities following the massive landslides that occurred on Venezuela's littoral in 1999. The main use of the military prior to 2002, however, was in the undertaking of domestic humanitarian operations in support of President Chávez's policies, and as a reservoir of educated and trustworthy personnel to staff key positions in civilian government ministries. Overall, the negative consequences of an expanded military role in the domestic arena were greatest in the area of military readiness. Organized violence per se was not yet a military issue in Venezuela.

The 11 April 2002 coup attempt

Although President Chávez's popularity had been declining throughout 2001, the successful general strike held on 10 December of that year demonstrated that the opposition, led by an unusual coalition of major business and labour federations, was finally coherent enough to raise a successful challenge to the government. The opposition's criticism of the Chávez administration centred on its policies on land use, education, organized labour and the economy, as well as a perceived foreign policy shift towards closer links with countries such as Cuba and Iraq, criticism of US foreign policy after 11 September 2001, and expressions of sympathy for the Colombian FARC guerrillas. President Chávez responded to his critics with characteristically tempestuous and aggressive language, heightening the tension between pro- and anti-government forces. The opposition's criticisms of the president found sympathizers in the armed forces, and a small number of senior military officers from all services began publicly to criticize President Chávez in a series of press conferences (Alvarez 2002a; *El Universal*, 25 March 2002). Although these individual actions were not a serious threat to the administration's grip on power, they did undermine the president's claim of unconditional support from the armed forces.

Opposition to President Chávez became especially trenchant after the administration began to make changes in the senior leadership of the state-owned oil industry. Although this had always been a prerogative of past governments, senior positions in PDVSA had traditionally been reserved for technocrats promoted from within with a leavening of outsiders with business experience. The appointment of Gastón Parra, an academic highly critical of PDVSA, to its presidency detonated a rebellion by the middle management that found support in civil society at large. A cycle of civilian protests against the government began as a means to pressure Chávez into reversing this decision. President Chávez went as far as summarily dismissing many senior technocrats, announcing the decision on his weekly radio show, *Aló Presidente*, which many took as an effort to heap insult on injury.

After it became clear that President Chávez would continue his efforts to seize political control of the oil industry, the civilian leaders of the opposition called for a new general strike on 9 April 2002. Highly successful, the strike was extended indefinitely by the leader of the national labour confederation, Carlos Ortega, on 10 April. Progressively larger anti-government demonstrations were held on successive days in Caracas, leading to a clash between the private-sector media and the Chávez administration over news coverage of the strike. Tragically, the massive anti-government march of nearly 500,000 people on 11 April ended in violence when protesters converged on the presidential palace. Here, they clashed with pro-government members of the Círculos Bolivarianos and were fired upon by unidentified snipers. An estimated twelve persons died and over one hundred were injured. Live coverage of the bloody events, shown in a split-screen format simultaneously with President Chávez's televised address to the nation, prompted the administration to close down private television transmissions. President Chávez also ordered the armed forces at this time to take military control of the capital, an order that rebel officers claim led them to begin the coup.

In the face of a worsening crisis, the military acted, although their intervention at first resembled a sit-down strike rather than a coup. There were initial reports on the evening of 11 April that a number of senior officers had attempted to broadcast a message against the government. Censorship of television and radio broadcasts began to break down as the coup gathered momentum. The turning point of the rebellion occurred when the commander of the army, General Efraim Vásquez Velasco, stated in a televised address surrounded by his officers that he would not obey presidential directives to suppress anti-government demonstrations and ordered all his troops to remain confined to base. In his speech he characterized President Chávez's directives as illegal, and in short order senior generals in the Guardia Nacional (a militarized national police force charged with internal security) and admirals in the navy echoed his sentiments in radio and television broadcasts. Active-duty officers who served in the government, such as the minister of finance and the vice-minister of citizen security, resigned their positions. Although President Chávez claimed in his national address of 11 April that he would hold out in the presidential palace with his honour guard and supporters to the bitter end, General Rincón Romero, inspector general of the armed forces, announced his resignation in the early hours of 12 April (Weffer Cifuentes 2002). A transitional government soon formed under Pedro Carmona, leader of the national business federation FEDECAMARAS.

General Vásquez Velasco's refusal to obey the president made it appear that the armed forces had turned decisively against the Chávez administration, yet the military rebellion never extended very far beyond the upper ranks of the officer corps. Venezuelan investigative reporter Patricia Poleo, in her published account of how the coup was hijacked by conservative elements of the civilian opposition, reveals that the rebellious elements of the armed forces controlled almost no combat troops. Although some senior officers admitted after the rebellion that they had been conspiring since the summer of 2001, they did not secure support from officers outside Caracas. The strategic military installations in the city of Maracay, where Venezuela's armoured, airborne and air forces are concentrated, never accepted the new government, and rebel military control in Caracas was spotty at best (Mayorca 2002a, 2002b). The military consensus in favour of deposing President Chávez rested on the shared conviction among officers that they should not be involved in repressing civilian anti-government demonstrators. Once the unconstitutional nature of the transitional government became clear, this consensus fell apart.

Pedro Carmona's interim government committed a number of key political errors during its brief existence. First, it was drawn from a narrow right-wing slice of the political spectrum that excluded key elements of the opposition to Hugo Chávez, most notably organized labour. Images of the well-heeled participants in the televised self-proclamation of Pedro Carmona as president quickly confirmed the sectarian upper-class nature of the new government, particularly to poor and working-class Venezuelans where pro-Chávez sentiments are concentrated. Second, Carmona's decree dissolving the National Assembly and the Supreme Court made it clear to many military officers that the new government was completely unconstitutional and not prepared to meet even minimum democratic criteria. Third, Carmona erred in the military arena, appointing as minister of defence an admiral who had very little authority within the officer corps rather than a senior army general. He also selected a recently cashiered officer, Admiral Molina Tamayo, as head of presidential security. These appointments, which also contravened military views on seniority and merit, angered a number of senior officers who had initially supported the Carmona government (Zapata 2002a).

In another critical miscalculation, nobody in the Carmona administration thought of replacing the troops in charge of security at Miraflores, the presidential palace. Once pro-Chávez demonstrations and riots began on 13 April 2002, loyal presidential security troops ejected the Carmona administration from Miraflores and allowed President Chávez's ministers to enter, reconvene the National Assembly, and temporarily swear in the vice-president, Diosdado Cabello, as interim president. As Pedro Carmona sheltered in a nearby military base, the junior and mid-ranking officers who actually commanded the combat units of the armed forces made it clear to their superiors that they would only support efforts to restore constitutional rule. This paved the way for a swift return of Hugo Chávez Frias to power on 14 April 2002 (Poleo 2002; Romero 2002a).

Consequences of the 11 April coup for Venezuelan civil–military relations Even though military participation in the domestic arena was the leading cause of the 11 April coup attempt, it was President Chávez's orders to the military to employ violence against civilian demonstrators which precipitated the rebellion. On the face of it, the rebel military officers argued that they were disobeying illegal and unconstitutional orders from the president to repress demonstrators. Even if the motives of some of these officers are suspect, they took advantage of the crisis created within the armed forces by these orders to pursue their agenda of removing Chávez from power. Either way, domestic roles for the military have led to substantial negative consequences for the armed forces, loyal and disloyal alike. In the long run, it has also meant that the Chávez administration cannot fully rely on the armed forces to defend the regime, opening the way for greater civilian participation in the use of force for political purposes.

The anti-Chávez faction, concentrated among senior officers, was hard hit by its defeat during the rebellion. Its members' association with the Carmona government is likely to have discredited them among their subordinates, and the Chávez administration has been pursuing a policy of legal action against these officers. Initially, military prosecutors detained fifty-eight officers, twenty-four of whom are generals or admirals. In the army, these detentions were largely concentrated in the logistics and aviation branches, an indication of the president's success in shuffling his opponents in the military into positions where they did not command significant numbers of troops (Trinkunas 2002b: 165–72). As the generals who participated in or sympathized with the 11 April coup attempt were cashiered, a substantial number of them have joined the civilian opposition or formed their own political interest groups (Hernandez 2003).

The government's legal strategy against the rebellious officers suffered a severe setback, however, when the Tribunal Supremo de Justicia (the Supreme Court), in a decision handed down in August 2002, declared that there had been no act of military rebellion during 11–14 April, and rejected the government's indictment of four senior officers on this charge. Since then, the government has continued to pursue legal avenues to punish officers involved in the April 2002 coup, but with mixed success since the most potent charge, that of military rebellion, has been rejected in most cases by the high court (Alvarez 2002b).

The government has had more success in pursuing administrative channels to punish or sideline rebellious officers. Many of the officers who participated actively in the 11 April coup attempts were involuntarily retired by the ministry of defence. Together with pursuing a policy of rapid rotation and promotion of politically reliable junior officers to senior positions, the Chávez administration secured renewed control over the armed forces. This control was strengthened by the presence of several of Chávez's military academy classmates in control of the army (*Tal Cual*, 3 September 2002). At least some observers in Venezuela report that as many as 980 officers have been removed from the armed forces since 1991 (Olivares 2003). The accelerated promotion of officers based on political loyalty rather than professionalism increased dissatisfaction with the government among the institutionalist wing of the military.

The success of Chávez's punitive tactics in the wake of 11 April eventually produced a reaction within the armed forces. A substantial number of officers affected by the administrative manoeuvres began an open-air vigil at a plaza in the Altamira neighbourhood of Caracas in October 2002. They criticized the government both for its left-wing political policies and for its politicization of the armed forces. Other officers and enlisted personnel joined them, and their numbers eventually exceeded one hundred. Their peaceful 'sit-down strike' attracted large numbers of civilian supporters who joined them in Plaza Altamira, provided food and shelter, and helped to stand watch against the government efforts at dislodgement that President Chávez publicly threatened to order more than once (La Rotta Moran 2002; Pérez Rodríguez 2002). This movement continued unabated until the conclusion of the larger general strike in February 2003.

From the perspective of civil–military relations in Venezuela, the most troubling aspect of these developments was the popular adulation that rapidly developed around the rebellious officers and the increasingly political nature of their pronouncements. Not only did they call repeatedly on President Chávez to resign, but they also began to take a leadership role in the political opposition to the administration, going as far as holding joint events with the Coordinadora Democrática, a civilian opposition umbrella organization. As the 'peaceful' military rebellion extended for months, the accusations against the government became more pointed, including attempts to link Chávez to support for al-Qaeda terrorism, a clear attempt to influence US government opinion on developments in Venezuela.[3]

Pro-Chávez forces emerged from the rebellion with a mixed record. Senior officers closely identified with the president's programme, such as General Rosendo, the commander of the armed forces unified command (CUFAN), sided with the rebels on 11 April (Zapata 2002b). As a result, almost the entire military high command was replaced in the days following President Chávez's return to power, and there was a further shake-up of the armed forces leadership in the summer of 2002. The coup attempt did allow the government to place officers that it considered most loyal, such as General Garcia Carneiro, into the key control positions in the armed forces. These officers have done a great deal to ensure the quiescence of most military officers in political matters. Their high visibility has made them the target of virulent protests by civilian opponents of the government, however, including *cacerolazos* (banging on pots, tables and glasses) whenever they appear in public places such as restaurants and civilian aircraft. This civilian distaste for these particular military officers has the potential to turn into a broader civilian disdain for the armed forces, once the most prestigious public institutions in Venezuela.

The institutionalist majority in the Venezuelan armed forces emerged as a key actor, one that will remain a threat to the Chávez administration in the long run. By standing by during the overthrow of the president in the first place, it showed that it was willing to place limits on the actions of the president and prevent him from using force to achieve his political objectives. Its support for democratic principles and the constitution also shows, however, that Venezuelan armed forces were not willing to support an outright dictatorship (Olivares 2002b). The Chávez administration's need for military support in order to remain in power has meant that it has intensified its vigilance over the armed forces, ironically using many of the same tactics that were used against the pro-Chávez military in the wake of the 1992 coup attempts. He has reportedly revived the strategy of 'divide and conquer' to pit the Guardia Nacional and the army against each other, just as democratizers did in Venezuela in the 1960s (Romero 2002b, 2002c).

The credibility of the civilian opposition to President Chávez was undermined by its anti-democratic actions during the 11–14 April period, and this will have a negative impact on its future relations with the military. The hijacking of the transitional government by the most conservative elements in Venezuelan civil society, their mistakes in handling civil–military relations and the subsequent failure of the coup can only create doubts within the officer corps about the wisdom of working with the opposition. More importantly, the unconstitutional decrees of the Carmona government confirmed for many officers the truth of President Chávez's claims about the opposition – namely, that it is led by a right-wing conspiracy between a corrupt oligarchy and the owners of the media. It also confirmed that an important element of the civilian opposition does not view the Chávez administration as legitimate and is more than willing to subvert the state's control over organized violence to overthrow the government.[4]

The December 2002 general strike and beyond

Government restraint on the use of the armed forces in internal security roles broke down during the sixty-three days of the general strike that began on 2 December 2002. Organized by the Coordinadora Democrática, the Confederación General de Trabajadores (General Confederation of Workers, CGT) and FEDECAMARAS (the federation of business chambers), the general strike was intended to force President Chávez from power, either through his resignation or his acquiescence in a recall referendum (*El Nacional*, 5 December 2002). President Chávez's popularity among the general public plummeted, with approval ratings dropping to 29 per cent (Giusti 2002). To survive the general strike, President Chávez turned to the armed forces to provide internal security, distribute goods and services, and assist in the restoration of oil production.

Political tension between the government and the opposition reached a peak when President Chávez ordered the armed forces to take over the Caracas metropolitan police force, which was under the control of the opposition mayor, Alfredo Peña. The government accused the police force of being partial to the opposition because it protected their demonstrations from clashes with pro-Chávez activists, such as the Círculos Bolivarianos. The government went so far as to accuse the metropolitan police of deliberately targeting its supporters. The armed forces prevented the police from operating and put troops on the streets of Caracas to ensure their control of the city. This striking use by the government of the armed forces to intervene in domestic politics formed the backdrop to the decision to call a general strike (Cardona Marrero 2002; Ruiz Pantin 2002).

The December 2002 general strike received broad backing from civil society, and economic activity was nearly paralysed in certain sectors. It gained real momentum when the management and workers of the state-owned oil company, PDVSA, joined the strike, critically undermining Venezuela's ability to export oil (Castro and Ventura 2002). Estimates of the impact on the Venezuelan economy varied wildly, ranging from an 80 per cent stoppage rate reported by the opposition to a 20 per cent rate reported by the government (Salieron 2002). During the height of the general strike, Venezuela was even forced to import gasoline from Brazil, an operation for which its port facilities had never been designed since it was a long-established leading oil producer.

Initially, the Coordinadora Democrática hoped to force Chávez to resign, but eventually settled on a strategy of forcing him to call for a referendum on his presidency. Venezuela witnessed the longest period of social mobilization since its transition to democracy in 1958, as literally millions turned out in anti-government demonstrations. The government turned out its own supporters in counter-demonstrations, and social and political tension rose to such an extent that OAS Secretary-General Cesar Gaviria committed his personal prestige and authority to a prolonged negotiation process between the government and its opponents (*El Universal*, 28 December 2002). Most of the opposition placed its hopes in a proposed referendum on President Chávez scheduled for 2 February 2003. Over 1.5 million signatures were gathered and delivered to the Consejo Nacional Electoral (National Electoral Council, CNE), as required by law, and the CNE began the process of organizing a nationwide referendum (Martinez 2002). This process continued even in the face of the obstacles placed in its path by President Chávez, such as the denial of additional funding for electoral organization and the refusal to provide military support and security to the electoral process, as had occurred in every election since 1958. Only the decision of the Tribunal Supremo de Justicia declaring the 2 February referendum non-binding and the board of the national electoral council invalid brought the process to a halt (Alvarez 2003). Discouraged, the civilian opposition called off the general strike on 3 February 2003.

The armed forces enabled President Chávez to remain in power during the general strike. The armed forces, particularly the Guardia Nacional and the army military police, acted to quell civilian opposition demonstrations on a number of occasions, and the military was used to intimidate civilian food producers participating in the general strike (Gonzalez 2003; Camel Anderson

2003a, 2003b, 2003c). The armed forces occupied the police stations of the Caracas metropolitan police force, preventing the civilian police from operating. The military occupied oil facilities and assisted in breaking the production strike by PDVSA workers. When the oil tankers of the Venezuelan merchant marine refused to load oil or operate, they were boarded by navy marine commandos and their crews were reportedly intimidated (*El Universal*, 8 December 2002). After President Chávez took the step of breaking up the existing organization of PDVSA and firing almost half of its employees, military officers were brought in to support the pro-government minority of oil workers and managers who returned to work (Camel Anderson 2003a, 2003b). Finally, as supplies and services ran short in most metropolitan areas of Venezuela, the navy was used to ship supplies from neighbouring countries, and the army was used to organize street fairs in which citizens could buy basic necessities and access health and government services (*El Universal,* 13 January 2003). With the rest of the state largely inoperative, wavering (the Supreme Court) or actively opposing Chávez (CNE), only the armed forces allowed the government to continue operating with some measure of physical security, access to resources and the threat of violence to compel its adversaries to end the general strike. It is very significant, however, that the use of the armed forces in internal security missions was limited to specialized units, such as the Guardia Nacional, army military police and the naval commandos, rather than to units of the regular military as a whole.

The growth of civilian organized violence during the Chávez administration

Since 2001, Venezuela has witnessed an unusual expansion in civilian organized violence which parallels the breakdown of civilian control of the armed forces and the expansion of the domestic role of the armed forces. Even though crime rates have risen during the 1990s, what is most threatening to democracy about the present situation is the degree to which civilian actors are organizing themselves to deploy force for political and criminal ends (PROVEA 2003). Amnesty International and Human Rights Watch have both denounced the growing violence and impunity in Venezuela (Human Rights Watch 2003; *El Universal*, 28 May 2003). The restraints on the security forces have increasingly broken down, and the judicial system has not been able to cope with the resulting violations of human rights. This is very unusual for a country that had not experienced significant political violence between 1970 and 1992, and which was often seen as a model of respect for democracy and civil liberties in Latin America during this period. Even though the breakdown of civilian control and the growth in civilian use of violence have occurred in parallel, there is little causal connection. Rather, all actors are reacting to the inability of the Venezuelan political system to resolve conflicts peacefully, and the result is a society that has become increasingly praetorian in nature.

Human rights organizations, both international and in Venezuela, report increasing use of violence as part of criminal activity, as well as a general rise in certain categories of crime. The police forces, which had not had enough resources to control criminal activity effectively prior to the political crisis, have been overwhelmed by demands on their members to provide security during numerous political demonstrations. In Caracas, police activities have been further hindered by the Chávez administration's decision to use the armed forces to take control of the metropolitan police force on charges that it favoured the opposition. According to PROVEA, a long-established Venezuelan human rights organization, there have also been increasing numbers of arbitrary detentions and executions by the security forces. Particularly notable are the use of death squad tactics by state police personnel against criminal organizations, now found in five (of twenty-two) Venezuelan states (PROVEA 2003). There has been little judicial progress in dismantling these organizations, although fourteen members of the Portuguesa state police were imprisoned in 2003 (ibid.). The inability of the judiciary to cope with this activity, and the paucity of resources to address it, contribute to general sense of impunity (*El Universal*, 5 January 2003).

The wave of massive demonstrations against the Chávez administration, the counter-demonstrations by government supporters and the attempts by the police to contain them have all provided new opportunities for political violence. Pro-government civilians, encouraged by government political leaders, have encouraged a physical division of the city of Caracas which parallels its class structure in an effort to deter the largely middle-class opposition from conducting protest marches in poorer neighbourhoods and adjacent to government buildings. The tactic has occasionally led to injury and death, most notably in the incident that sparked the 11 April coup, but also during the efforts to deliver signatures supporting a presidential recall referendum to the National Electoral Council in December 2002. The opposition has reacted by deliberately convening marches in pro-government neighbourhoods, including one in the Caracas suburb of Catia that resulted in one death and twenty-one injuries from gunfire in May 2003, and another demonstration in the poor neighbourhood of Petare, which led to multiple injuries and the destruction of a police office by pro-Chávez counter-demonstrators (*El Universal*, 28 May 2003; *El Nacional*, 16 June 2003). Attacks on the media, often accused of anti-government bias by civilian supporters of President Chávez, have become

Venezuela

so frequent that some journalists have successfully sought protection from the Inter-American Court of Human Rights (COFAVIC 2003).

During the Chávez administration, opposition leaders have persistently accused pro-Chávez neighbourhood political organizations, the Círculos Bolivarianos, of acting as a paramilitary organization, and they have accused elements of the armed forces of providing training and equipment to these groups. The government has consistently denied this charge. These organizations are reported to have participated in political violence in the wake of the 11 April coup attempt, and opposition leaders often accuse them of inciting violence during political protests (Human Rights Watch 2003). Urban guerrilla organizations have emerged in poorer sectors of Caracas, most notably the Tupamaros and Carapaicas. These groups have a radical agenda that places them at odds with the anti-government opposition. They have gone so far as to appear in televised broadcasts and hold news conferences where their members display military-style assault rifles, camouflage and black masks (*El Universal,* 15 June 2003). The government disclaims all connections to these organizations, but the Tupamaros and Carapaicas have publicly proclaimed their dedication to defending the Bolivarian revolution. There are also reports that, at least in the western states that border Colombia, anti-government paramilitary organizations associated with local cattle ranchers have begun to emerge to combat both pro-Chávez organizations and FARC incursions from Colombia.

Venezuelan human rights organizations have also reported a notable increase in the psychological sense of insecurity, far in excess of the actual reported increases in criminal and political violence. The reaction among the civilian population has been to acquire increasing numbers of weapons. There are also burgeoning reports of neighbourhood and apartment-building self-defence organizations emerging in middle-class zones of Caracas, often based on home owner and condominium associations. This reflects the class divisions that have deepened during the 1999–2002 period, and the fear of attack among the middle class accentuated by the often violent language used in the public remarks made by President Chávez regarding the opposition (PROVEA 2003). The development of neighbourhood self-defence organizations may be a first step towards more overt use of political violence by anti-Chávez civilians.

The effects of organized violence on Venezuelan society

There is little evidence that the growing use of organized violence for political purposes can be attributed to the remilitarization of Venezuelan politics. Rather, the remilitarization of politics and the rise in organized violence are a consequence of the growing gap between the Chávez administration and the opposition, neither of which sees the other as legitimate. In the absence of legitimacy, both the government and the opposition have tried to lay claim to the most powerful organization in society, the armed forces. So far, neither side has entirely won this tug of war, yet the struggle has clearly had a deleterious effect on Venezuelan democracy. The armed forces have not been a reliable source of compulsion and force for either the government or the opposition, and the result has been increasing civilian-on-civilian violence with the expected negative impact on democracy. As Koonings and Kruijt argue in Chapter 1 of this volume, the effects of organized violence on democracy are: a growth in fear and distrust among political and social actors; an atomization of civil society; and decreasing legitimacy for the regime and the government. All three of these outcomes are now clearly present in Venezuela's politics and society.

The heated and often apocalyptic rhetoric that the government and the opposition use to refer to each other is more than a political tactic; it is also a reflection of the growing fear with which political actors regard each other in Venezuela, as both PROVEA and COFAVIC, local human rights organizations, have noted. The most recent example of the impact of this phenomenon can be found in the prolonged negotiations that followed the conclusion of the 2002–03 general strike. These discussions, focusing on restoring political peace in Venezuela and addressing the terms under which the government would hold a referendum on President Chávez's term of office, revealed two sides with almost no common ground politically. The participation in these negotiations of the secretary-general of the OAS, Cesar Gaviria, on a daily basis over a period of months is unprecedented in the history of the organization. His statements during this process confirm the depths of mistrust among participants. At their conclusion, the negotiations produced an agreement with little substance, and it was almost immediately disavowed by important political actors from both the pro- and anti-Chávez movements.

In addition, fear and distrust among social actors are also clearly documented by the growing use by civilians of violence to achieve political ends. The psychological sense of insecurity experienced by many Venezuelan citizens and the growth in organized and armed groups are reflections of this phenomenon. The re-emergence of urban guerrilla organizations is especially troubling evidence of the breakdown of the state's monopoly of the use of force. This may lead to a spiral of organization and violence as political actors each engage in an arms race to protect themselves and deter their opponents. The armed forces have attempted to remain at the margin of the growing violence in Venezuelan society, and even the 11 April 2002 coup attempt was notable for the fact that almost all violent acts that occurred during this period involved civilian rather than military use of force.

The impact of the remilitarization of politics and the rise in organized violence on civil society is mixed. On the one hand, there has been an explosion of politically motivated organization as pro- and anti-Chávez elements compete for political space and public support. Venezuelan human rights organizations, whose profile was relatively low during the Punto Fijo period, have acquired new visibility, enhanced by their annual and semi-annual reports that document the growth in violence and impunity in Venezuela. On the other hand, non-political elements in civil society are apparently being starved of resources. A recent report notes that three hundred NGOs (of over two thousand registered), many of which were focused on ameliorating poverty, have ceased to function for lack of resources (Camel Anderson 2003a, 2003b, 2003c). Given the poor performance of the economy during the past two years, this means that there are fewer resources to address a large and growing phenomenon. The use of the armed forces to distribute supplies in poorer areas of Venezuela helps to address poverty, but it may undercut the development of community-based NGOs that use local knowledge to address local problems.

The greatest effect of current political and criminal violence, however, is on the legitimacy of the government. Pro- and anti-Chávez factions in Venezuela see in each other an existential threat. The government points to the 11 April coup attempt and the general strikes that have been convened against it as evidence of the opposition's goal of overthrowing the regime. In light of this, they discredit every proposal made by the opposition and reject all efforts to reach political consensus. The president's references to the opposition as a 'squalid oligarchy' and 'destabilizers' summarize effectively the government's view of the opposition. The opposition points to the repeated violations of the Venezuelan constitution by the government, ongoing violations of legislative procedures to favour government legal proposals, widespread corruption and impunity, and government repression of political demonstrations as evidence that the country is no longer democratic. From their perspective, since President Chávez's political agenda leads to dictatorship, the regime is not legitimate and must be removed, legally or otherwise. The mutual withdrawal of legitimacy by each side is of particular concern since the government has few policy successes to point to that could bolster popular support for the regime, particularly since the limited economic growth achieved in 2000 and 2001 has been erased by an 8.9 per cent decline in GDP in 2002 and an estimated 12 per cent decline (or more) in 2003 (Sarmiento 2003).

Conclusions: explaining the remilitarization of politics

In the highly politically charged atmosphere that has characterized the Chávez administration, the Venezuelan armed forces have not actively sought an expanded role in domestic affairs. Rather, they initially responded to the president's request to support government programmes, and later became the centrepiece of a political tug of war between the government and the opposition. Although there has always been a development role enshrined in armed forces organic laws and in the 1999 constitution, the preferences of the military have usually run in other directions, as is revealed by their preferences in terms of acquisitions: French main battle tanks, Italian missile frigates, and US jet fighters. It was not until newly inaugurated President Chávez ordered the development of Plan Bolívar 2000 that the armed forces expanded their efforts in domestic affairs. President Chávez ordered each of the expansions in the armed forces' domestic role that followed, particularly during the general strike. Moreover, the ability of elected officials to manipulate the military promotion system on the basis of personal loyalties and politics, even after the 11 April 2002 coup, and their ability to prosecute officers and punish them administratively, indicates that the likelihood that the remilitarization of politics in Venezuela has an institutional source is low.

The failure of the 11 April coup indicated that, even though discontent in the officer corps is broadly based, the sentiment in favour of military intervention in politics was limited to a small number of senior officers, now expelled from the institution (Rios 2002a). A sufficient number of junior and mid-ranking officers supported the constitutional government to ensure the return of President Chávez to power. This preference for constitutionalism is confirmed by the arguments that pro- and anti-Chávez military leaders used during the coup. The coup leaders clearly couched their actions in constitutional terms, arguing that they refused to obey illegal orders issued by the president to fire upon peaceful demonstrators. Credibly or not, they explained their role in forming the failed interim government in terms of filling the vacuum of power left by President Chávez's resignation. They also immediately transferred power to a civilian interim administration, another sign of their unwillingness to take power directly (Alvarez 2002a, 2002b, 2002c). The pro-Chávez officers who intervened against them and restored the president to power also argued that they were acting on constitutional grounds, a claim repeatedly made by their leader, General Baduell (Rios 2002b). Furthermore, the fact that the armed forces did not intervene against the president during the 2002–03 general strike, a period of intense social conflict, also argues that the officer corps would prefer to avoid politics (although it may also indicate that Chávez's manipulation of promotions and assignments is especially effective). In any event, pro-Chávez military officers still base their support for the president on the constitution. What is most disturbing and remains a great threat to Venezuelan democracy is the persistent appeal by civilians on both sides for support from the armed forces, which recalls the 'knocking on the barracks door' phenomenon that Alfred Stepan (1971) described in the case of Brazil during the 1960s.

Notes

1 The views presented in this chapter do not necessarily represent the views of the Naval Postgraduate School or the Department of Defence, and are entirely my own.

2 Retired officers belonging to the Frente Institucional Militar (FIM), a group opposed to President Chávez, have consistently argued that military preparedness has been negatively affected by President Chávez's policies. General Garcia Ordoñez, then a senior army general and commander of the Armed Forces Joint Command (CUFAN), stated in May 2000, however, that participation in the Plan Bolívar 2000 involved less than a third of his forces' duty time and thus had little impact on readiness. Officers in the US Military Assistance Group in Venezuela told the author in June 2001 that the truth lay closer to the arguments of the FIM.

3 See the website of dissident military officers, < www.militaresdemocraticos. com>.

4 For an example of the government perspective on the 11 April coup, see the National Assembly's report, *Informe de la Comisión Parlamentaria Especial para investigar los sucesos de Abril de 2002.*

8 | A failed state facing new criminal problems: the case of Argentina

MARCELO SAIN

Democratization and new forms of violence

When, on 10 December 1983, Raúl Alfonsín assumed the presidency of the republic, Argentina at last left behind a past marked by political violence. Since the mid-1950s, with the political prohibition of Peronismo, the military endorsement of this exclusion, and the acceptance by almost the entire non-Peronista partisan faction of this state of affairs, the country had been sinking into a situation of crisis and recurrent political conflict (López 1994; Cavarozzi 1987). The distinctive feature that characterized the Argentine political process that was developing throughout these years was the growth and extensive institutionalization of military power as a political actor. In this context, the armed forces were transforming themselves into a highly corporate power player, with a large degree of institutional autonomy within the political system. This was related not only to the recurrent military intention to consolidate its position as a tutelary actor on the political scene, but also, and in particular, to the weakness of the civil partisan leadership, which accepted, encouraged and maintained that role as necessary and legitimate.

On 24 March 1976, the military junta, consisting of the commanders-in-chief of the three branches of the armed forces, assumed government and initiated the most violent and transformational military dictatorship in the history of Argentina. This dictatorship represented a significant change in the workings of military power, not only through its self-defined and self-maintaining tendency of military interference in the political system, but also by its remarkable reconstitution of the conditions of social domination and the redefinition of the role of the state (and the social and political reconstruction that this operation implied) within the framework of the cruellest experience of state terrorism observed in the Southern Cone. On this occasion, the goals of the military corporation within the so-called Process of National Reorganization (PRN) were not exclusively confined to the coercive disarticulation of the social-political structure that gave sustenance to 'populist' society, but also extended towards the creation of new structural bases and the shaping of new dominant social subjects – all in combination with political repression and socio-economic transformation (Collier 1979).

The collapse of the PRN and Alfonsín's assumption of the presidency at the end of 1983 meant the closing of the cycle of political violence that had been present throughout the previous decades, and the beginning of an institutional process of democratic construction in which the political autonomy of the armed forces was broken, and the subordination of the military to political power was established (Sain 2000). The profound social, economicand political changes that took place in Argentina during the 1980s and 1990s, however, prompted the emergence of new forms of social conflict, produced through the convergence of a number of social and institutional conditions. In these years, Argentina went through a profound process of social disintegration and differentiation, as reflected in the growing deterioration in the quality of life for the middle and lower classes, the breakdown of family groups, the breaking off of traditional ties of community solidarity, the consolidation of a highly regressive structure of income and wealth distribution, and the submission of vast social sectors to poverty, need and vulnerability. Conversely, this same period also witnessed a significant growth in the concentration of economic power and wealth in the hands of the social elite (CEPAL 2001). This situation, as a whole, moulded a complex and heterogeneous social structure in whose bosom has taken place a significant growth in the social exclusion and marginalization of important social sectors.

Out of a total population of 36,233,947 Argentines in 2003, 58 per cent live below the poverty line, 28 per cent in a situation of extreme poverty, and 44 per cent are wage earners without entitlements to state or private retirement funds. On the other hand, of the economically active population, 20 per cent are in a situation of underemployment and 18 per cent are unemployed. But what is significant in this panorama is the distribution of wealth among the different social sectors. In effect, the richest 30 per cent of the population control 65 per cent of the national wealth, while the poorest 30 per cent of the population control barely 8 per cent of the wealth; and the 40 per cent of the population that make up the middle classes control 27 per cent of the national wealth (*Clarín*, 27 April 2003). In short, during the last two decades Argentina has been transformed from a society characterized by full employment, labour stability, highly regulated work and a high rate of social integration into a society characterized by long-term structural unemployment, the deepening of permanent poverty and the appearance of new forms of poverty, thus defining one of the most retrogressive social situations in the whole of Latin America (García del Delgado 2003). In this context, the most significant, intense and encompassing expression of the violence that has emerged out of this complex social context has been the growing and increasingly complicated criminal violence unfolding at the domestic level – mainly in the largest cities – as well as the appearance of new forms of organized crime. Of course, the social situation just described also derives from certain institutional conditions.

The expanding social pauperization produced in Argentina has not been the direct cause of the rise and growing complexity of crime. Rather, in its determination, a number of social, cultural and economic conditions have come together which have favoured the shaping of violent situations and the growth as much of common criminality – in particular of violent crime – as of organized crime (Arriagada and Godoy 1999). Among these conditions, what stands out, of course, is the state's increasingly failing ability to regulate, mediate and resolve basic social conflicts, particularly its incapacity to prevent and to successfully deter criminal activities in their various manifestations. It is a crisis whose most visible feature is the collapse of the criminal justice and prison system, and, in particular, of the police system owing to the systematic and recurrent exercise of illegal violence that is endorsed or carried out by the government or some of its agencies (Méndez 2002).

Like other regional experiences, the political democratization of Argentina provided the setting for a failing state: that is to say a state that has displayed an incapacity to guarantee the effectiveness of its laws, regulations and policies throughout its territory and its system of social stratification, thus moulding with it a scenario in which the relation between state and society comes to be characterized, in many of its aspects, by a low degree of institutionalization (O'Donnell 2002). The aforementioned failings were based upon two characteristics, which have been present ever since the establishment of democracy: (i) permanent political misgovernment in matters of public security on the part of governmental authorities; in addition, and as a consequence of this, the recurrent delegation of the administration of these matters to the police, all of which has resulted in a systematic absence of security policies and strategies appropriate to the challenges imposed by the emergence of new forms of social conflict, particularly the rise and increased complexity of criminality; (ii) the inefficiency of the security and police systems in recognizing the rise and increasing complexity of crime, and, as a result of this, their inability to prevent, confront and successfully deter its different manifestations. This includes the intervention of certain agencies or sectors of the state – especially those of the police – in the production and reproduction of particular modes of crime through complicity, direct participation or disregard. Let us now consider some of these aspects.

A failed state

The new criminal problems in Argentina

The rise in crime Throughout the last few years in Argentina, violence and crime have risen significantly. The crime rate (that is to say, the perpetrated crimes registered per 100,000 inhabitants) has risen since the 1970s. But in the course of the 1990s, this rate surpassed the highest levels reached in previous decades (Dammert 2000; Golbert and Kessler 2001). In 2001 there were 3,182 criminal acts registered, whereas in 1990 there had been 1,722. In other words, during the last few years the rise in crime has been almost 100 per cent. The greatest increase occurred between 1998 and 1999, with a jump of 349 registered criminal offences per 100,000 inhabitants. The official statistics indicate that 'the evolution throughout the 1990s of the crime rate against property registered in the country was very similar to the total number of presumed criminal offences, registering likewise a reduction similar to that which occurred from 1990 to 1991, growing progressively from this moment until 2001, to arrive at 2,114 per 100,000 inhabitants', and also that 'in the case of crimes against the person, the development throughout the decade presents a rising tendency of a gradual character, reaching in 2001 a rate of 569 registered crimes per 100,000 inhabitants' (Dirección Nacional de Política Criminal 2002b: 12).

Moreover, in the largest Argentine cities the rise in registered crime in recent years has been accompanied by a significant increase in levels of violence. During 2001, in the city of Buenos Aires, 40 per cent of the population were victims of crime on at least one occasion, while 60 per cent had never been victims of crime. The percentage of the population that has fallen victim to crimes against property rose to 29 per cent. The proportion of violent robberies, however, was reported at 9 per cent. This is a crime that makes a strong social impact, since it involves the direct use of physical violence against its victims. Between 1998 and 2001, non-violent crimes relatively diminished, whereas violent crimes rose. In effect, violent robbery accounted for 8 per cent of violent crimes in 1998, but by 1999 had risen to 12 per cent. From that year on, however, it began to decline slightly, from 10 per cent in 2000 to 9 per cent in the following years. Nevertheless, if we take the national crime rate in 1998 as a benchmark, we see that the general tendency during these years was one of growth. Moreover, the lower figure of 8 per cent is nevertheless still very high as compared with international parameters (Dirección Nacional de Política Criminal 2002a: 10, 11). The crime levels are highest in the province of Buenos Aires. In 2002, there were 347,566 crimes committed, which included 1,964 homicides, 720 rapes, 134,654 robberies without injury or death, 10,832 robberies resulting in injury or death, 79,735 thefts, and 2,309 kidnappings (*Clarín*, 6 July 2003).

On the other hand, in recent years, in greater Buenos Aires, where more than 75 per cent of the crimes committed in the province are concentrated, the patterns of victimization have been similar to those of the city of Buenos Aires, although the levels of victimization and of criminal violence have been higher in the latter. In 2000, 39 per cent of the population fell victim to one sort of crime or another, while 61 per cent were unaffected by any type of crime. The proportion of the population which in that year suffered crime against property reached 34 per cent, while violent robberies made up 12 per cent of crimes. In 1998, violent robbery comprised 11 per cent of the total crime rate, and the following year made a remarkable jump up to 15 per cent (Dirección Nacional de Política Criminal 2001: 6ff). Something similar is taking place in the city of Rosario, which is another of the country's metropolises. In 1998, 46 per cent of the population were reported to have fallen victim to crime, a greater proportion than in the other cases mentioned. Thirty-six per cent were victims of crime against property, while violent robbery affected 12 per cent, which is less than the 13 per cent registered in 1999, but higher than the 7 per cent recorded in 1997 (Dirección Nacional de Política Criminal 2001a: 8ff). Finally, in the city of Córdoba, only 35 per cent of the population had suffered crime in 1999, of which 9 per cent were victims of violent robbery (Dirección Nacional de Política Criminal 2000: 8ff).

On the other hand, these tendencies have developed into a social and institutional scene that is characterized by the retreat or evaporation of the state in vast regions of urban territory, as well as in considerable sectors of its social structure. The result of this is that the effectiveness of the law is extended irregularly, giving rise to certain '*favelizado*' territorial spaces within these large cities. This absence of state regulation is replaced by interactions based on violence, and by extended criminal networks. In these communities – in the context of permanent unemployment, lack of regular income, the retreat of the welfare state and the explicit repressive intervention of the police and/or the condoning of blatant criminal activities – the traditional social ties have unravelled, giving rise to a social logic that dramatically combines incipient forms of social solidarity with everyday acts of violence and criminality. In many of the *villas* (slums) of the principal cities of Argentina, these conditions have favoured the formation of autonomous local power holders and have permitted the articulation of violent forms of social domination, exercised generally by criminal groups or bands operating in the new *favelas*, whose activities predominantly revolve around the distribution of drugs. 'The [drug invasion] is, along with the lack of employment, the dominant preoccupation in the *villas* of *Capital Federal* (the province of Buenos Aires) and *Gran Buenos Aires*

(Metropolitan Buenos Aires,' Javier Auyero appropriately noted, to which he adds: 'the distribution of drugs and alcohol nourish a cycle of distrust and interpersonal violence; a cycle that, without clear origins or aims, permeates the entire atmosphere of *villa* life and impacts on its basic routines ... ' (Auyero 2001: 17). The highest number of violent criminal acts, in particular the greatest number of homicides, is concentrated as much in the interior of these territories as in the *barrios* and in neighbouring zones.

The growing complexity of crime In the context described above, it is not only common crime which has increased, but also the criminality perpetrated by criminal organizations, which have at their disposal ample logistical and operational capabilities, and whose illegal activities aim at the generation of a high level of economic profit. These groups are strategically dispersed. In some cases they possess an international reach, and in others a national or regional one. Furthermore, the degree of organizational complexity, the division of functions, the professionalism and the operational coordination between different groups and sub-groups that comprise the organization accord them relative social importance.

The trade in illegal drugs – in particular cocaine and marijuana – constitutes the most important illicit activity with the greatest profit for these crime centres (Emmerich 2000). Over the past few years, traffic in and distribution and local consumption of these drugs have been increasing remarkably, particularly in the case of cocaine from Bolivia and marijuana from Paraguay and Brazil (UNDCP 2000). Argentina is not a producer of the aforementioned narcotics, nor do the principal international routes of drugs destined for international markets pass through its territory. The marijuana and cocaine that are trafficked, stored and distributed in Argentina are manufactured in neighbouring countries, such as Paraguay and Bolivia, and are brought into the country over the northern frontier and the north-east border by groups of local or foreign traffickers who, although not organized into cartels, are nevertheless growing more and more concentrated (Observatoire Géopolitique des Drogues 2000). After crossing numerous provincial jurisdictions, the shipments of drugs finally arrive in the large cities and are distributed in the retail market in a decentralized and dispersed manner. According to official and international estimates, a notable rise in the traffic and local consumption of narcotics occurred in the 1990s – an increase of between 10 and 30 per cent, although other estimates suggest that over the last fifteen years the general consumption of prohibited drugs has quintupled (Barbano 2003; *Clarín*, 28 July 2003). As in other countries of Latin America, two-thirds of drug consumption in Argentina is of cocaine and related products, and the rest is of marijuana, tranquillizers and inhalants (UNDCP 2000).

On the other hand, the trade in and illegal sale of arms does not constitute a criminal activity that is highly profitable – its significance is that it is the source for the arms that are used in most acts of criminal violence. The bulk of this illegal market is in small, light firearms, such as pistols, stolen from or illegally sold by the police, from stockpiles of legally confiscated or disused firearms that have not been destroyed and instead have been illegally reintroduced into the black market.

According to information provided by the Ministry of Security for the province of Buenos Aires, the significant growth in violent criminality is accompanied within the boundaries of this provincial jurisdiction by an increase in the trade, carrying and illegal use of firearms with criminal intent. According to the Centro de Operaciones Policiales (Centre of Police Operations) and to the Ministry of Security's Subsecretaría de Planificación y Logística (Subsecretariat of Planning and Logistics), 380,069 criminal offences were registered within the provincial jurisdiction in 2000, of which 12,882 (or 3 per cent) were committed with firearms. In 2001, of 308,878 registered criminal offences, 15,631 (5 per cent) were perpetrated with firearms, while in 2002, out of 361,718 acts of crime, 18,920 (5 per cent) involved the use of firearms (Ministerio de Seguridad de la Provincia de Buenos Aires 2003). It is valid to say, therefore, that, based on this official information, between 2000 and 2002 the total number of crimes registered diminished slightly while the percentage of crimes perpetrated with the use of firearms doubled. In 2002, the provincial police seized 10,647 firearms in various operations, but 73 per cent of these seizures took place within the jurisdiction of greater Buenos Aires, where the highest incidence of violent crimes occurs. During that year, the increase in the confiscation of firearms was 11 per cent, although between 2000 and 2002 this increase was in the order of 39 per cent. Of the firearms seized by the police in 2002, 86 per cent were handguns, the type used most in the violent crimes perpetrated in metropolitan Buenos Aires (*La Nación*, 15 June 2003).

The theft and dismantling of automobiles, and the illegal sale of car parts, constitute one of the fastest-growing, most complex and most profitable criminal activities in recent years in Argentina's large cities, particularly in the province of Buenos Aires. This criminal problem involves, in addition, the highest levels of violence, and the theft of automobiles is one of the principal causes of homicide. In addition, it entails complex interrelationships between the different groups that participate in this business; that is to say, those in charge of stealing the vehicles, those who manage the dismantling and subsequent sale of car parts, the so-called 'recovery companies', and the police. The majority of the 'dismantlers' (*desarmaderos*) are located in metropolitan Buenos Aires, although the sale of car parts extends to embrace a wider area. In the province of Buenos Aires, another aspect of this mode of crime is the 'recovery' of stolen vehicles, an activity carried out by numerous companies – legal or clandestine – that are headed by former police chiefs, and based on information and favours exchanged with different police chiefs still in active service. Throughout 2002, in the province of Buenos Aires, more automobiles were stolen than were imported by the provincial car dealers (*PuntoDoc* 2003). At present, it is estimated that an average of 11,000 automobiles are stolen each month throughout the province, about half of which are dismantled and sold off as car parts in the black market. This activity generates more than $400 million, although other estimates suggest that this illegal market has a turnover of some $700 million, just within the province itself. Around 25 per cent of stolen automobiles are recovered by companies specializing in this business. The rest of the stolen vehicles are 'duplicated' (*doblados*), which means they are illegally re-registered using the documentation of other vehicles of the same model which have been destroyed. Luxury automobiles are more often smuggled to neighbouring countries (*Clarín*, 15 May 2003; *Página/12*, 6 July 2003).

Another mode of organized crime that has begun to develop over the past few years, particularly in metropolitan Buenos Aires and throughout the rest of the province, is the robbery of goods in transit, perpetrated by so-called 'pirates of the asphalt'. It is a non-violent crime of a largely local character, which generates a high profit. It is carried out by relatively complex groups, which not only organize the robbery but also manage the storage and retail sale of the goods. In the province of Buenos Aires, 1,864 incidences of 'asphalt piracy' were prevented in 2000, whereas in 2001 this level was reduced to 1,491. In 2002, however, the number of registered crimes of this type rose to 2,357 (Ministerio de Seguridad de la Provincia de Buenos Aires 2002).

Finally, another novel mode of criminal activity that has grown considerably, principally in the province of Buenos Aires, is the abduction of individuals. During 2002, in the province of Buenos Aires, 146 abductions were recorded, of which fifty were abductions for the purpose of extortion, and ninety-six were abductions for the purpose of obtaining a small ransom (Subsecretaría de Planificación y Logística 2003). To a great extent, abductions organized for extortion occur with police sponsorship. They have also developed as a form of neutralizing certain political attempts to introduce changes in policing, or as a way to pressurize governmental authorities in order to obtain additional income or to neutralize political interference (Sain

2003a; Sánchez 2003). All this has recently been presented as clear evidence that a number of abductions have been carried out by mixed bands of common criminals and policemen in active service (*Pagina/12*, 29 July 2003).

The development and spread of the aforementioned criminal activities – drug trafficking, the dismantling of cars for the sale of car parts, and robberies perpetrated by 'pirates of the asphalt' – are the result of a certain degree of police participation in the composition of, and the protection enjoyed by, these criminal gangs. In the main cities of the country, and in greater Buenos Aires in particular, the ability of these gangs to create operational bases in certain neighbourhoods, and to create highly developed logistical structures and intelligence capabilities, is due to the protection provided by certain sectors of the police, and their direct complicity in the criminal business carried out by these groups (Sain 2003b). Moreover, the most developed and best organized of these criminal groups are increasingly becoming autonomous of police management or regulation, and maintain with the police a type of relationship that combines different levels of complicity, competition and/or confrontation (Barbano 2003).

Political misgovernment, deficient policing and social insecurity

The spread and complexity that the crime problem in Argentina has acquired have made quite evident the existing institutional deficiencies in the country's system of security and, in particular, the deficiencies inherent in governmental decision-makers and the police agencies that comprise them.

In general, the government authorities have maintained a lack of interest in and an ignorance of matters of public security, as well as the changing problems of crime and the intricacies of the police function, and have abandoned the task of the administration of all these issues by delegating it to the police. In tackling these tasks, the police, on the other hand, have followed the ensemble of directions, conceptions and practices autonomously fashioned and reproduced over decades inside their own institutions. In most cases, this impromptu delegation has been based on a pact – implicit or explicit – in which the governmental authorities agree to refrain from interfering in the institutional life of the police in exchange for a guarantee of certain politically acceptable levels of public security (Sain 2002; Míguez and Isla 2003).

Nevertheless, over the last few years the growth and increased complexity of criminal activities, in addition to rising insecurity (objectively and subjectively perceived) in the everyday life of the nation, have served to undermine this manner of organizing and executing public security. In this context, what is evident is the profound anachronist structure and disjointedness – organic, functional and doctrinal – of Argentina's system of policing and public security in the face of recent changes in criminality (Sain 2003c). Likewise, this situation has proven favourable to the institutional reproduction of police practices on the borders of legality, and to the maintenance of a system of direct and indirect regulation of certain criminal activities by some groups within the police itself.

The system of public security in Argentina, of which the police form one particular dimension, was based on a set of traditional parameters that are the outcome of a long historical process (Maier 1996; Maier, Abregú and Tiscornia 1996; Andersen 2001; Sozzo 2002). The Argentine police force was basically shaped as an institution at the service of state governments rather than of communities, within the framework of a conceptualization of security as rooted in the protection provided by the state and not in citizens' rights and liberties, a strongly 'statist' view. Likewise, in the time of the authoritarian regimes the military governments assumed iron control of the police and, more recently, positioned the police as key actors in the control and repressive internal discipline directed by the armed forces. All this served to bring about a comprehensive organizational and functional militarization of the police forces. It also gave rise to the institutionalization of highly illegal and clandestine practices and orientations in the working of the police (Andersen 2001; Vallespin 2002), which has not been subjected to any type of reform or reorganization on the part of successive governmental administrations since the restoration of democracy. Thus, Argentinian police, far from establishing themselves as a civil and civic force, instead conducted themselves as guardians of the political order, and as a militarized police, more sensitive to the orientations and interests of the government in power and its respective leaders than to the law. This historical process has resulted in the establishment of a police system that to date has been inefficient in preventing and guarding against the new manifestations of crime. It is a system that is also inefficient in its ability to structure a mode of policing that can successfully regulate crime, the most significant consequence of which has been the establishment of a stable network of policemen who are financed through gifts and funds that originate from diverse tolerated criminal activities, which are protected and even carried out by the policemen themselves, and endorsed politically (Latorraca, Montero and Rodriguez 2003).

The inefficiency of the police corresponds to the profound doctrinal backwardness that dominates Argentina's police agencies, as well as to their anachronistic organizational and functional policies in the development of crime prevention and control. With some exceptions, these agencies display a series of institutional defects that lie at the base of their inefficiency (Sain 2003c; Waldmann 2003). In the same way, these anachronisms have proved favourable to the reproduction of institutional behaviour and forms of organization and functioning that are outside the law, and to the maintenance of a system of direct and indirect regulation of certain criminal activities on the part of some members of constituent groups within the police force. Within the ambit of policing a set of habitual institutional practices that are widely and arbitrarily exercised is reproduced and legitimized. These practices are exemplified by 'maltreatments, tortures, the refusal to exercise one's protective function, blackmail and extortion, corruption, arbitrary detentions, falsification of evidence, collecting money in return for police protection, as well as the participation in criminal activities and the concealment of such complicity' (Stanley 2001: 239). Traditionally, the regulation of crime exercised by certain sectors of the police involved the protection of and participation in activities such as prostitution, illegal gambling and petty crime. Over the last few years, however, these relations of protection, sponsorship and direct participation have extended to the more complex forms of crime already described in this chapter.

This is the picture, then, of the institutional situation that has been eroding society's confidence in the state, its judicial and governmental authorities, and, in particular, its police force. In 2000, 69 per cent of the population of metropolitan Buenos Aires that had fallen victim to crime declined to file a police report, for which 44 per cent cited as the reason: 'the police might not have done anything'. (Only 30 per cent of crime victims filed a police report.) It is the opinion of 52 per cent of the population of this region that the police are not doing a good job in controlling crime, and only 32 per cent of the population feel that the police are doing a good job. At the same time, 31 per cent of this population describe the quality of the police's crime prevention actions as 'average', while 13 per cent are of the opinion that it is 'bad', 2 per cent that it is very bad, 4 per cent that it is abysmal; and 20 per cent feel that the police fail to take any preventive actions whatsoever. Likewise, 56 per cent of the capital's population believe that the national government is not doing anything with regard to the issue of security, and 28 per cent feel that the government is doing something but not enough (Dirección Nacional de Política Criminal 2001). The situation is similar in the federal capital, in Rosario, Córdoba, and other large cities throughout the country.

In this way, then, the objective rise in crime and the greater complexity of criminal activities in the last few years, the notable increase in violent crime, the significant growth in the widely acknowledged state corruption, the participation of the police in the conduct of a large portion of the criminal activities taking place in the country and the consequent diminution of public confidence in the police – all this has contributed greatly to an increasing sense of insecurity in a country regarded as safe until a little over a decade ago (Dammert and Malone 2002). Equally, in this context, another factor that fundamentally underpins the widespread feeling of insecurity and the erosion of public confidence in the state is the police's involvement with and connivance in certain criminal activities (Muleiro 2003). In short, faced with this new public security scenario, Argentina has, in this sense, a failing state; that is to say, a state with noticeable deficiencies in the elaboration of a new understanding and diagnosis appropriate to the new problems of security, and relevant to the construction – based on its doctrinal, organizational and operational tenets – of an up-to-date and efficient system of public security. The effect of these deficiencies has been to generate a situation in which the state is debilitated in its ability to exercise a monopoly of force by groups that oppose it and vie for this monopoly. The result is a state 'incapable of gaining compliance to all its laws and regulations and not only promulgating them' (Waldmann 2003: 15).

Finally, in this political mismanagement of security and in the autonomy of the police lies the state's failure to control, to attenuate and to prevent the new forms of violent crime, particularly those that derive directly from the state's ineptitude in exercising its power to police those modes of crime that are being favoured, permitted or carried out by some sectors of the police force itself. And one should not lose sight of the fact that the reversal of these defective tendencies would not necessarily guarantee lover levels of crime, if it is not pursued within the framework of social policies that tend to reduce the levels of marginality and exclusion of important sectors of Argentine society, while reconstituting the state's internal regulatory functions.

9 | Urban violence and drug warfare in Brazil

ALBA ZALUAR

Introduction

Despite the relative absence in Brazil of large-scale social and political violence over the past century or so, this country has always displayed a gap between the formal institutions of the rule of law and citizenship rights and the ambivalent domain of social processes and practices not controlled by them. Over the past few decades this has facilitated the rise of new forms of violence, particularly in the urban context and directly related to the spread of the distribution and consumption of illicit drugs.

In this period worldwide production of and trade in illicit drugs have increased dramatically. It is said that the illegal drugs market is today one of the biggest economic sectors in the world economy, economically, politically and socially embedded in almost every country in the world. As a result, transnational and localized organized crime have increased violence in certain areas. These activities include other criminal activities such as robbery and the theft of goods that will be used as currencies for buying drugs and precursors (Zaluar 1994; Geffray 2001; UNDCP 1997). They also follow networks already established for other illegal activities such as smuggling, governmental corruption and gun trafficking (Luppo 2002). In a context of poor economic growth, more people may be attracted to the risks of the crime business, organizing their activities so as to curtail detection and prosecution.

Among the illegal drugs, cocaine is today associated with a lifestyle that sets great store in money, power, violence and the consumption of goods with a trendy trademark. Owing to very high prices of the drug, its trade has become a source of enormous and rapid profit, as well as significant violence. At the same time this is the main reason for corruption in institutions such as the police, the judiciary, the legislature and government. In Brazil, institutional corruption, disrespect for the law, inefficiency and arbitrariness in the justice system have gone hand in hand with increasing urban violence.

In this chapter, I analyse the nature of drug-related urban violence in Brazil against the background of this institutional failure, but also in relation to persistent patterns of inequality and social exclusion that characterize the country despite its considerable modernization in terms of consumption patterns, lifestyles and social values. I will therefore argue that the combination of accelerated urbanization and persistent poverty has left many poor young men in a state of vulnerability. The institutional mechanisms of organized crime have offered them opportunities for what I have called 'perverse integration' (Zaluar 2000, 2001). I will take up this idea in the final section of the chapter.

A brief history of social and institutional violence in Brazil

Brazil has a long history of social – institutional and private – violence, but not of political violence, as has been the case in other Latin American countries. In fact, social violence also diminished in the first decades after the Second World War but increased again amazingly from the end of the 1970s onwards. Political violence – not altogether absent from Brazilian history from colonial times – cannot by itself explain this recent spurt of interpersonal and private violence. Elections in Brazil have historically been propelled by clientele arrangements and multiple mediators: the Brazilian rural patron, the *coronel* (colonel), had to please minor grandees and his followers as well as the central government. Votes were then bought with favours, but also with real local improvements as well as constraints upon the voters. *Coroneis* received this title because they had troops of *jagunços* or armed men at their service within the boundaries of their properties. Personal vengeance and blood feuds were common. In fact family warfare characterized the history of Brazilian violence up to the twentieth century, especially in the north-east and the hinterlands, for centuries the most violent areas of the country. Judges had hardly any autonomy in these localities and decisions usually benefited the powerful, whose crimes went without punishment. Only in Rio de Janeiro, the capital, did courts achieve some independence. Therefore, impunity has a long history in Brazil. Policemen were trained to comply with and submit to the powerful proprietors, repressing only the poor, the blacks and the natives. Relationships between central government and provincial (after 1889, state) oligarchies, however, made negotiation and manipulation more important than open and violent conflicts. As a result, elections in Brazil have been less violent than in other Latin American countries, even though sometimes the results have not been accepted.

The military regime between 1964 and 1985 perpetrated a certain degree of collective violence, especially institutional violence, during which 333 people died as a result of state terror, one hundred times fewer than during the Argentinian military dictatorship (Skidmore 1988; Zaverucha 1994). Yet there has never existed in Brazil anything similar to the phenomenon of *la violencia*, the war without rules which devastated the Colombian political parties and civil population during the1950s. Nor has there been the enduring phenomenon of urban and rural guerrillas, or the paramilitaries that underpinned the peculiar pattern of violence in Colombia. Unlike in other countries, the Brazilian political system continued functioning during the whole military period, despite severe restrictions over the better part of this period. The government continued to use corruption along with clientelism as a strategy to control the politicians, who still had some powers of decision-making.

Nevertheless, the very fact that the military dictatorship used and abused torture, illegal arrests and censorship facilitated the emergence of organized crime. Some of the officers who had adhered to those unlawful practices became members of extermination and extortion groups, or became involved with *bicheiros* (racketeers controlling the illegal *jogo do bicho*, the 'animal game' lottery) and drug traffickers (Gaspari 2002). The military who committed such crimes were protected by the National Security Law, which was not abolished until 1988, and by the Amnesty Law of 1979 that prohibited their indictment and punishment (Zaverucha 1994). Finally, since there have been no or few reforms within the justice system, and especially no changes in police practices with regard to the poor, one might say that the effects of the military regime are still present in the functioning of these institutions which do not practise respect for the civil rights of the poor and excluded population

Urban violence, crime and drugs

From the late 1970s onwards, criminal violence increased quickly and significantly in state capitals – Cuiabá, Vitoria, Recife, São Paulo and Rio de Janeiro – and some medium-sized towns in the hinterlands of a few Brazilian states, mainly Pernambuco, São Paulo and Paraná. In the metropolitan region of Rio de Janeiro, the homicide rate tripled during the 1980s, growing from twenty-three deaths per 100,000 inhabitants in 1982 to sixty-three per 100,000 in 1990, a period in which the population of the city stabilized. This happened mainly in the peripheral and poor municipalities of the metropolitan region, however, because police investigation is particularly difficult there. In 1994 the rate reached seventy-four per 100,000 and then started declining until 1999, when it was forty-one per 100,000.

A careful study of police inquiries and judicial cases during 1991 in Rio de Janeiro showed that 57 per cent of the homicides that year were linked to drug traffic (Soares et al. 1996). This is just one more indication that the growth in the homicide rate has been linked to the increased entry of guns and drugs into the country, since both began at the same time during the late 1970s.

Another indicator of the correlation between gang warfare and murders is the age of the victims. Although violent death rates have increased all over the country, the most common victims are not children but adolescent and young males from the metropolises and the richest regions of the country. This rapid growth in homicides particularly affected young men between 15 and 29 years old. They were killed in crimes taking place in public places involving people who did not know each other. During 1991, official statistics indicated that 12.5 men had died for each woman within the 20–39 age cohort in the metropolitan region of Rio de Janeiro. Most of the agents of this violence were young males; they were also the main victims (Campos 1988).

In 1980, according to data from the Ministry of Health, 59 per 100,000 men between 15 and 19 years old died of gun injuries in the state of Rio de Janeiro; in 1990, 190 per 100,000 died the same way; in 1995, 184 per 100,000. The rates for men aged between 20 and 24 were even higher. In 1995, in the city of Rio de Janeiro, 6,399 people were victims of violent deaths of which 45 per cent were homicides. In the metropolitan region, 17,684 deaths by external causes were registered, of which 55 per cent were homicides. As a point of comparison, deaths from nutritional deficiencies affected 382 persons in the same year.

Exactly the same pattern is found in disputes over the division and defence of territories and the paying off of traffickers and robbers as that which developed during the violent competition between gangs in the ghettos of Los Angeles, Chicago and New York at the beginning of the twentieth century. But impunity in Brazil is certainly another factor in the increase in the mortality rate among small traffickers, because homicides are hardly investigated at all and crimes related to illegal drugs are fiercely repressed in poor areas.

Nevertheless, in 2003 Rio de Janeiro was far from being the most violent capital in the country. Data from the Ministry of Justice's Secretaria Nacional de Segurança Pública (National Secretary of Public Security) shows this city to be seventh in intentional homicides, fourth in robberies, seventeenth in rape, eighth in robbery followed by death, eighth in extortion from kidnapping, and thirteenth in deaths in traffic accidents. Furthermore, a comparison between towns of more than 20,000 inhabitants shows that the ten most violent are found in the hinterland of the states of São Paulo and Pernambuco, where the most important area of marijuana production is situated.

The view that Rio de Janeiro is at the centre of organized crime is misleading and an aspect of the fierce parochial competition that nowadays exists in Brazil. One of the main routes of cocaine in the country passes through Rondônia, Mato Grosso, Paraná and São Paulo, states in which violent death rates and incidences of the HIV virus, through the intravenous use of drugs, reached the highest levels in the country, doubling during the 1980s (Bastos 1995). Official data from the State Secretaries of Justice, based on police reports, indicate that, in the metropolitan region of São Paulo, the proportion of intentional homicides grew tremendously during the 1980s and 1990s (Adorno 1995). Of these deaths, 47 per cent involved young males between 15 and 24 years of age. In the municipality of São Paulo, the increase was more than 90 per cent, from 3,516 in 1984 to 6,697 in 1994. These figures are even more impressive if one adds deaths caused by policemen. At the beginning of the 1980s, there were approximately 300 deaths per year in São Paulo due to encounters with the military police. At the end of the decade, there were 585 deaths per year, and in 1991 there were 1,140 deaths. These figures were not included in the homicide rates. The number of deaths among policemen also increased over the years. Even though they include deaths off duty, the figures are quite clear: 26 military policemen died in 1982 and 78 died in 1991 (Caldeira 2000).

Explaining the paradox of violence

What general factors explain this increase in violence over the past two decades, which, paradoxically, witnessed the transition from authoritarianism to democracy and showed significant progress in terms of democratic consolidation?

Instead of economic growth, during the democratization process there was an economic, moral and political crisis, fuelled by rapid inflation. Brazil has a varied and modern economy, but its political and juridical institutions have not evolved accordingly. Not only has the country maintained one of the most unequal income distributions in the world, but there are also great inequalities in terms of access to public welfare or justice provisions. Even after the promulgation of the 1988 constitution, which formally guarantees civil rights to the poor, they continued experiencing violations of their rights, though less so than before.

Thus, the hard core of discrimination in Brazil is in the institutional sphere, i.e. in the violations of the rights of the poor that depend on the workings of the justice system (Zaluar 2001).[1] Corrupt policemen form what one could call 'extortion groups', a name more appropriate than 'extermination groups', for policemen who kill young traffickers are demanding their share of the traffic money. But the majority of the poor youngsters are still killed in gang warfare. This is one of the main reasons why one cannot describe the present wave of violence as being simply an effect of the existing genealogy of violence. In this section I examine the interlocking mechanisms of social inequality in the urban domain and the failure of public institutions to uphold the rule of law. Both mechanisms boil down to a persistent pattern of social exclusion preparing the ground for organized criminal violence.

Economic hardship and social exclusion Inflation, which ravished the country until 1994, is not an exclusively economic phenomenon; psychological and moral factors are also involved. It has therefore had perverse effects on the attitudes and values of the population, especially among the wage-earners who gained nothing from it. High inflation erodes mutual trust, without which there is no stable social relationship between economic agents. Furthermore, inflation was considered a form of stealing from the salaried, and depreciated governmental credibility, fostering a governance crisis in the country. Psychologically, it was used as a justification for crimes against property. Finally, high inflation facilitated the functioning of organized crime inside the country, in so far as it helped to create the mirage of 'easy money'. Those who had started practising increasingly more daring economic crimes were helped by the growing problems with record-keeping and controls over public budgets and bills. This facilitated corruption and money laundering, activities that are very important in establishing criminal connections but which have not been properly investigated up to now.

It is also a fact that, in order to compensate for the wage losses provoked by unemployment, low salaries, inflation and the new consumption demands, poor families put children and adolescents out to work in order to increase their income. Several studies point to the growth of this category of work and to a greater rate of unemployment among youths. Nevertheless, the majority of these youngsters – many of whom work informally in the streets – never join criminal groups, despite their vulnerable position. Only a small number get involved with gangs of traffickers or robbers. Basic needs or the wish to help their families are not sufficient reasons to explain why some join gangs and others do not, though the need to earn money remains a major motive for their actions and personal decisions. In fact, few poor people opt for a criminal career. In field research undertaken in a poor neighbourhood of Rio de Janeiro, It is estimated that around 1 per cent of the total population (380 people out of a population of 39,000) belonged to the trafficker gangs, and about 1,200 people were involved in occasional thefts and mugging (Zaluar 1994).

The existence of a new form of informal market is another element in the Brazilian paradox. Informal markets have always existed in Brazil and have been an important source of income for those with few work qualifications or no jobs. These informal markets have developed personal networks and rules governing the occupation of public spaces in the urban centres. Yet over the past decades, those who work in them have been joined by street vendors who sell several counterfeit products, some of which are smuggled in from other countries,[2] and diverse types of goods stolen from trucks, residences and pedestrians. Informal trade, which traditionally has been a way out of unemployment, has hence become tied to organized crime. This becomes even clearer when one examines its connections with gold-selling shops, car repair shops, wrecked-car lots and antique dealers, some of which have become collection points for stolen goods. It has been discovered recently that even some legal truck transport businesses are part of the truck robbery network. There has been little systematic investigation of these networks so far, however, although the police have sometimes harshly repressed the last in the line: those who sell on the streets.

Impunity and institutional failure Equally important in understanding the growth of violent crime in Brazil are the strategies of corruption; the unequal functioning of the justice system due to the organizational practices created and maintained by those working in it; and the obsolete penal code adopted by consecutive governments since the foundation of the republic in 1889. Together, they created 'islands of impunity', to borrow an expression conceived by Dahrendorf (1992).

Once again, the interconnections between political power and institutions remain the crux of the matter. Although the judiciary is nowadays an independent power (too independent, some say), the executive appoints members of the audit system, those who monitor and audit their expenditure. The executive also designates judges of first instance courts as well as the heads of civil police departments and military police commanders. Both are sources of easy corruption because neither has the necessary autonomy and will to combat violations of the law efficaciously. Reform of the state is only slowly coming about.

The very inefficient and unjust functioning of the justice system in Brazil has played an important role in the crisis of morality and the weakening of the ethos of work, and has allowed criminals to become entrenched in the country. An incredibly high percentage of homicides are not properly investigated and their authors are never identified. A study of the criminal justice system in São Paulo (Adorno 1990) has found greater percentages of conviction among those accused of robbery, theft and drug traffic than among those accused of homicide and assault. Another study revealed that only 1.38 per cent of the homicides committed against children and adolescents up to seventeen years old were effectively investigated, with the victims and the suspects identified, leading to judicial cases that resulted in sentences (Mesquita 1996). Yet another study showed that of 4,277 homicide bulletins only 4.6 per cent had noted the author and the motive for the crimes. In Rio de Janeiro, another study shows that 92 per cent of homicide judicial cases were returned to the police because they were poorly investigated; in other words, only 8 per cent of the murders registered by the police in the form of an inquiry were in fact judged (Soares et al. 1996).

Workers and bandits alike have a moral view of crime that relates it to necessary punishment. Nevertheless, the dynamics of interactions I will describe below transform this view into a cynical, instrumental and manipulative version of the law on the part of those who have been indicted. Luck, manipulation of judicial actors and the due process of law, occasional pressures and bribes before, during and after the judicial process, the regular corruption of policemen, intimidation of possible witnesses by the use of guns or terror exerted on neighbours, and a very lucrative business offer incentives and justifications for the crimes committed, including murder.

As institutions, the police and the justice system have a considerable negative reputation. When someone assesses them positively, he or she is almost certainly referring to a specific person, such as a policeman known to them or a judge who has presided over a fair decision. Prison and police precincts are equated to 'schools of criminality'. The justice system as a whole is seen as 'propelled by money', as are most of the country's organizations nowadays. Policemen still have the power to begin an inquiry by registering the *auto da prisão em flagrante* (flagrant arrest report) or any other proof necessary to the judicial process. Sometimes they also maintain the practice, in contravention of existing institutional norms and the constitutional rights of Brazilian citizens, of torturing prisoners, mainly poor and black people, in order to extract confessions from them about their supposed criminal acts.

Impunity is another effect of their frail professional ethos and precarious status as investigators. Many bandits never get caught, which they regard as a stimulus to repeat delinquent acts. And since money may guarantee impunity, either because a policeman will not register the act and thus not start an inquiry, or because well-paid lawyers know how to avoid judicial processes, joining drug traffic gangs becomes even more attractive (Zaluar 1998). When questioned, the indicted may lie, for there is no oath in Brazilian justice. Therefore, the whims and wishes of the traffickers may be decisive for the outcome of a youngster's career (Zaluar 1994; Lins 1997).

Drug trafficking in Rio de Janeiro

I have suggested before (Zaluar 1994) that the underlying workings of the war on drugs have helped to put Brazil on the cocaine route to Europe, while opening a widespread market for it. Illegal drug traffic was never a major social problem in Brazil until the late 1970s. Then cocaine started to be trafficked on a large scale, following the new routes chosen by the Colombian cartels and the Italian-American Mafia. Along these routes cocaine cargoes were sent to Europe and to the USA. Passing through several Brazilian states and cities, including Rio de Janeiro and São Paulo, the route engendered new consumer markets for drugs. From the beginning of the 1980s, there was a clear market strategy aimed at changing the habits of drug consumers in those cities. Formerly the illicit drug market involved almost exclusively marijuana, which was an underground and drop-out drug and never had great economic importance; nor did it attract a rigid repressive policy. Then cocaine started to be offered at prices that represented good value.

The traffic itself changed. It was no longer conducted on an intimate basis in a face-to-face relationship with the 'man of the truck' who brought marijuana from Pernambuco, its main producer. A new, complex, diversified and very well-armed organization, in which any commercial or personal conflicts were settled with guns, arrived on the scene with a virile power cult. This created the conditions that enticed many lower-income youths to involve themselves in a localized but very deadly war (Zaluar 1994, 2001). Today, the drug trade has become synonymous with warfare in most Brazilian small towns and big cities.

There are several new and diverse networks that connect Brazilian states (São Paulo, Mato Grosso, Rondonia, Paraná, Minas Gerais, Espírito Santo, Rio de Janeiro) and others that connect Brazil with producing countries (Paraguay, Bolivia, Peru, Colombia) by which cocaine and guns reach their destination inside towns and cities. Conversely, stolen goods such as automobiles, trucks, jewellery and domestic appliances – robbed from their owners on highways, roads, streets or in residences inside those states and used in non-monetary exchanges for illegal drugs – also reach their final destination without difficulty. This quiet, hidden style of trafficking contrasts with the noisy and murderous one at the selling points inside the *favelas* of Rio de Janeiro, Vitoria, Belo Horizonte, Recife and São Paulo.

Even if not coordinated entirely like a Mafia hierarchy, the drug trade in Rio de Janeiro has an efficient horizontal structure by which a shanty town that runs out of drugs or guns immediately gets them from allied shanty towns: either through the networks of the CV (Red Command) or the TC (Third Command), the two best-known organizations for drug and gun traffic. These networks or *comandos* agree upon the demarcation of a geographically defined territory, which includes diffusion points, from which other linkages are established on the basis of horizontal reciprocity. This has both positive and negative aspects. For even though guns and drugs are readily lent to allies, the violent reciprocity of private vengeance becomes imperative. Because of such exchanges, adolescents die not only in wars for the control of trading points but also for any act that threatens the status or pride of youngsters trying to assert their virility – the so-called *sujeito homem* (Lins 1997).

There is a hierarchy of shanty towns, some of them functioning as distribution centres for retail trade, while others act as small dealers' trading points. In the first, exceedingly well-armed crews dominate the local population with extremely ruthless security rules. In the second, the level of insecurity varies, depending on the relationship between drug crews and local military policemen, or the neighbourhood and the police. Because of this, the Favelado Federation of the Associação de Moradores (Dwellers' Association) estimates that around 20 per cent of all *favelados* (people living in shanty towns) have left their homes.

Drug traffic has developed divisions between shanty towns so close to each other that their internal streets and constructions merge. Although neighbours still recognize the areas by their former names, now they are officially considered as one complex. In one of these complexes (called O Alemão – the German), after the death of the leader who unified several *favelas*, there was not only a state of war between the respective gangs linked to different traffickers, but neighbours were forbidden to cross the artificial borders between them. Many adolescents have been killed just because they have passed from one of the areas controlled by the belligerent networks of the crime business to another.

In any event, among some of the youngsters, those who hang out on the streets, traffickers and their organizations are well valued. Their symbols – TCK trade marks for the Terceiro Comando or Nike for Comando Vermelho – are used as ways of identifying themselves with one or the other. Adolescents say they belong to one of them as if they were soccer team supporters. They also absorb the warrior ethos with all its consequences by saying they have enemies everywhere and need guns. Finally, they display a deep loathing of policemen and a fear of being judged stool pigeons. This latter entails a high risk of being killed and the enormous shame of losing esteem from gang mates. At the same time they talk about the hatred they feel for dealers who have killed friends, close relatives or innocent neighbours. Some of the heavy users, who have connections with dealers, also speak of their loathing of the dependence acquired from sniffing cocaine, the most common heavy drug used. The present opposition to traffickers may be explained by the fact that recently there has been a change in the hierarchy of the Comando Vermelho: the former leaders, mostly now in prison, were succeeded by younger traffickers who were more unruly and had fewer connections with local residents. Most of these young bandits inspired only fear and terror among neighbours.

Small dealers in Brazilian shanty towns, despite their military apparatus, in fact help those higher up in the hierarchy – those who produce and trade in tons of the illicit drugs – to accumulate capital elsewhere. Little is yet known about such people in Brazil: who they are, how and where they live, and how they make their contacts in the underworld of crime.

The warrior ethos and warfare

There is a masculine warrior ethos bred in drug gangs that helps one to understand the growing appeal of violence in such places. For youths have been partly socialized in this setting (Elias and Dunning 1992: 10–11) sharing the codes through which they search for respect and consideration from members of the drug gang. Many think this social construction and management of masculinity is a natural component of social interaction, for they have friends or relatives who have been part of the drug trade networks. Since these youths try not to breach its main rules, they become conformists and lose autonomy, and are thus called *teleguiados*. But poor youths may acquire, in their neighbourhoods, instruments of power and pleasure (guns and drugs) that come from elsewhere. This is possible because of institutional failures and social values that push them to the pursuit of sensation and easy money. For youths, the main source of pride lies in the fact that they are part of the gang, use guns, join in robbing and looting, become famous for this, and, if they have the proper 'disposition', may someday ascend in the hierarchy of crime (Zaluar 1994; Lins 1997). Thus strategies for recruiting youngsters – calculated according to how many permanent dealers (from ten to thirty) the trading point needs – are based as much on the prospect of earning easy money as on the youth's fascination for power and fame.

In any event, there has always been ambivalence in the terms employed by the youths to denote criminal actions. Terms like 'vice', 'delay' or 'devil condominium' express the opposite of morally valued work (Zaluar 1994). They are applied to explain why someone is trapped in a vengeance circle, in blood feuds as well as in police persecution. 'Revolt' is the positive term used to denote those who won't accept low wages and hard work, based on a simple conception of social justice and male pride that defies economic exploitation. But injustice can also be another cruel bandit or corrupt policemen. Dope hustling is generally cited by disillusioned pushers as a domain of distrust and animosity, however, where there is no respect except for the other man's gun. It is also a sexually charged, virile world. All the men carry guns; to carry a gun is to 'walk mated' or to 'have your iron in your belt'. To show off your weapon, or 'to pull your stick out', is a common characteristic of such urban outlaws, and one that can often prove fatal. Instead of 'robbing', they talk of 'mounting' their victims, an expression used both for mugging people on the streets and for breaking and entering houses. To kill somebody is to 'lay them down'. The prime audiences for such displays are apparently the women they are trying to impress with their power and the money in their pockets. Women confirm this:

> ... So a guy goes and puts a gun in his belt, thinks he's really cool, picks up a whole bunch of women, makes a baby in one of them, and dies overnight. Sometimes the older guys get women involved in this who have nothing to do with the scene, and they think it's all going to be cool, like it's going to be like that famous guy with all kinds of women, with gold necklaces, and they're going to have it easy, go to a nice motel in a fancy car and all that ... Most women like outlaws ... because of the guns, they figure if anybody messes with them, they're going to get it ...

Here may lie the crux of the matter: exaggerated male pride and a thirst for unbridled power in a historical context of moral and institutional crisis, with inefficient restraints on the highly lucrative, expanding market for illicit drugs. Internally, for the crew, there is a fierce hierarchy of power. In order to keep control of a cocaine outlet, a 'front man' or 'chief' must be constantly vigilant. He must make sure his competitors are not taking too big a slice of the action by selling more or better goods or acquiring more arms. He has to deal with his national and international suppliers as well as local military policemen, who commonly receive part of the profits, or else he gets ripped off, his spot is taken, or he is simply wiped out by competitors from both inside and outside his gang, inside and outside prison (Coelho 1988; Zaluar 1985, 1994). Money in the drug business is highly concentrated at the top. Half of the profit goes to the 'man in the front' or 'trafficker', 30 per cent to the 'manager', who does the accounts, and various percentages to the 'vapour', who remains at the trading point and distributes the small amounts of cocaine to the *aviões* (aircraft), the very young dealers who finally take the dope to the customers. [3] The latter are those most commonly arrested and prosecuted. Most of the time they just receive *cargas* (loads) to sell, for which they become entirely responsible. They may sell them after increasing their weight with cheap substances in order to raise profits; they may consume most of them, which makes them vulnerable to being killed by the trafficker. The death penalty is the sentence for those who repeatedly do not pay the trafficker or who excessively adulterate the merchandise.

The political place occupied by traffickers is not, then, clear cut. They may be praised for the respect they have for neighbours or for the many social activities they patronize inside the shanty towns. Contrariwise, they may be loathed because of the way they seduce or order girls to have sexual relations with them, as well as for the continuous threat that their guns represent in any case of conflict or suspicion of betrayal involving traffickers, unarmed inhabitants and policemen. Still, youngsters say that the criminal crews provide more security for their members, since they assure juridical assistance that increases the chance of not being sentenced the higher the youngster is in the gang hierarchy. Since money can buy defence, and guns offer the protection that emerges from fear, they say it is useful to commit more crimes in order always to have money, guns and respect, as well as protection inside the gang. In fact, their preference for armed robbery is due to the possibility of silencing witnesses by terror, inflicting fearful respect on accomplices and bribing policemen, multiple ways of escaping arrest and making conviction more difficult. In reality this calculation may prove ineffective in so far as it does not eliminate completely the likelihood that a poor or less important bandit may go through the experience of being beaten up, tortured or extorted for a sum of money they cannot provide. Or someone who is making a lot of money may provoke the suspicions of both the trafficker and the corrupt policemen. The situation may become, as they say, 'sinister'. They may be killed by either one of them. Their guns and the riches they have just acquired may be removed from them, or they may be taken to jail if policemen prefer to show dedication or to increase the stakes in the corruption game. They may also be accused of crimes they have not commited as a way of improving statistics at the police precinct. Besides, power relationships and the division of labour, sometimes very exploitative, also restrain criminal activities.

Local gangs wage violent fights over women during or after dances organized by youngsters during which they listen to new styles of music that recommend violent confrontation with the 'system'. The story of the war between Zé Pequeno and Manoel Galinha is well known. Manoel Galinha was a handsome working man with a beautiful girlfriend, who was coveted by Zé Pequeno, a gang leader who expanded his drug business at the point of a gun. [4] He wanted to 'have it all', to take over all the drug outlets in the neighbourhood. He also wanted Manoel's woman. Manoel decided to organize his own gang and take revenge. A war started and lasted for several years, involving other gangs even after the main protagonists were killed. Hundreds of young people died in the process because the chain of personal vengeance is especially bitter between drug dealing gangs (Zaluar 1985, 1994) and because drugs and arms enter the country so easily. [5] There are many crews and individuals striving for power and position within the trade. The same kind of struggle is waged over women, weapons, dope and stolen goods. As one disillusioned young 'vapour' said: 'Dealing dope is a business of getting even. Pushers have always got an eye on other men's goods, even their women. They'll kill just to get another man's woman.'

Since the end of the 1970s, gun possession has created, for those youngsters involved in the drug trade war, a military power that has shaken the foundations of authority. Schoolteachers as well as local leaders have had their authority diminished *vis-à-vis* the youths with the power of money and guns (Guimarães and de Paula 1992; Zaluar 1988, 1994). Today children are sometimes unable to go to school or attend the various projects that train them in sports, arts and the professions because of warfare between neighbouring shanty towns. Even the experienced and politically concerned adults who have worked in the countless neighbourhood organizations (Zaluar 1985) have lost power and are now trying to recover it with the support of local government. The legislative assembly of Rio de Janeiro has recently completed an inquiry by its Committee against Violence and Impunity which identified eight hundred leaders of poor communities murdered, expelled or co-opted by traffickers in greater Rio de Janeiro between 1992 and 2001. [6] Half of them were associated with the bandits. Three hundred others had to leave the shanty towns and one hundred were killed because they refuse to be intimidated (*O Globo*, 20 June 2002).[7] An unidentified community leader asserted that more than two hundred directors of shanty town dwellers' associations had been executed by traffickers during the 1990s. He also claimed that policemen had been negligent when investigating these cases and suggested that the Public Ministry should undertake a thorough investigation of these associations. This has not yet been done. A recent case reveals the dynamics of intimidation and murder. A healthy ex-marine, president of the Federação de Favelas do Estado do Rio Janeiro (Shanty Town Federation of the State of Rio de Janeiro, FAFERJ), died of a stroke on 15 April 2002. Four days earlier he had had a heart attack, half an hour after he was forced by traffickers to legitimize the investiture of the president of the dwellers' association appointed by them in a shanty town. He had previously received death threats (ibid.).

Traffickers have also succeeded in penetrating several voluntary and public organizations and in intimidating drivers and personnel to take drugs or guns in their vehicles from one part of the city to another without arousing suspicion. Those who have undertaken military service in the Brazilian armed forces and are not part of the gangs are compelled to give military training to young dealers or 'soldiers'. Furthermore, traffickers from the criminal organization that prevails in São Paulo – Primeiro Comando da Capital (First Command of the Capital) – started their dealings in *favelas* in Rio de Janeiro as partners of the Comando Vermelho. At least seventy men escaped justice by moving from São Paulo to Rio de Janeiro and joining dominant dealers in six shanty towns there in order to enter the highly profitable business of dealing dope. With them they brought terrorist tactics that were first used on 11 September 2002 and culminated in January 2003. Then the Comando Vermelho circulated a printed manifesto in which it ordered that all shops should remain closed on 24 February 2003 until midnight the following day, otherwise '... they will disobey an order and be radically punished ... no way, we want our rights, we are not kidding, those who are kidding are the politicians with this total abuse of power and robbery, let the Judiciary open up the gates of the prisons and act according to the law before it is too late'. The reason for this was a loss of privileges inside prison, including the use of cell phones, restaurant food, daily visits by lawyers, girlfriends and relatives able to enter without being searched. The revolt, during which buses were burned and several policemen killed, lasted three months. As mysteriously as it had begun, it ended. The main leaders are now in high-security prisons outside their state of origin. Other leaders were caught when the focus of investigation finally moved to the national and international sphere. Unfortunately for the state police forces the focus is still the petty criminals and small dealers who will not say a word about their connections and suppliers so as not to be killed.

Conclusion

Three main dimensions of violence have been considered: the institutional inertia that explains persistent civil rights violations and the malfunctioning of the justice system; the importance and limits of macro social explanations, such as poverty and social exclusion, for violent criminality; the micro social processes that involve young poor men in drug trafficking. Together, these factors shape a state and a society where the rule of law is deficient. Since in countries such as Brazil there has always been a gap between formal civil rights and real ones, one must focus not only on the letter of the law but also particularly on social processes not controlled by it, such as the informal rules or social practices that govern the dynamics of drug-related crime and gang warfare in Rio de Janeiro and other large cities in Brazil.

Notes

1 Leonardo Dias Mendonça, Brazil's main cocaine trafficker, benefited from a scheme supposedly organized by a federal deputy in Brasília to certify the concession of habeas corpus for the trafficker. The deputy controlled the court schedule so as to establish in advance which judges would be presiding over the sessions. He waited to present it during a session in which judges who would not approve the concession were absent. Federal police investigations showed that many people had participated in such operations.

2 The petty smugglers from medium-sized cities in the state of São Paulo who brought in goods worth around US$150 by bus were caught by the federal police and rioted, burning their products (*Estado de São Paulo*, 22 December 2002).

3 'Vapour' denotes the man capable of quickly disappearing, responsible for distribution to the sellers. He is the one who takes care of the selling point and administers its personnel. He is second to the manager, who is the financial administrator and keeps the books.

4 The first gang that fought with Zé Pequeno, who led the most powerful gang in the neighbourhood, was the *caixa-baixa* (lower-case), a band of young thieves that brought valuable stolen goods back to him. Because of the high cut taken, they killed Zé Pequeno and took over the hustle after a fierce struggle. They were nearly all killed off in a subsequent battle with the Comando Vermelho. This ring has a policy of seeking support from the local population and therefore fights local thieves who mess up its business. It also follows a strict rule of capital punishment for men, women and adolescents who squeal, betray or kill for personal motives.

5 A total of 722 young people were killed during fifteen years of warfare in this neighbourhood.

6 There were 547 shanty towns in the city of Rio de Janeiro in 2000. Almost 1 million people lived in them, out of a total city population of 5,897,000. Almost one hundred are now urbanized as normal districts (called *favelas bairros*).

7 Reported by Deputy Carlos Minc, president of the commitee.

10 | Youth gangs, social exclusion and the transformation of violence in El Salvador

WIM SAVENIJE AND CHRIS VAN DER BORGH

Although the Salvadorean peace process is generally seen as a relative success story in terms of ending civil war and political violence, it has been strikingly ineffective in stopping other forms of violence. Relatively high levels of violence still characterize Salvadorean society, but its manifestations in the public sphere have changed. One of the most eye-catching illustrations of this is the demobilization of guerrilla armies and the rise of youth gangs in the post-war period.

Different explanations for the causes of this transformation are put forward, including the existence of a post-war security vacuum, the post-war 'fallout of political violence', and the continuing structural violence. We will argue that everyday forms of violence in illegal and semi-legal neighbourhoods of San Salvador should be analysed in the context of continuing social exclusion. Violence in these neighbourhoods is not, however, the immediate consequence of social exclusion and marginalization. Rather, violence and social exclusion are strongly intertwined and hard to separate. He we identify three intermediary mechanisms for the reproduction of violence: frustrations caused by social and economic hardship, the normalization of violence, and the presence of perverse social organizations. A prevailing and especially visible illustration of these are the Salvadorean youth gangs that readily use violence for numerous objectives. Exploration of the symbolic and political dimensions of this violence demonstrates the significance and usefulness of violence in constructing group and individual identities, status and power.

This chapter starts with a brief overview of the statistics on violence in El Salvador, which indicates that in the first five post-war years (1992–96) the number of homicides increased considerably; this was followed by a steep decline. Nevertheless, the figure remains high, in terms of both historical and international standards. In the second section an outline is given of the transformation of violence in El Salvador. We argue that both violence and social exclusion have been central elements in Salvadorean history, although their public manifestations have changed over time. In the third section we discuss different sets of explanations for these changes, concluding that the relationship between social exclusion and violence needs to be scrutinized. In the fourth section, based on recent empirical data, intermediary mechanisms are discussed which link social exclusion with the occurrence of violence in the marginalized neighbourhoods of San Salvador. The final section addresses the phenomenon of youth gangs, highlighting the political and symbolic dimensions of the violence used by these gangs.

Statistics on violence and homicides

There is a lack of accurate data on contemporary violence in El Salvador. The most relevant statistics concentrate on homicides, but even these statistics are incomplete, not always reliable and based on different methodologies. Most important are the statistics of the Public Prosecutor's Office (FGR), the Institute of Forensic Medicine (IML) and the National Civilian Police (PNC).[1]

The homicide rates[2] reported by these institutions give an impression of general levels and trends. According to the figures of the Pan-American Health Organization and FGR, the homicide rate per 100,000 inhabitants increased from 30 in 1969 to 69.8 in 1990.[3] Thereafter, there was a considerable increase between 1990 and 1995, and a steep decline in the period between 1996 and 2000. The FGR reports the number of homicides per 100,000 inhabitants as 138.9 in 1994, while this goes down to a 'war-time level' of 56.6 homicides per 100,000 inhabitants in 2000. The IML figures for the metropolitan area of San Salvador show a similar trend: the number of homicides peaks in 1995 and declines afterwards. The PNC reports the lowest numbers: 36.9 for 1999 and 37.4 for 2000.

The homicide rate in El Salvador is among the highest in Latin America. According to Cruz and González (1997) El Salvador already had one of the highest homicide rates in Latin America in the 1970s. In 1994, when the homicide rate for Colombia was 146.5 and Cuba and Mexico had a rate of 12.6 (World Health Organization 2002), the FGR reported a rate of 138.2. In 1995 El Salvador still had the second-highest rate of homicide in the continent after Colombia (IUDOP 1996). In 2002 the WHO reported a global homicide rate for the year 2000 of 8.8 and a rate of 19 for the region of the Americas; meanwhile the FGR reported a rate of 56.6 and the PNC 37.4 (PNUD 2002).[4]

On the basis of a survey undertaken by the University Institute of Public Opinion (IUDOP) in 1998, it has been estimated that over a period of one year, among the adult population of 3.2 million in El Salvador, 96,000 had been victims of beatings, 29,000 had been hurt by knives, machetes, etc., 22,000 had been injured by firearms, and 285,000 had been threatened with death (Cruz et al. 2000: 30–1).

Summarizing the foregoing, one can conclude that, although the data are

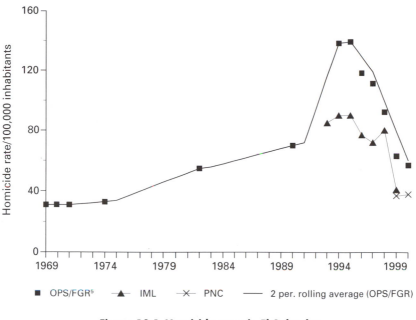

Figure 10.1 Homicide rates in El Salvador

incomplete, El Salvador has a tradition of high homicide rates and, compared to other countries, this is still the case. The data point at a considerable increase in the number of homicides in the four to five years after the peace accords, as well as a steep decline in the years between 1996 and 2000. But homicides are only a small part of the picture. Many people are victims of beatings, injured by a variety of weapons, or have received death threats. Information about the perpetrators and their motives is extremely limited.

The depoliticization of violence in El Salvador

The characteristics of violence in El Salvador have changed over time. Until the 1970s violence was more or less institutionalized and served the interests of the Salvadorean oligarchy, among other things by preventing land reform and political change. Alvarenga (1996) describes how in the period between 1880 and 1932 armed groups connencted to the state and powerful landowners exercised violence, especially in the countryside, to suppress rebellions and to guarantee a constant supply of cheap labour. In this period the state and the Salvadorean oligarchy 'came to rely more and more on coercion to maintain the stability and expansion of the new economic order' (North 1981: 22). With the *matanza* (massacre) of 1932, 'terror as a method of social control reached its maximum expression' (Alvarenga 1996: 29).[6]

The main cause of the Salvadorean civil war, between 1979 and 1992, was socio-economic inequality, which was sustained by a militarized and author-itarian political system that mainly served the interests of a small oligarchy linked to the agro-export sector.[7] Attempts at economic modernization led to economic growth through industrialization and some diversification of agricultural exports in the 1960s and 1970s, but did not lead to further redis-tribution of income and land. Large sectors of the population, particularly the rural poor, were further excluded economically. Political modernization failed because of the strong position of the conservative factions of the military that backed the interests of the oligarchy. The decades preceding the civil war can be characterized as exemplifying a process of economic and political modern-ization that failed to include the interests of large sections of the Salvadorean population.

The rise of the revolutionary movements in El Salvador is generally seen as a reaction to the 'institutionalized violence' that served the interests of the eco-nomic elites and which sustained the socio-economic inequalities. The peace agreements, signed in 1992 by the Salvadorean government and the guerrilla movement Farabundo Marti National Liberation Front (FMLN), focused on re-forms in the security sector (especially the military and police) and the political system, while paying scant attention to socio-economic issues.[8] These agree-ments were successful in ending political violence and civil war and bolstered the process of democratization, but they were unable to improve security and to foster the inclusion of the poor into social and economic life.

The National Republican Alliance (ARENA) party – representing the in-terests of old and new economic elites – came to power in 1989 and imple-mented a policy of macroeconomic stabilization and structural adjustment, which represented, according to Rosa (1993), one of the century's most ambitious efforts to redefine the Salvadorean development model. Although the economic model has led to economic growth in the 1990s and to some poverty reduction, poverty is still a structural problem and large sections of the population are excluded from basic services such as healthcare and safe water (Rivera Campos 2000: 216–18).

Since the end of the civil war manifestations of violence in the public sphere have changed, just as Salvadorean society itself has changed profoundly in comparison to its status in the 1970s. The inability to address the historical problem of social exclusion is of crucial importance in understanding the un-relenting violence. The persistence of social exclusion, defined as the process through which individuals or groups are wholly or partially excluded from full participation in the society in which they live (Haan and Maxwell 1998; Savenije and Andrade-Eekhoff 2003), is a breeding ground for of violence, whereas the use of violence leads to feelings of insecurity about society itself and limits possibilities for full participation.

Explaining the transformation of violence in El Salvador

In debates on the ongoing violence in El Salvador there are roughly three sets of explanations. The first focuses on the failure of state agencies to curtail violence and to provide security to the state's citizens. In this view the existence of a security vacuum in the years following the signing of the peace agreements was the result of a weak new national civilian police force that still had to be built up, while some of the old forces had already been dismantled. At the same time this new police force was confronted with a sharp rise in criminal activity. This may explain the rise and fall of homicides after the civil war, as after 1996 the new police force had grown and problems related to the demobilization of former combatants had diminished.[9] There are no accurate data on the composition and perpetrators of this violence, however, and after the years of transition there are still relatively high levels of violence.

A second explanation focuses on the social processes by which the political repression and violence of the civil war have become embedded in daily interactions. Bourgois states that one explanation for contemporary violence is the fact that political repression has generated 'everyday violence through the systematic distortion of social relations and sensibilities' (2001: 19). In his view, social relations in the post-war area have been affected by the political violence of the war. Binford (2002: 214) criticizes this idea of 'the post-war fallout of wartime political violence', arguing that greater emphasis should be placed on the fact that the peace agreements did not address the socio-economic roots of the conflict.

A third set of explanations focuses on sustained social exclusion through inadequate economic policies, protracted and increasing socio-economic inequality, and widespread marginalization. Some authors use the concept of structural violence in order to describe the suffering resulting from unequal social structures. Bourgois (2001: 222–3) talks about a continuation – 'if not the exacerbation – of structural violence in the post-war transition in El Salvador', and considers that this structural violence is expressed through symbolic and everyday violence. Binford (2002: 215) states further that everyday violence should be seen also as 'a function of poverty and exploitation in the present (structural violence) – resulting from Peace Accords that hardly touched the pre-conflict economic class structure'. He states further that the 'unfavourable peace settlement, which preserved unequal structural relations', is an important factor in explaining the high levels of post-war violence (ibid.: 201).

Although these explanations can be useful in understanding contemporary forms of violence in El Salvador, it is also true that the civil war ended eleven years ago. Instead of continuing to blame the civil war for contemporary violence, the challenge is to improve our understanding of how everyday violence and continuing social exclusion are interrelated and reinforce each other (Binford 2002; Bourgois 2001). It is the 'preserved unequal structural relations' which still haunt a considerable proportion of the Salvadorean population and which need further scrutiny. Rather than conceptualizing this exclusion as a form of 'structural violence' and pointing at the political and economic structures at the macro level that 'cause' violence at the local level, however, the challenge is to improve our understanding of how social exclusion and everyday violence are also interrelated and reinforce each other at the local level and in the daily lives of the inhabitants of marginalized neighbourhoods.

Structural, political and symbolic violence

It is of great importance to look at unequal social structures in understanding the suffering, hardship and insecurity of marginalized people, but to call these structures 'violent', as the notion of structural violence does, leads to a blurring of the concept of violence. The notion of violence should be seen in connection to the behaviour of actors, principally 'as some kind of behaviour, either physical or symbolic, that is carried out with the intention to harm someone' (Berkowitz 1993: 11).[10] This means that someone (an individual, a group or institution) is acting intentionally to cause harm to some target (other individuals, groups, institutions). If the violence is deliberately planned, it has a more instrumental quality; if it arises in a course of action as an immediate reaction to an aversive stimulus, it has a rather impulsive quality (Savenije and Lodewijkx 1998; Berkowitz 1993). Violent acts committed under the influence of alcohol, drugs or frustration have a more impulsive character, and a planned assassination attempt is an example of instrumental violence. The primary objective of violence, deliberate or not, can be of an economic, social, political or symbolic nature. Violence can be used to acquire or protect resources or to send a message to a broader audience than the immediate victims, and in this respect violence has a more symbolic character. In practice these aspects can be found in different combinations. For example, the act of beating up and robbing a local resident by youth gang members can serve the objectives of gaining a reputation, releasing frustration and obtaining material gain.

The idea that violence has symbolic aspects requires some further explanation, as it is generally associated with Bourdieu and the notion of internalized legitimizations of inequality and oppression (Bourgois 2001) concealed in normal social practices (Scheper-Hughes 1997). Bourdieu (2000) defines symbolic violence as a consensual coercion in which the dominated share the definition of the situation of the dominator and therefore perceive it as natural. Symbolic violence in this sense can refer to the power to influence the way people think, perceive and legitimize – for instance – their situation of marginalization and exclusion.

Bourdieu's definition emphasizes the *power to* influence and to create consensus even without the use of physical violence. In this chapter, however, symbolic violence will be interpreted as the use of violence with the intention of sending a message to a broader audience by harming persons or objects that have a special significance and emotional value for the addressees, thus targeting them indirectly.

Violence in marginalized neighbourhoods in San Salvador

The symbolic dimension of violence is one aspect that comes to the fore in the poor districts of the capital city. This section draws on a study conducted by Savenije and Andrade-Eekhoff (2003) on the experiences of violence in daily life in five illegal or semi-legal neighbourhoods in San Salvador.[11] The results were astonishing in two respects: the regularity with which violence occurs, and the extent to which people find it 'normal' to live with violence or use it for their own purposes.

Incidence of violence In a household survey[12] the respondents were asked about the life conditions of their family, their perceptions of the concomitant risks of living in the neighbourhood, and the experiences of the family members with violence. Asked about the risk of being assaulted in their own community, 14.8 per cent reported that they found it somewhat to very probable that they would be assaulted by daylight and 33.7 per cent at night in their own community. For strangers the situation was still more dangerous: 36.2 per cent of the respondents found it somewhat to very probable that strangers would be assaulted by daylight, and 69.3 per cent at night (see Table 10.1).

If asked about violence in their communities, the residents considered delinquency, youth gangs from other communities, alcohol and drugs as the principal problems. But if questioned about the experiences of victimization of family members, the respondents gave a slightly different picture: 40.6 per cent of households had at least one member who had been the victim of physical violence the year before the survey took place; some of violence occurred outside the community but more than half took place in and around the community.

TABLE 10.1 The perceived risk of being assaulted in the community (%) of respondents

Victims	During the day		At night	
	Somewhat to very probable	Not probable	Somewhat to very probable	Not probable
Local residents	14.8	85.2	33.7	66.3
Strangers	36.2	63.8	69.3	30.7

Source: Savenije and Andrade-Eekhoff 2003

The respondents also reported a high incidence of domestic violence in this period: 56.5 per cent mentioned at least one incident of violence against children, and 15.6 per cent between adults of the same household (ibid.).

What catches the eye is the diversity of violence that the people in these communities suffer: domestic violence, violence related to youths and neighbours in the community, and violence related to delinquency are common problems. Violence related to drugs and delinquency inside the community, however, is reported as less problematic.[13] Although the residents do not mention their neighbours and the youth of their own community as major sources of violence, their experiences of victimization indicate that they are.

One of the findings of Savenije and Andrade-Eekhoff (ibid.) is that the relationship between social exclusion and violence is symbiotic in the sense that one engenders the other. The study identifies three mediating mechanisms by which social exclusion is linked to the occurrence of violence: (1) through the frustration it generates, (2) the normalization of the use of violence, and (3) the existence of perverse social organizations. Below each of them will be briefly described.

Frustrations Living continuously in situations of poverty, in shacks without basic services such as drinking water and sewage systems, in overcrowded areas, without the legal right to live there, generates frustrations. Not only the frustration of everyday life – for instance, having little money to cover necessary expenses, having to wait in line for drinking water, the noise of the neighbours, the lack of even a little privacy, and so on – but also the frustration of not being able to overcome this situation of poverty and exclusion.

In the social psychological literature is it basically accepted that frustration is somehow related to the occurrence of violence (Berkowitz 1993; Geen 2001). A recent formulation of this association states that frustration is specifically related to the occurrence of impulsive and expressive violence, through the feelings of discontent that it generates (Berkowitz 1993).

It is through the experiences of everyday frustration that social exclusion can be related to the diverse forms of everyday violence, be it domestic violence directed at partners, children or the elderly, or violent encounters between neighbours about the faltering water supply, noise, etc. The residents recognize this phenomenon and call it '*el desquite*' (literally 'taking it off'). They concede that at times they vent their negative emotions on others who are mostly weaker or more dependent than the aggressors. One resident admits: 'Well, some of the parents [do beat] their children when maybe they are unable to cope. Any little thing that the girl or boy does, and they get reprimanded in a very ugly way, really strong, and maybe the children cannot be blamed for what is going on' (Savenije and Andrade-Eekhoff 2003: 150).

The normality of violence Social life in these neighbourhoods is permeated by the threat of violent interactions. Neighbours and youth play an important part in the creation of this atmosphere. A member of a committee for the development of the community tells how the threat of violence impedes their functioning: 'If we dare to reprimand a neighbour we run the risk, first, of being insulted. After that he threatens us, and if we still go on ... well, nobody does anything for fear that the threats will be carried out. That's reality' (ibid.: 104). As will be explained below, the presence of other actors such as youth gangs and drug sellers and users augments the potential for violent exchanges.

There is a threat of violence not only in the narrow streets of the neighbourhood, but also between the walls of the little houses or shacks. A social worker in one of the communities comments: 'Husbands beat wives; mothers beat their children or children their mothers; that happens a lot; it always happens' (ibid.: 117). It is not only the relationship between adults which contributes to this atmosphere, but also the violence directed towards children. A teacher at the local nursery school articulates it thus: 'We think it is a natural thing, so normal that nobody thinks about it' (ibid.: 123). The experience of the investigators corroborates this impression; in 4.6 per cent of households children were hit during the half-hour in which the survey interview took place. Domestic violence is a 'normal' phenomenon in two senses: first, it happens very frequently; second, people consider it an adequate and justified form of behaviour, although not all the victims accept this. A member of a committee for the development of the community expresses this very eloquently: 'When he threatens to beat me or his daughters, I say to him: "You can do with them what you want because they're yours. But you don't touch me'" (ibid.: 145). This 'normality' makes it difficult for other people to intervene to stop the violence taking place, although everybody knows it happens: 'But you cannot interfere, because these are family problems. So you just hear what goes on, nothing more' (ibid.: 125).

The fact that violence is considered appropriate behaviour can be attributed to the inability to find alternative methods of educating children or of resolving conflicts with others. One participant in a focus group expressed preoccupation with the activities of certain NGOs and government agencies protecting human and children's rights. This, he argued, made raising children more difficult: 'You cannot bring up your children in the right way. There is a fear of mistreating the creatures because someone will call the police and then you'll be taken to jail' (ibid.: 124).

Perverse social organizations Another way in which social exclusion and violence are articulated is through the presence of perverse social organizations. Moser and McIlwaine (2000, 2001) distinguish between forms of social capital that are productive for the community, and forms that are harmful for the community as a whole, while benefiting the interests of their members. The former will be called productive and the latter perverse social organizations.

Drugs sellers in some communities use their houses as storage places, and the narrow streets as the area where they meet consumers and as a route for the transport of drugs. The residents suffer the presence of drugs users, who sometimes rob them and passers-by. In other communities the presence of youth gangs (*maras*) generates an atmosphere of threat and fear. These gangs normally consume and sell drugs, but this is generally not their principal activity. Mostly they hang out together, have parties, fight other gangs, and are involved in petty crime. Their ready use of violence generates fear and apprehension not only here but also in society at large.

Perverse social organizations form a parallel power structure in marginal neighbourhoods, and often wield more influence than the productive ones. Their power derives from their readiness to use violence, the possession of arms, the number of people involved, and the quantity of money they manage. The drug sellers use violence to protect their business and youth gangs to control their neighbourhood, but also to fight other gangs and to commit petty crimes. Productive social organizations, such as the committees for community development, are often severely handicapped in confrontation with these perverse ones, if they lack the full backing of state institutions such as the police. Nevertheless, it is exactly in these socially excluded neighbourhoods that the police are often absent and where their relationship with the residents is at best problematic.

The presence of perverse social organizations causes fragmentation of the protective social structures and undermines productive social control. Sometimes the residents perceive themselves more as potential victims of others than as actors with the right to take care of their common interests. The risk of opposing these organizations can be great, as one of the residents explained by sketching the relationship with the local youth gang:

> Because they are the untouchables, the all powerful ones here in the community, nobody does nothing against them, against the gang members [*mareros*] ... So, if they want someone to go away, they slander him and then he goes; they take people out, kill them, rob them, rape them ... They say they protect the community ... But that's a lie. They themselves commit the crimes. They themselves attack the community. Here they rape anyone. (Savenije and Andrade-Eekhoff 2003: 163–4)

In the next section we will take a look at one of these perverse social organizations: the youth gangs or *maras*.

The mara *phenomenon*

Youth gangs have a very visible presence in poor marginalized neighbourhoods, which they consider their territory and which they defend against members of other gangs. Their widespread use of violence is greatly feared in contemporary El Salvador. Their relationship with the community is complicated. Gang members say that they protect the community and its residents against criminals and outsiders, but they also use threats and violence against the same residents. From the residents they expect above all non-interference in their affairs, but nevertheless solicit monetary contributions and 'war tax'.

After a brief introduction to the youth gangs, we will analyse their use of violence, focusing on two aspects: its symbolic value and its instrumental character in obtaining and protecting a local power base.

*Youth gangs (*maras*): the practice of violence* Salvadorean youth gangs have a history that precedes the peace accords. Only in the early 1990s, in the poor, overcrowded and marginalized neighbourhoods, did the number of youths involved rapidly increase, and this captured the attention of the general public (Cruz and Portillo 1998; Ramos 1998; Savenije and Lodewijkx 1998; Smut and Miranda 1998). The deportations of Salvadorean gang members from the United States that started in 1992 transformed the dynamic of local youth gangs (Smut and Miranda 1998; *Homies Unidos*, in Cruz and Portillo 1998). The situation in which different neighbourhoods had their own gangs that fought those near by (Savenije and Lodewijkx 1998) changed into one in which most Salvadorean gangs became parts (*clikas*) of one of the two super-gangs with roots in Los Angeles, which fight each other to the death. The super-gangs are known as Barrio 18 and Mara Salvatrucha ('MS 13').

On 20 January 2003 the national newspaper *La Prensa Gráfica* published a police report stating that in the first twenty days of the year ten people had already died in fights between youth gangs. It also reported that in 2002 eighty-two gang members had died in the 'gang war'. Of the deceased gang members fifty-eight were older than twenty, twenty-two were between sixteen and twenty, and two were between ten and fifteen years old. Furthermore, Cruz et al. (2000) found that one of the most stable predictors of a conviction for homicide and of recidivism among prison inmates was membership of a youth gang.

According to police estimates, in June 2002 there were approximately three hundred youth gangs (mostly *clikas* of the super-gangs) with 5,906 gang members (*La Prensa Gráfica*, 20 January 2003). Other estimates are much higher; for instance, Cruz and Portillo (1998) mention unconfirmed police figures of 20,000 at the end of 1996, and Ramos (1998) gives estimates of between 10,000 and 12,000 gang members.

Protection against rival gangs is the principal justification given for the existence of gangs by their members. The most serious offence a gang can commit is to enter a rival's territory, wipe out their symbols and graffiti, and kill or harm one of the members. Being in a rival gang is sufficient reason for being attacked and killed (Santacruz Giralt and Concha-Eastman 2001; Santacruz Giralt and Cruz Alas 2001; Smut and Miranda 1998). Violent encounters with rivals take place when gangs accidentally meet each other, or they are planned in advance. Mostly, however, the objectives of these confrontations are not immediately clear. Youth gangs do not have the capacity to erase their rivals and take possession of the neighbourhoods they consider as enemy territory, as happens in conventional warfare.

Besides this inter-group rivalry, gang members also use (threats of) violence for material gain in acts of pretty crime and drugs trading. Now and then they are also accused of involvement in major crimes such as drugs trafficking, bank robbery and kidnapping, but these accusations have to be regarded with caution. It is probable that the organizational demands of these activities exceed the capacities of most youth gangs. Gangs can become seriously delinquent, however, as members develop these capacities and obtain the social capital necessary to engage in more professional criminal activities (Savenije and Andrade-Eekhoff 2003).

The symbolic aspects of gang violence Killing or harming a member of a rival gang simply because he is a member of a rival gang, without knowing him personally, makes sense only if the symbolic aspects of these violent acts are brought to the foreground. In order to do so, it is necessary to look behind the isolated acts of violence. Killing or harming a rival gang member is equivalent to damaging the reputation, status and honour of his entire gang; for this reason, to bump into a member of a rival gang in itself provokes and justifies an attack. It is not important who gets wounded or killed as long as he is related to the rival gang, although the symbolic value of an attack and the harm caused are higher when the victim is an important gang member or leader.

An important aspect of gang violence is that it is mostly directed at a broader audience of rival gangs, but also at other *clikas* of the same gang and the local community. The antagonistic relationship with the other gang cannot easily be explained as inter-group conflict over scarce material resources, for instance gang territory. The territories of gangs are mostly the neighbourhoods in which most members live, where they grew up, went to school, played and fought together. It is 'their neighbourhood' in the sense that they have lived part of its history, share the same experiences and identity. It is not a resource that one can possess and which other gangs can take.

The violence aimed at other gangs is not brought into play simply to protect or desecrate a territory, to eliminate or harm an enemy; these are only means to a higher end. A member of the Mara Salvatrucha says: 'Because he [the victim] is one less of the other gang. We win points for that ... in other words, for each person from the other neighbourhood, because just like that they win points when they kill a homeboy [sic] of ours' (Santacruz Giralt and Cruz Alas 2001: 65). The aggressor who kills gains 'points', for himself and for his gang, in a game much greater than the actions of individual gang members. The gang struggles to achieve a reputation as a dominant, courageous and dangerous gang. Violence is an instrument to achieve this recognition by showing direct and clear superiority over rivals.

Individual members contribute to this greater struggle, but at the same time fight for a position of status and respect in their own gang. For youths that live in situations of social exclusion, in poor and marginalized neighbourhoods, the gang can become an important source of belonging and of otherwise unobtainable recognition (Cruz and Portillo 1998; Santacruz Giralt and Concha-Eastman 2001; Santacruz Giralt and Cruz Alas 2001; Savenije and Andrade-Eekhoff 2003; Savenije and Lodewijkx 1998; Smut and Miranda 1998). The cost of these forms of belonging and social recognition can be high as gang members continuously run the risk of being attacked and assassinated by rivals. Only in their own territory, under the protection of their gang, are they relatively save. The benefits are important too, however: in a survey of 1,025 gang members carried out by Cruz and Portillo (1998), 84.3 per cent of the gang members reported that, because of their membership of the gang, they had gained respect, 83.9 had gained friends, 77.5 had gained power, and 71.4 had gained protection. For lots of youths from the marginalized neighbourhoods the benefits outweigh the costs: 'many feel that it is better to have a reputation for being aggressive or violent than to be marginalized and ignored' (Santacruz Giralt and Cruz Alas 2001: 66). In other words, the normalization of violence and membership of a youth gang can function as an antidote to the frustrating daily experiences of socially excluded youths.

Gang violence and local power The gangs often treat their neighbourhood as their empire where they can do what they want and where nobody can stop them. Occasionally they ask for a contribution when residents enter or leave the neighbourhood or demand a 'war tax' from the owners of small retail outlets and repair shops in the community, intimidate the residents so that they do not contact the police, sell and consume drugs in the alleyways, steal things from neighbours, etc. The relationship between youth gang members and local residents is at times one of fear and intimidation, but also one characterized by family relationships, shared history and common fate. In one of the neighbourhoods studied by Savenije and Andrade-Eekhoff (2003), twenty families were 'temporally' living outside their community for fear of the youth gang that reigned there.

An important objective of the violence directed against neighbours in the community is to impose and reinforce the power of the gang in their territory. Threatening or attacking residents of the same poor and marginalized neighbourhood can provide only small material gains, but the non-material gains, in terms of an increased capacity to influence the behaviour of others, can be great. Calling the police when the gang is fighting, consuming drugs or intimidating neighbours is out of the question because a very violent reaction can be expected. The relationship between the youth gang and the community has been characterized by one resident with the term 'all powerful ones' (*todopoderosos*). Another resident explains why they fear them so much: 'Because they are aggressive. They respect nothing. When they are on drugs they go crazy [*andan perdidos*] ... If they hold a grudge against somebody he may get shot or cut up with a machete' (ibid.: 101).

Youth gangs also have non-violent means of exercising control, but these are usually backed up by the threat of violence. For instance, asking the neighbours for a contribution when they walk in the street, apart from generating a little money, instils fear in the residents and makes the presence of the gang clear. The residents sometimes refuse to give money, but not always. Small shops are asked to pay a 'war tax'; refusing would certainly have serious consequences for the owner. No one can complain openly about the problems and nuisance caused by the gang without coming into serious conflict with them. People simply have to bear it, and also to pay for it.

The symbolic aspects of gang violence become clear once again when one considers that such violence not only 'punishes' but also serves as a reminder to other residents of what may happen to them if they do not respect the order imposed by the gang.

Conclusion

Twelve years after the peace accords were signed in El Salvador, violence is still an integral part of daily life for the residents of marginalized neighbourhoods in San Salvador. The actors and their motives have (partly) changed, but violence has remained widespread. In order to understand the recurrent violence in marginalized neighbourhoods the connection with social exclusion is crucial. We explored three mediating mechanisms that link social exclusion and violence: frustration, the normalization of violence and perverse social organizations. The first mechanism concerns frustration with the conditions of everyday life. In combination with the second mechanism it points at an inability to deal with personal stress or resolve conflicts in a peaceful manner. Violence has become an integral element of processes of socialization, thus becoming a relatively normal instrument. Perverse organizations emerge in this context, which shows that the normalization of violence can influence social and political life in the communities at large. This means that at the community level violence has its own dynamic and momentum, but this dynamic finds fertile ground in a context of limited opportunities, marginalization and exclusion from participation in broader society.

The context of limited opportunities to participate in society is of crucial importance in the understanding of everyday violence. For young people who grow up in a context of limited socio-economic opportunities, and where the use of violence is a normal phenomenon, membership of a youth gang can provide them with a feeling of power and identity that may not be obtained in other ways. The material objectives – such as money, goods or drugs – of the violence used by these gangs are in many cases of limited importance, and in themselves an insufficient explanation for the violence. A combination of political and symbolic aims is fundamental in explaining the use of violence by members of youth gangs. Violent confrontations with rival gangs are a way to establish the reputation and identity of both the gang and its individual members. At the level of the neighbourhood, the (threat of) violence is a means to exercise control over the territory and residents of their neighbourhood. The violence of youth gangs can be seen as both a consequence and an aggravating factor of social exclusion, while at the same time it is a form of resistance to its humiliating effects.

Notes

1 According to Cruz and Gonzalez (1997) the FGR has the most complete and systematic data available.

2 Cruz and Gonzalez (1997) estimated the homicide rates for 1969 to 1990 using the records of the Pan-American Health Organization (OPS) and thereafter of the FGR. Cruz et al. (2000) elaborated these estimates for the years 1997 and 1998 using the data of the FGR. PNUD (2002) reports FGR data for the years 1999 and 2000. Cruz and Gonzalez (1997), Cruz et al. (2000) and PNUD (2002) also report IML data for the years 1993–99. This last publication also includes PNC data for 1999 and 2000.

3 There are good reasons for supposing that the archives of the war years show an important level of under-registering. If one takes seriously the estimate that the civil war caused 75,000 deaths in the twelve years it lasted, this gives an average of 6,250 deaths a year and a homicide level of 130 per 100,000 habitants (Cruz and Gonzalez 1997).

4 This comparison gives a general indication, because the FGR and OPS data are based on different methodologies.

5 The figure for 1998 is an estimate, because the records do not include the months May and June (Cruz, Trigueros and Gonzalez 2000).

6 It is estimated that between 15,000 and 50,000 peasants were killed.

7 For the roots of the Salvadorean civil war: see Paige (1998); Stanley (1996); Williams (1994); Montgomery (1995).

8 The peace accords contained a socio-economic element, including a land-titling programme for ex-combatants of both sides, as well as a socio-economic forum of government officials, employers and employees.

9 See Costa (1999) and Spence et al. (2001) for a discussion on problems relating to the establishment of a new Salvadorean police force. For a discussion on the problems of judicial reform, see Popkin (2000).

10 In the social psychological literature on violence and aggression both concepts are mostly intimately related.

11 The five communities were selected from a list of 357 illegal or semi-legal neighbourhoods that represent 27 per cent of the population of the metropolitan area of San Salvador.

12 The survey consisted of 238 questionnaires; depending on the size of the community, between fifty-two and sixty-five families per community were surveyed.

13 It should be mentioned that the questions about violence related to drugs use and the drugs trade were those with the most answers in the 'no response' category.

11 | Violence and fear in Colombia: fragmentation of space, contraction of time and forms of evasion

LUIS ALBERTO RESTREPO

The social order, the tranquillity and the progress of a nation have their ultimate foundation in fear. Such is, in essence, the teaching of classic thinkers such as Hobbes, Locke and Rousseau.[1] The fear of violence of 'every one against every one' induces individuals to confer to a third party the power and authority to exercise centralized force and to uphold rules, sufficient to dissuade individuals to return to the exercise of private violence. To replace the terror of anarchical violence with the fearful respect for a predictable force in order to guarantee the security of all is, then – at least in the view of those philosophers who ascribe to the idea of individuals as originally existing in a state of nature – the primary purpose of the social contract. In this sense it could be said that all modern societies are 'societies of fear'.

If we assume this perspective, we could inversely say that where the state is unable to offer security to its subjects, society tends to become submerged in violence that is more and more Hobbesian, of every one against every one. This is, to a certain extent, the present situation in Colombia. And, of course, the anarchical overflow of the violence is able to instil fear in every degree: from the simple precaution that imposes a general silence and distrust to fear and panic in the face of imminent threats, or to permanent anxiety about uncertain dangers, which leads to diverse forms of flight and evasion.

Violence and fear in Colombia

Violence produces fear; but the roots of both, and their operational range, are not the same. Violence is an objective phenomenon that one can describe and quantify, whereas fear is a subjective reaction against any threat. It is mediated by imagination. Our capacity to imagine anticipates for us real or possible violence, producing within us a profound fear of death.

If we want to investigate the fear that rules in Colombia, we should first get an idea of the magnitude of the violence that besieges the country today. There operate in Colombia three powerful 'military machines', each more preoccupied with conquering territory at the cost of the unarmed population than with gaining its sympathy. In the first place there are two well-armed guerrilla organizations: (1) the Fuerzas Armadas Revolucionarias de Colombia-Ejército Popular (FARC-EP), with a ground force of about 18,000 combatants, to which one must add a thousand urban militiamen (*Análisis Estratégico*, 11 April 2002); and (2) the Ejército de Liberación Nacional (ELN), which has some 6,000 armed fighters. In addition, there are small remnants of the Ejército Popular de Liberación (EPL) and of the Movimiento 19 de Abril (M-19). Also, the Autodefensas Unidas de Columbia (AUC) or paramilitaries can count on around 11,000 armed militants. On the other hand, there are also powerful criminal organizations, which sometimes act on their own account and on other occasions operate in cooperation with the paramilitaries or guerrillas. In some districts in several cities, hired killers and armed youth gangs proliferate. To this picture it is necessary to add the security forces of the state, which not infrequently operate at the margins of the law, increasing the general insecurity. In sum, there is in Colombia an ensemble of powerful, violent organizations that are able to instil fear and panic.

Some numbers can give us an idea of the violence ruling Colombia. In 2002, the number of homicides reached 28,837. Between 1996 and 2002, a homicide was committed in Colombia every twenty minutes. During 2002, the number of kidnappings rose to 2,986. Between 1996 and 2002, a kidnapping was committed every 3.2 hours. Every two days a child is kidnapped. It is estimated that in 2002 alone 75,730 families had to leave their homes because of the violence, and that in the last seven years 939,155 Colombians (an average of 368 persons per day) were uprooted from their land. In 2002 the number of terrorist attacks grew to 1,171 (<www.dnp.gov.co>).

The situation regarding children is illustrative of the existing violence in the country. According to investigations made between 1996 and 1998 by the Defensoría del Pueblo (Human Rights Ombudsman)[2] on the participation of children in the armed conflict, 18 per cent of the minors interviewed had killed at least once. Sixty per cent had seen someone killed and 78 per cent had seen mutilated bodies. Twenty-five per cent had seen someone kidnapped, and 13 per cent had themselves been kidnapped. Eighteen per cent had seen someone tortured. Forty per cent had used a firearm against somebody at least once, and 28 per cent had been wounded (<www.colomb iastreetkids.org>).[3]

We can say, then, that in Colombia one finds the state's monopoly of legitimate force for the sake of collective security deeply debilitated. From this point of view we could perhaps speak of a partial collapse of the state, although in the Colombian case it would not be unreasonable to ask to what extent something can collapse that had never been upheld in vast regions of the country.[4] In any case, faced with the weakness and precariousness of the state, wide sectors of society have taken justice into their own hands.

Social distribution of the violence

Let us nevertheless place Colombian violence within the context of the geographical and demographic dimensions of the country. The armed conflict and criminal violence are scattered over a territory of 1,138,914 km², which is equivalent to twenty-eight times the size of the Netherlands, and almost five times the area of Great Britain. In addition, three branches of the gigantic Andean mountain range divide Colombian territory, and around a sixth of the country is covered by tropical Amazon forest, along with other wooded zones in the interior. That is to say, the country as a whole constitutes an extensive territory, fragmented by steep or impenetrable geographical features, still barely populated by around 42 million inhabitants (approximately thirty-seven inhabitants per square kilometre), with an insufficient road network that hampers communications.

These geographical and demographic conditions have been, and continue to be, formidable obstacles to national integration and the full expansion of the state, and also impede a uniform diffusion and perception of the violence within the national territory. Owing to the armed conflict, the situation is much more uncertain and difficult in the countryside than in the cities. There are now scarcely any rural areas where there is no presence of irregular armed groups. Common crime is more prevalent in the great urban centres, however, although numerous cities have also been affected in the past by murders and selective disappearances perpetrated by vigilante groups, and more recently by sporadic terrorist acts by guerrilla groups.

In numerous rural areas the armed organizations turn up only occasionally: they often come only to carry out some operation – a kidnapping, an assassination, an incursion – and then leave again. Yet this mere possibility is enough to spread insecurity, anxiety, lasting fear and uncertainty among the population. In the zones where armed groups habitually pass through, local peasants face a dangerous dilemma. It is not easy to distinguish between a guerrilla, a paramilitary and a soldier. If some of them ask for food, a place to rest, or support, the farmer cannot refuse for fear of possible reprisals. But if he renders aid, this may result in one of the opposing groups considering him an auxiliary of the enemy. In fact, the paramilitaries as much as the guerrillas try to justify many of the murders and massacres with this sort of reasoning. In this way, the silence, the isolation and the mutual distrust that prevails in these regions preclude the peasant from retiring early to his home. It is as if the fear of a physically violent death has imposed in advance the death of society.

But the most serious situation is the one suffered by the regions and small towns disputed by guerrillas, paramilitaries and the army. At the moment, the bloodiest fighting rages freely in six rural zones: (1) in the south, where the state and the self-defence groups clash with the FARC; (2) in the north-west, in Cordova and Urabá, where the army, the self-defence groups and the FARC maintain a presence; (3) in the centre of the country (Magdalena Medio), where an intense dispute between all the actors is developing; (4) in the north-east, in Arauca and on the border with Venezuela, where the self-defence groups and the state have begun to confront the presence of the ELN and the FARC; (5) in the Oriente Antioqueño, whose dominion is disputed among all the actors; and (6) in the zone of confrontation that is being opened in Magdalena and Cesar, in the extreme north of the country, around the Sierra Nevada and the Serranía del Perijá (Valencia 2002: 260–1). All these zones constitute strategic centres or corridors in the war. In all of them intense clashes will rage over the next few years, and sustained offensives and counter-offensives will be launched, affecting the entire territory and particularly the civilian populace (ibid.: 261). The violence in these zones has produced an uninterrupted flow of internal refugees who continue to arrive at the urban centres.

When they are not the victims of a massacre, the settlers – almost always poor farmers – see themselves frequently forced to leave everything: houses, crops, animals, their few possessions, and all the landmarks of their memory. In a caravan of misery and neglect, the displaced persons arrive in the urban centres, which for them constitute unknown and hostile country. The cities, which are not prepared to receive so many new inhabitants, view them principally with distrust, as possible allies of one or another party in the conflict. Many therefore end up becoming nomads without a destination.

A classic example of this current situation is offered by the department of Arauca, located in the north-east part of Colombia, along the border with Venezuela. In 1968, the FARC created here 'Front 10'. In 1976, the ELN established its 'Front Domingo Laín'. The petroleum wealth of the region enabled the ELN to turn itself into the richest group, independent in its organization, by means of a combination of tactics: blackmailing the petroleum multinationals for certain favours in return for not kidnapping their personnel and not blowing up their pipelines; blackmailing local politicians and their families into transferring to them a significant proportion of the municipal budgets, which are nourished by petroleum royalties; introducing coca and poppy crops. From 1997, FARC's Frente 10, and later Frente 45, decided to dispute the ELN's territory, and in 2000 paramilitaries also began to enter the area. Official spokesmen claim that in Arauca there are some 2,000 FARC combatants operating, another 1,000 from the ELN, and around 800 paramilitaries. In addition, from the beginning of September 2002 until 30 April 2003, the Uribe government declared Araucan a Zone of Rehabilitation, and entrusted the army with the task of restoring law and order. This was no easy task, for many Araucanos, above all politicians and civil employees, ended up complying with the dominant forces in the region as a result of guerrilla pressure coupled with lack of protection from the public force. In Arauca today it is difficult to know who works for whom. One is dealing here, then, with a society that in the full sense is one of caution, reciprocal distrust and fear. For this reason, at the end of the period of rehabilitation there were no clear signs that the measure had produced significant positive results.

Nariño, on the border with Ecuador, is in a similar situation. The department had been an untroubled region, almost bucolic. But for the past five years, guerrilla and paramilitary groups, along with drug traffickers, have been disputing control of this province among themselves, and in particular contol of Tumaco, the regional port. In Darién, on the border with Panama, and in the western Urabá region in the province of El Chocó, clashes between combatants from the same side also occur frequently, since the thick forests of the region offer a place of retreat from enemy attacks, and a privileged corridor for the transportation of contraband arms coming from Central America, and for the traffic of drugs towards the isthmus.

Perhaps the most dramatic case of zones in dispute is presented by the districts situated north of Medellín, where the ELN, the FARC, the paramilitaries, the hired killers of narco-trafficking, the delinquent youth gangs, the local self-defence groups, and, in certain cases, the public force fight for control of a densely populated urban territory. The first groups were formed here between 1985 and 1986, through the initiative of the guerrillas of M-19, who set up the so-called Camps for Peace and Democracy (Campamentos para la Paz y la Democracia). When, in 1990, that organization was reincorporated into civil life, some of these groups became hired killers in the service of Pablo Escobar, while others formed gangs of ordinary delinquents. Besieged by these bands in their own *barrios* of origin, other youths organized themselves in self-defence groups. And, in the mid-1990s, the FARC and the ELN began to form urban militias there. In this context, there developed towards the end of 2002 the only episode of urban warfare that has taken place in Colombia. Combined forces of the army and the police took by blood and fire Commune 13, situated in the western half of the centre of Medellín, from where the soldiers are said to have cleared out the guerrillas. Inhabitants in the rich southern part of the city found out about the engagement only through news reports on television and in the press.

The situation in the disputed zones contrasts with the apparent tranquillity that is experienced by people who live in regions controlled either by the guerrillas or the paramilitaries. The FARC maintains a strategic rearguard in a wide zone of the eastern mountain range, in the confluence of the departments of Meta, Caquetá, Guaviare and Sur de Cundinarmarca. The AUC dominate a region consisting of Alto Sinú and San Jorge en Córdoba, Urabá Antioqueño and Bajo Cauca. The rearguard of the ELN, which today is debilitated, is situated between Bajo Cauca and Sur de Bolívar. Guerrillas and paramilitaries impose strict order. They establish a tribute system and a simple and expeditious scheme of security and justice. The FARC eliminate common crime and everything and everyone they consider to be paramilitary or close to the paramilitaries, while the latter drive away or assassinate real or suspected guerrillas, teachers, religious leaders, union leaders and spokesmen, and, in some regions, drug addicts and homosexuals.

The big cities find themselves in an intermediate situation between the horror of the contested countryside and the apparent tranquillity of regions where an illegal, armed organization predominates. In these urban centres one notes a greater presence of *la fuerza pública* (forces of the law). Aside from the previously described episode in Medellín, up to now there have been neither open clashes nor massive pressure exerted by illegal groups on a vast sector of the population, as has occurred in the rural zones. The conflict manifests itself rather in isolated activities, such as selective assassinations, forced disappearances, kidnappings, and occasional terrorist attacks. The disappearances and murders are ordinarily carried out by paramilitary groups against specific persons and social sectors, although on occasions guerrillas also resort to similar tactics, particularly kidnapping.

Nevertheless, these crimes seem not to to disturb the tranquillity of the rest of the urban population. Perhaps repetition of these types of crimes over several decades has resulted in the desensitizing of Colombians, or has made them passive in the face of a phenomenon against which they feel impotent. The terrorist actions that guerrillas occasionally mount in cities such as Bogotá, Medellín, Cúcuta and Villavicencio certainly produce panic, but their impact is fleeting; people are obliged to continue their daily activities, and it is impossible to predict where and when the next attack will happen. Among the many examples of these atrocious actions, we may single out the homemade missiles that were fired at the governmental palace on 7 August 2002, the day of the presidential inauguration. The attack, which destroyed the exclusive club El Nogal in Bogatá, left thirty-six people dead and 162 wounded. A similar attack took place in Barrio de Neiva, next to the airport, destroying numerous houses accommodating people with few resources.

Over the entire country there hangs a vague sense of uncertainty about the future, a feeling that seems to be diluted in periods of relative tranquillity but returns to the surface powerfully with each new criminal atrocity. As already indicated, the cities are more exposed to common crime than the zones controlled by illegal organizations, since the *fuerza pública* cannot apply summary justice as they can. Medellín is once again a case in point, and also a fitting example of the unequal distribution of violence in Colombia. This city of 2 million inhabitants displays the highest rates of violence in the country and one of the highest in the world. The rate of homicides reached 177 per thousand in 2002.[5] In the poor northern *barrios*, where the *fuerza pública* has difficulty penetrating, there are around four hundred youth gangs, which, through force, have divided among themselves control of the territory. Meanwhile, just to the south a relatively calm, amply organized, industrious city, with a high degree of civic spirit, thrives.

Besides this geographic distribution, the violence also has a specific social distribution. The guerrillas, as much as the paramilitaries, select their victims. By means of extortion and kidnapping, the guerrillas influence the upper and middle classes, and above all politicians and government officials such as senators, mayors and governors. In this way FARC tries to consolidate its dominion in its zones of influence, and to weaken the state from these regions.

Paramilitary action is directed at all those who exercise some kind of independent and critical orientation or leadership. By the early 1990s, paramilitary groups had systematically liquidated, in collusion with sectors of the *fuerza pública*, several thousand militants and leaders of the Unión Patriótica (UP),[6] a political group launched by the FARC during the peace negotiations with the government of Belisario Betancur (1982–86). They also assassinated three presidential candidates of the left,[7] in addition to numerous journalists, reporters, trade unionists, teachers and intellectuals. Trade unionists and journalists have been among their main victims. According to a report produced by the Escuela Nacional Sindical (National Trade Union School), between 1991 and 2001 as many as 1,752 trade unionists were murdered, of whom 371 were directors and 1,381 were rank-and-file members. Most of these killings were committed by paramilitaries. The number of journalists killed is also dramatic: some forty journalists assassinated over the past ten years, at least fifty kidnapped since 1999, and another thirty or so forced into exile[8] (Escuela Nacional Sindical 2002). According to the union leaders, 117 members were murdered in 2002, and twenty in 2003 (*El Tiempo*, 19 June 2003).

As shown in this summary, various forms of violence have been besieging Colombian society for quite some time, overwhelming the state's capacity for control. Society is teetering on the brink of anarchy, facing terror, uncertainty and anxiety.

Fear and its impact

Fragmentation of space through fear In the first place, fear of violence has gradually come to curtail, fragment and annul many of the vital social spaces of Colombians. Since the 1970s, when crime began to increase in the cities, urban inhabitants have limited their movements, and to select streets and zones in which they can travel without danger. At night, Colombians tend to retreat to the security of their own homes. In short, citizens have experienced an impoverishment of those networks of free social relations that make life more enjoyable and strengthen so-called social capital. Fearing robbery, kidnap or attack, high-ranking civil employees of the state and the wealthier social sectors live in exclusive residential estates closed to the public and guarded by private watchmen; they travel at great speed in bullet-proof cars, and are obliged to change their routines continually. One might even say that the city and their houses are their prisons, between which they commute like fugitives on the run.

The middle classes, on the other hand, take precautionary measures to the extreme: they instal security locks in their houses, do not open their doors to strangers, travel with the windows of their cars closed, and they try not to go out at night. The upper classes have tried to reduce or to eliminate completely the need to travel by highway or to stop in recreational areas for fear of being kidnapped individually, or taken in one of the mass kidnappings first practised by the ELN and later also by the FARC.

In fact, until the installation of the present government automobile trips or pleasure outings to rural areas – one of the great benefits offered by the picturesque Colombian countryside – had almost entirely ceased. Overland communication between many municipalities was reduced for fear of guerrilla roadblocks. Those who dared to make such journeys would use potentially risky highways only until two or three o'clock in the afternoon at the latest, or turn back if after ten minutes no other vehicle had appeared travelling in the opposite direction. There are cities, such as Pasto and Calí, which remain besieged for fear of guerrilla roadblocks. For the past five years none of the inhabitants of Pasto has ventured out of the city by any of the four access roads; fear of roadblocks, extortion and kidnap have confined people to the urban centre. The situation is similar in Calí, at least in relation to the routes that lead towards the Pacific coast and the mountains.

The guerrilla roadblocks have also affected the economy. The internal market, above all between Medellín and Bogotá and Medellín and the Caribbean coast, has been seriously disrupted. The guerrillas frequently stop large lorries, rob the merchandise, and later set fire to the vehicles. From a political and administrative point of view, the guerrilla siege of the main highways takes the country back to the regional fragmentation that was predominant in Colombia fifty years ago, when vehicles that travelled between cities were scarce and one could say that the country was made up, to a certain extent, of an aggregate of city-states. Since August 2002, the present government has strengthened the vigilance exercised by the *fuerza pública* on the highways. Simultaneously, it has launched large-scale security operations on some of the principal routes, particularly at holiday times, so that Colombians will resume using them. The massive exodus of automobiles at such times, and the atmosphere of national celebration that accompanies it, is a good indicator of the accumulated frustration. Although very costly for the nation, these joint caravans of private and public security vehicles have become a symbol of the yearned-for recovery of the national territory. But of course they are still a false symbol. The country is far from finding a stable solution to the guerrilla blockades on the roadways, to the frequent kidnappings of travellers and the destruction or robbery of vehicles and merchandise.

If we consider that about 15 million Colombians reside in cities that on average have half a million inhabitants, this means that approximately 35 per cent of the national population are not suffering a situation of permanent fear. Yet all are obliged to increase their precautionary measures against crime, experience a growing distrust of strangers, and are increasingly found cloistered in the city and in the home, looking towards the future with uncertainty.

Contraction of time through fear The violence and the fear do not simply fragment space. They have a deeper impact: they undermine hope and they foreshorten the horizons of individual and collective futures. The past stops being a useful guide. Existence therefore tends to contract into an anxious present. For at least thirty years in Colombia, every day has brought repetitions of the same acts of violence: assassinations, massacres, kidnappings, terrorist attacks, and the destruction of transportation routes, bridges and power plants. These are shown every night on television news bulletins, like an interminable national nightmare. Colombians have become impotent observers of the daily elimination of compatriots, and of the blind destruction of the national work of decades. And this obsessive reiteration of tragedy sinks into the national memory, dimming future prospects.

Under the impact of violence and fear, the future seems limited. Life projects become provisional. Faced with the risk of having to leave everything behind, or of becoming a target for kidnappers and assassins, the upper and middle classes restrain their desire to improve their living conditions, to change their home or vehicle, to acquire a good television set or a better stereo. Life is lived only from day to day, and the home tends to turn into a transitory refuge. Personal savings are not invested, but rather are spent on recreation, or kept under the mattress, or sent outside the country.

The same occurs on a national level. Productive investment in economic activity has diminished. Political activity is no longer concentrated on great projects of national construction, but rather on short-term strategies and measures to deal with insecurity and conflict. In fact, the positions adopted by the presidential candidates, in favour either of peace negotiations or of greater military pressure, appear to have exercised a notable influence on voting in the last two presidential elections. And national opinion has become polarized around these immediate themes, leaving the grave structural problems of the country and the enormous challenges that the international context creates on the sidelines. As already mentioned, the past also loses its value. It offers no guidelines on how to escape the spiral of violence. A blocked future and a past without value transform time into an absolute present.

Even so, it is necessary to note that this contraction of the future in Colombia is also unequally distributed. For instance, Bogotá, the national capital, where 7 million Colombians, representing 17 per cent of the total population, reside, is a shining exception. For the past decade, the city has been the scene of significant projects. Perhaps no other city in Latin America has, over the last decade, experienced such a large-scale and rapid modernization of the physical infrastructure, and such a remarkable change in customs and citizens' expectations, as Bogotá. This transformation has been possible thanks to the past four mayors, who have succeeded in providing the city with a new vision and sufficient financial resources for its development. Medellín has made similar accomplishments over the past decade, although at the moment it seems to be entering a relative decline.

It is worth noting at this point some additional considerations regarding perception of the collective future. In well-organized societies, appreciation of the future depends on accumulated social capital – that is to say, the governing relations of reciprocal confidence between citizens. On the other hand, in societies that are weakly articulated, such as those of Colombia and Latin America in general – whose social fabric appears, moreover, to be unravelling owing to poverty, crime and violence – the collective perception of the future is much more bound to the government of the day and to the confidence it is able to instil. In Latin America the messianic temptation of *caudillismo* is ever present, threatening frustration and a new loss of heart.

In Colombia, changes in the national spirit related to the last three governments have been manifest. The Samper government's (1994–98) crisis of legitimacy induced deep pessimism in the upper and middle classes of the country, as well as in vast sectors of youth. In fact, it permitted the sharpening of conflict and the diffusion of different forms of escape, on which more shortly. For this reason, President Pastrana (1998–2002) was received by the upper and middle classes as a saviour who opened the doors to hope again. In these social sectors, his government managed to restore a certain feeling of self-esteem and national dignity. But mismanagement and the failure of peace negotiations with the insurgent organizations instilled a new sense of pessimism towards the future. The inevitable reaction of the voters was acceptance of the military challenge posed by the armed organizations and a massive vote for a show of authority and attempts at national revival. Symptomatic of this new situation in the country are the incipient reactivation of the economy[9] and the upswing in construction activity.

Nevertheless, it is not impossible that one is witnessing only a brief cycle, and that, in a few months, amid the rigours of the war, a deep pessimism will once again re-emerge. If so the present hope for the future will have been shown to be nothing more than an illusion.

Forms of flight

The suffocating narrowness of an existence in which they are imprisoned by fear induces Colombians to attempt diverse forms of escape or flight. The most obvious mode of flight is changing one's place of residence – displacement – either within the country or abroad. In the western hemisphere, Colombia is the country with the greatest number of internally displaced individuals (*El Tiempo*, 1 June 2003). According to figures compiled by official and private sources, every year between 300,000 and 350,000 peasant farmers are displaced from their lands. The estimate of the total number of *desplazados* varies markedly from one source to the next, depending on whether the statistics have been compiled since the beginning of the displacements, in 1985, or only over the past three years, when the issue has attracted more urgent attention from the state. The total number varies, therefore, from 772,873 to 2,914,853 individuals (*El Tiempo*, 26 May 2003).[10] The latter figure represents around 7 per cent of the national population. Approximately 74 per cent of *desplazados* are children. In the last ten years, 700,000 have been displaced owing to internal political violence in Colombia. On the other hand, fear of current and future violence has impelled many Colombians of all social classes to emigrate. Since the 1990s, Colombia has become, along with Venezuela, Ecuador, Nicaragua and El Salvador, one of the largest net exporters of people. In 2000, the International Organization for Migration estimated that as many as 1 million Colombians had abandoned the country in the last four years (OIM 2001).

Of course, many have left in search of better economic opportunities. We should note, nevertheless, that this emigration still has to be seen as indirectly related to the uncertainty of a future of probable violence. Many other Colombians from the upper and upper-middle classes have left the country expressly motivated by the fear of falling victim to extortion or kidnapping, having received threats of this sort or having already been victims of certain crimes. Among the emigrants are found numerous successful entrepreneurs, and many young professional couples who, faced with the uncertain future of the country, choose to search for new horizons abroad. In these cases Colombia is losing not only the investment made in raising and educating them, but also, and most unfortunately, the future that these young people are taking away with them. Their voluntary exile signifies an anticipated 'undercapitalization' of the nation's future. One must note, nevertheless, that in the majority of cases the emigrants who flee the country end up once again facing economic uncertainty, cultural displacement and lasting discrimination in their chosen places of refuge.

These forms of spatial flight or escape – internal displacement and emigration – are self-evident. But next to them other, subtler forms of inner emigration proliferate, bound up not with space but with time. Many Colombians, above all young urbanites, try to allay anxiety about the future through vain attempts to reduce the perspective of time to the present, and to dilute it with some form of artificial stimulus. This form of escapism takes many forms, of which we will mention only a few. One is the increase in indulgence in alcohol, drugs and sex. In recent years, small liquor shops have proliferated near the universities, where young people, both men and women, meet early to drink beer with the intention of escaping from the present. Of course, this is not a unique feature of Colombians. Rather, it seems characteristic of an age and of a civilization, mainly Western, disinclined to work without respite in the pursuit of happiness. But the siege conditions of war, the underlying fear of violence and an uncertain future exacerbate this eagerness to exhaust the possibilities of existence in an eternal present, forgetting the past and ignoring an uncertain future that will perhaps never come. Such behaviour is not very different, in this sense, from that of the hired killers of Medellín, youths from poor families who have inherited the gangster culture of Pablo Escobar and his followers, and have learned to gamble with life in the risky intensity of the present, believing that in any case they lack a future. With a shiny pair of Reebok sneakers, a fine Yamaha motorbike and a pretty girl, these youngsters defy death.

We could also mention here many other phenomena, such as the proliferation of satanic sects or the rise in suicides among youths, related, among diverse factors, to the occlusion of the future by the violence. All attempts to evade time have their origins in a firm will to forget: to forget the past, to deliberately deny the future, and to flee from the present. Many of these phenomena are related to poverty and the lack of a future, but all have their roots, in the first place, in the little value that human life has in an environment of violence as unbridled as that of Colombia.

Finally, I should mention one last form of flight, which is closely related to the cultural traditions of the nation. This subtle form of evasion has to do with the real or the apparent superficiality of Colombians, which expresses itself in their inexhaustible humour, their ability to generate laughter out of the worst tragedies, and in their obsession with music, dance and celebration. These characteristics of the national culture are not new. Perhaps ever since colonization and the dawn of the republic in the nineteenth century, many Colombians, mainly from the popular classes, have found humour and revelry to be the best ways in which to mock the cruel attacks of poverty, suffering and death. Perhaps for that reason, violence, war and the uncertainty of the future, rather than plunging Colombians into bitterness, have instead contributed to fortifying these features of the national character.

A visitor could mistake this trait for a crazy joy – oblivious to current risks, and irresponsible in the face of future challenges. Nevertheless, it is possible that, beneath the apparent happiness, there flow subterranean currents of sadness and lack of hope for the future, which Colombians anxiously try to escape by reaffirming the force of life. Perhaps this is not about consciousness, but rather about a painful understanding of one's own impotence to change the present. Perhaps laughter and the fiesta are not signs of superficiality, but rather serve to disguise a tragic awareness of our complex reality.

In a recent short story by the Colombian writer Laura Restrepo, one of her characters, a young French woman who is helping those displaced by violence, makes the following poignant remark: 'Here in your country I have learned that when things have no solution, the best remedy is to go away and dance ... There is no other country in the world more beautiful than this ... No, there is not; nor one as deadly' (2001: 71).

Notes

1 Hobbes starts with the proposition that man was originally in a pre-social and pre-political state of 'nature', where everyone was at war with everyone else. In order to escape widespread insecurity and fear, individuals established among themselves a social contract, which handed over authority and the monopoly of force to a sovereign. For Locke the contract is established so as to prevent even the possibility of war and insecurity, and for Rousseau the social contract is established in order to put an end to inequality, insecurity and the conflict generated by the institution of private property. In all three positions, fear of anarchical violence is replaced by the fearful respect of the citizenry for the centralized and regulated force that is the sovereign.

2 A state organization charged with defending the rights of the population.

3 Owing to the difficulties involved in attempting to speak directly with the children, the information that the *Defensoría* presents is generalized.

4 In the answer to this question can, perhaps, also be found the reason why the Colombian nation has not disintegrated, a victim of its own conflicts, perhaps because that which never was a solid unit cannot shatter into pieces.

5 <www.lachiva.com/2003/abril/10/3585homicidos.htm>.

6 The numbers vary notably, depending on the source. Official figures from the state estimate between 1,700 and 1,800 victims, whereas the UP estimates 3,000 militants. In 1997, the Inter-American Commission for Human Rights blamed the action taken by the UP against the government for the death and disappearance of nearly 3,000 of its militants (*El Tiempo*, 19 June 2003).

7 Jaime Pardo Leal and Bernardo Jaramillo, leaders of the UP, and Carlos Pizarro, ex-commander of M-19.

8 Data provided by a delegation of the Instituto Prensa y Sociedad and Reporteros Sin Fronteras, which visited Colombia from 22 to 30 October 2001, to investigate the working conditions of the journalists.

9 For the first time since 1997, the economy grew 3.8 per cent in the first trimester of 2003.

10 Occupied with this problem are the NGO called Consultoría por los Derechos Humanos y el Desplazamiento, the Red de Solidaridad Social de la Presidencia, the International Committee of the Red Cross, the Human Mobility section of the social clergy of the Colombian Episcopal Conference, the United Nations High Commissioner for Refugees, and a member of the Inter-American Court of Human Rights, responsible for the chapter on displacement in the *Informe Nacional de Desarrollo Humano* 2003, under the auspices of the UNDP and the Swedish Agency for Cooperation.

12 | Epilogue: violence and the quest for order in contemporary Latin America

PATRICIO SILVA

This volume has highlighted one of the key paradoxes of Latin American societies today. On the one hand, we observe that over the last two decades serious and sometimes relatively successful attempts have been made to consolidate democratic rule in the region. Almost everywhere in Latin America, formal democratic systems are in place, while the probability of authoritarian regression is low in most countries, at least in the short run. On the other hand, these new democracies have in many cases proved unable to establish real democratic civil order. Since the mid-1980s democratic rule has been accompanied by increasing levels of social and organized violence in which 'armed actors' of all kinds have frustrated the efforts to achieve a peaceful social and political order. Instead, violent disorder has permeated many Latin American societies up to the present. As a result of this, in most Latin American nations important segments of the population have experienced an increasing feeling of insecurity in their daily lives (Frühling et al. 2003). This has resulted in many cases in growing demands on the state to take a tough stance with respect to crime fighting and to guarantee people's security on the street and even at home.

In recent years scholars have singled out a number of factors that could be held responsible for the widespread climate of violence in the region.[1] While for some the use of violence for all types of objectives represents an inherent and continuous feature of Latin American political culture, others argue that the current wave of violence finds its immediate roots in the authoritarian regimes of the 1970s and 1980s (e.g. Pinheiro 1996). From this perspective, the systematic application of state terrorism against citizens has resulted in the destruction of the state's legitimacy. Consequently, organized and unorganized actors have begun challenging the authority of the state and its claim to the monopoly of the legitimate means of coercion in society. Following the restoration of democracy from the early 1980s, the argument follows, most civilian governments simply proved unable to reverse this tendency to undermine state authority. In other words, the legacy left by authoritarian experiences from the recent past – when the illegal use of violence by the state and its 'uncivil' supporters was commonplace – has not disappeared. So today we observe the persistence of violence generated by the state and state-related actors, characterized by impunity and arbitrariness. In this manner, the new democracies have so far been unsuccessful in finding adequate mechanisms to control their own state institutions. Instead, the latter groom ties with organized crime and repressive activities, just as was the case during the authoritarian era.

Other scholars relate the emergence and strengthening of this new violence to neo-liberalism. The application of structural adjustment programmes and the subsequent transformation of Latin American economies and societies according to free market principles have resulted, in this view, in a dramatic exacerbation of social inequality. This growing gap between the 'haves' and 'have nots' has finally alienated poor sectors from the societal order, expressed in the recurrent use of violence to secure their livelihood and to challenge the state's authority. In this manner, the resulting social and political marginalization of the poorer sectors – expressed respectively in the explosive expansion of the informal economy and the manifest depoliticization of the population – not only generates violence but also hampers efforts within civil society to develop defence mechanisms against this violence.

Some scholars stress the weakness of the democratic fabric itself in the region and the ways in which the increasing levels of violence are related to the dynamics of democratic rule. The eruption of violence in the region has indeed coincided with a period of democratic restoration and consolidation. What is clear is that since the early 1980s most forms of violence, such as street criminality, organized crime and drugs-related conflict, seem to have been aggravated. It is still unclear to what extent the existence of democratic freedom itself has helped to generalize the sensation that crime and danger are around almost every corner, but some factors may point in this direction. To begin with, democratization has generated a free press that has systematically highlighted crime and violence in practically every Latin American country. Contrary to what constituted the norm under authoritarian rule, when the inability of rulers to deal effectively with everyday violence was generally not acknowledged by the controlled press, today even relatively insignificant cases of violence receive generous coverage by newspapers and television. Furthermore, the notion of the increase in all types of violence since democratic restoration is often based on statistics of registered crimes and criminal violence. So it could be argued that, at least in part, the increase in registered violence since the early 1980s could be the result of the fact that after the demise of authoritarian regimes a larger number of victims of violence have begun to go to police stations to report criminal acts or acts of violence. The reasons for this range from increased confidence in the police forces to the simple fact that citizens nowadays require proof of a formal report in order to claim compensation from insurance schemes, which have experienced a rapid expansion in Latin America in recent years.

Some critics of present-day Latin American democracy are also inclined to relate the growing levels of violence to the relative lack of popular participation in the decision-making process and the absence of transparency and account-ability of politics and governance in the region. This major deficiency in the institutional framework is supposed to have facilitated an increasing abuse of power by the political and economic elites, including fraud, corruption and state violence. It is perfectly reasonable to assume that these factors work against social and political stability in society, and hence result in violence. These deficiencies of democratic rule in themselves cannot, however, in my view, explain the phenomenon. For instance, they do not satisfactorily explain the fact that that during the previous authoritarian period – when participa-tion and transparency were by definition non-existent – the levels of violence not directly related to political struggles were generally lower than what we are experiencing today.

Finally, there are sectors that attempt to talk down the severity of the spiral of violence. They refer to the situation in other parts of the developing world, such as in Africa and parts of Asia, where the spiral of violence is seen as much worse than in Latin America. From this comparative perspective, Latin America is still perceived as a relatively safe place to live in the developing world. In the same vein, it has been pointed out that widespread societal violence has become a general feature of modern society. In the industrialized world too the level of violence has substantially increased in the last two decades or so. In other words, the globalization process must be factored into the equation; this has led, among other things, to the internationalization of organized crime in the form of powerful networks and cartels, such as those that are familiar from the drugs industry.

In any case, Latin American democracies are facing the enormous and urgent task of establishing the monopoly of the legitimate means of violence. In other words, governments must take control of the use of coercion to stem the increasingly 'privatized' nature that violence has acquired in recent years. This implies among other things disarming the citizenry in those countries – particularly those nations which in recent years have experienced bloody armed conflicts, such as Nicaragua, El Salvador and Guatemala – where large quantities of weapons (especially small arms) are still in the possession of civilian groups.

Therefore, at the end of the day it is the state and its institutions which have directly or indirectly received most of the blame for the high levels of violence existing in most Latin American countries. Some talk about state failure or even state collapse. This notion refers *inter alia* to the recurrence of political crisis in the region as a result of the poor management of state affairs and the economy by weak and corrupt governments. This has led to an increasing erosion of the legitimacy of the state in general, and of the political class in particular. In addition, for many the failure of both the judiciary and the police to enforce the rule of law and to condemn those who do not obey it stands as the most visible expression of the crisis of the state in Latin America. As we have seen in this volume, the malfunctioning of the army, the police and other security forces – which instead of defending the population from violence have often been among the main actors generating it – has substantially increased the sense of vulnerability experienced by an increasing number of citizens *vis-à-vis* the state and its armed institutions.

This tendency to blame the state can be criticized, however. Such a view may fail to acknowledge responsibility for the violence within society as a whole. In my opinion, the problem we observe today in Latin America with regard to violence indicates not only state failure but also societal failure. From this perspective it can be proposed that not only the state but also civil society has shown its inability to generate mechanisms to reduce the levels of violence and to renounce the use of force and physical confrontation as instruments for social and political struggle. So the paralysis and ineffectiveness shown by most Latin American states when dealing with the violence issue is in my view only a reflex of a broader kind of Durkheimian anomie affecting the entire societal order. For several reasons, both elites and popular sectors have been unable to establish effective institutional and legal schemes that could guarantee at least the basic functioning of the rule of law. Consequently, the phenomenon of violence in Latin America has not only a social and economic dimension, but represents in the first place a political problem. Apparently, key actors in society are not convinced that political negotiations and the achievement of consensus with respect to the organization of politics and the economy can be more advantageous for their interests than the use of violence. This means that, in terms of Linz and Stepan's (1996: 5) notion of democratic consolidation, democracy in Latin America is still 'not the only game in town', not, in this case, because of the attractiveness of authoritarian political alternatives but owing to the negation of non-violent consociation as an indispensable pre-condition for democratic governance.

In present-day Latin America it is not only the state which is weak, but also the main actors within political society, namely political parties. In the last two

189

decades, political organizations have rapidly lost their prestige and ability to aggregate social demands and to politically represent the will of their alleged constituency. This has resulted, among other things, in the structural weakness of most Latin American legislatures. Not only do they not properly control the acts of the executive, but they also do not adequately relate to the claims and aspirations of the electorate. Without the proper mediation of political organizations, in current Latin American societies people adopt individual or collective strategies for survival in which the use of violence has often become an indispensable component. In the process Latin American societies have acquired certain praetorian features in which social groups attempt to establish political power, not by convincing others or by generating broad-based consensus, but by imposing their will at any cost and by any means. This constitutes the 'politics of coercion', which is the goal (or if not that at least the effect) of organized violence within the framework of an 'uncivil society' (Koonings 2001; Koonings and Kruijt, Chapter 1, this volume).

The question of the 'newness' of the violence is still part of the ongoing debate. In my view, references to the so-called 'old' violence have tended to overly reduce the historical framework of analysis to the authoritarian regimes of the 1960s and 1970s. As a result, emphasis has mainly been laid on the political and military confrontations between the repressive forces of the state and leftist insurrectionary sectors. Although it cannot be denied that during those years the confrontation between the dictatorships and their opposition constituted in many cases the single most important source of societal violence, this does not mean that during those years most of the kinds of violence experienced today were not present in Latin American societies. The fact is that in those years the attention of both scholars and international organizations was mainly focused on the analysis of state terrorism, dirty-war practices, political kidnappings and guerrilla warfare, and so on. At that time, one could say, everyday violence had not yet been 'discovered' by social scientists as an interesting field of study, being confined, in part as a result of disciplinary boundaries, to a small group of criminologists and security experts. Even less well known is the map of violence – both urban and rural – in Latin American societies during the decades prior to the establishment of the military regimes.

If the issues and cases studied in this volume show anything, it is that the factors that have generated and reproduced violence over the past two decades are multiple in kind and diverse in intensity. In each country, a particular set of factors has been responsible. While in countries such as Colombia, Guatemala, El Salvador, Nicaragua and Peru civil wars and state versus guerrilla warfare have been at the root of the generation of societies dominated by fear and the use of force, in countries such as Brazil, Mexico, Honduras and again, of course, Colombia, drug trafficking has penetrated the social fabric and state institutions and has eroded public probity with quite destructive consequences for the legitimacy of the political authorities.

The regeneration of public institutions and the restoration of the people's confidence in the political authorities cannot be effectively addressed from a restricted national perspective. As many factors generating societal violence possess an international dimension (drug use and trafficking, transnational criminal networks and the like), the solution has to be approached in part from a regional level in which several Latin American states combine their efforts to tackle these problems.

So far Latin American citizens still demand and hope to obtain some type of social order which liberates them from living in fear of violence perpetrated by the state, armed groups and faceless criminals. It is this fear which inhibits the ability of many Latin Americans to have faith in their future and the future of their offspring.

Note

1 See Morrison et al. (2003: 102–7) for a recent though partial overview.

Epilogue

About the contributors

Chris van der Borgh is a lecturer at the Centre for Conflict Studies, Utrecht University. He has published on war and post-war reconstruction in El Salvador and is currently participating in a large-scale research project on peace and reconstruction in the former Yugoslavia and southern Asia.

Mario Fumerton holds a postdoctoral post at the Department of Cultural Anthropology, Utrecht University. He is the author of various articles and a recently published PhD thesis about the peasant self-defence organizations in Peru during the 1980s and 1990s.

Kees Koonings is associate professor of development studies at the Faculty of Social Sciences of Utrecht University. He is the author of books and articles on development issues, ethnicity, and militarism and violence in Latin America.

Dirk Kruijt is professor of development studies at the Faculty of Social Sciences of Utrecht University. He has published on poverty and informality, military governments, and war and peace in Latin America.

Francisco Leal Buitrago is professor of political sciences at the Universidad de los Andes and honorary professor at the Universidad Nacional de Colombia. He is the author of numerous books and articles on the decades-long violence in Colombia.

Piet van Reenen is professor of police studies at the Faculty of Law of Utrecht University. A former high-ranking police officer and adviser to the minister of internal affairs in the Netherlands, he has published mostly on police reform and policing extensions.

Simone Remijnse holds a postdoctoral post at the Department of Cultural Anthropology, Utrecht University. She is the author of various articles and a recently published PhD thesis about the indigenous self-defence patrols in Guatemala during the civil war.

Luis Alberto Restrepo is professor of international relations and a founding member of the Instituto de Estudios Políticos y Relaciones Internacionales (IEPRI), Universidad Nacional de Colombia. He has published on Caribbean societies and on violence in Colombia.

Marcelo Sain is professor of political sciences and research fellow in the research programme on Armed Forces, Security and Society at the Universidad Nacional de Quilmes, Argentina. Until 2003 he was the vice-minister of security, in charge of the police of metropolitan Buenos Aires. His numerous publications are about violence and crime in (the Southern Cone of) Latin America and on reforms in the security sector.

Wim Savenije is a research member at the Facultad Latinoamericana de Ciencias Sociales (FLACSO), El Salvador programme. He has published several articles and book chapters about youth gangs (*maras*) in Central America and is preparing a PhD thesis about the proliferation of *maras* in El Salvador.

Patricio Silva is professor of Latin American studies at the Faculties of Humanities and Social Sciences of Leiden University. His publications are mostly about the process of democratization in Latin America and the role of military administrators and civilian technocrats.

Harold A. Trinkunas is professor at the Naval Postgraduate School in California and is the author of a standard work about civil–military relations in Venezuela. He has published extensively on the Latin American armed forces.

Menno Vellinga is professor of Latin America studies at the University of Florida, Gainesville. His publications include work on the entrepreneurial class, the industrialization process, the political structure and the state, and – more recently – the long-term effects of drugs and violence in Latin America.

Alba Zaluar is professor of anthropology at the Universidade Estadual do Rio de Janeiro. A renowned specialist on the theme of urban violence and gang warfare in Brazil, she has published on *favela* culture, youth gangs, drug trafficking and urban violence systems in Brazil

Bibliography

Adorno, S. (1990) *Violência Urbana, Justiça Criminal e Organização Social do Crime*, mimeo, São Paulo: Núcleo de Estudos da Violência da USP.

— (1995) 'Discriminação racial e justiça criminal em São Paulo', *Novos Estudos CEBRAP* 43 (November): 45–63.

Agüero, F. and J. Stark (eds) (1998) *Fault Lines of Democracy in Post-Transition Latin America*, Coral Gables: North–South Center Press.

Alvarenga, P. (1996) *Cultura y Etica de la Violencia, El Salvador, 1880–1932*, San José: EDUCA.

Alvarez, I. (2002a) 'Deliberancia de la FAN Pone en Riesgo Seguridad de la Nación', *El Universal*, 25 February.

— (2002b) 'La Constitución Guió a Efraín Vásquez Velasco', *El Universal*, 14 August.

— (2002c) 'Cuatro Equipos para 20 Magistrados', *El Universal*, 14 August.

— (2003) 'Cero Comicios hasta Designación del CNE', *El Universal*, 23 January.

Alvarez, S. E., Evelina Dagnino and Arturo Escobar (eds) (1998) *Culture of Politics, Politics of Culture; Re-visioning Latin American Social Movements*, Boulder, CO: Westview Press.

Americas Watch (1986) *Civil Patrols in Guatemala,* New York and Washington, DC: Americas Watch Committee.

— (1992) *Peru Under Fire: Human Rights since the Return to Democracy*, London: Yale University Press.

Amnesty International (1991) *Peru. Human Rights in a Climate of Terror*, London: Amnesty International Publications.

— (1997) *Politically Motivated Criminal Charges against Land Reform Activists*, London: Amnesty International Publications.

— (1998) *Brazil, Corumbiara and Eldorado de Carajas*, London: Amnesty International Publications.

— (2002) *Guatemala. The Civil Defence Patrols Re-emerge*, London: Amnesty International Publications.

— (2003) *Report 2003*, Oxford: Alden Press.

Análisis estratégico (2002), 11 April (<www.viaalterna.com.co>).

Andersen, M. E. (2001) *La policía. Pasado, Presente y Propuestas Para el Futuro*, Buenos Aires: Editorial Sudamericana.

Antunes, P. C. B. (2002) *SNI & ABIN. Uma Leitura de Atuação dos Serviços Secretos Brasileiros ao Longo do Século XX*, Rio de Janeiro: Editora FGV.

Arévalo de León, B. (ed.) (2003) *Hacia una política de seguridad para la democracia*, 1–3, Guatemala: FLACSO/WSP International.

Armas, M. (2003) 'Recortan Asignación para las Regiones', *El Universal*, 15 February.

Armon, J. R. S. and R. Wilson (1997) *Negotiating Rights: The Guatemalan Peace Process*, London: Conciliation Resources.

Arnson, C. J. (ed.) (1999) *Comparative Peace Processes in Latin America*, Washington, DC/Stanford, CA: Woodrow Wilson Center Press/Stanford University Press.

Arriagada, I. and L. Godoy (1999) *Seguridad Ciudadana y Violencia en América Latina: Diagnóstico y Políticas en los Años Noventa*, Santiago de Chile: United Nations/CEPAL / ECLAC, Serie Políticas Sociales 32.

Asamblea Nacional (2002) 'Informe de la Comisión Parlamentaria Especial para investigar los sucesos de abril de 2002'.

Astorga, L. (2004) 'Mexico, Drugs and Politics', in Vellinga (2004), pp. 110–28.

Auyero, J. (2001) 'Introducción. Claves para Pensar la Marginación', in L. Wacquant, *Parias urbanos. Marginalidad en la Ciudad a Comienzos del Milenio*, Buenos Aires: Manantial.

Avilés, W. (2001) 'Institutions, Military Policy, and Human Rights in Colombia', *Latin American Perspectives,* 116, 28(1): 31–55.

Bagley, B. (2004) 'Globalization and Transnational Organized Crime: The Russian Mafia in Latin America and The Caribbean', in Vellinga (2004), pp. 280–306.

Bagley, B. M. and W. O. Walker III (eds) (1994) *Drug Trafficking in the Americas*, Boulder, CO: Lynne Rienner.

Barbano, R. (2003) 'Los Narcos en el Espejo', *Clarín, Revista Viva*, Buenos Aires, 29 June.

Barreira, C. (1998) *Crimes por Encomenda*, Rio de Janeiro: Relume Dumará.

Bastos, F. I. (1995) *Ruína e reconstrução: Aids e drogas injetáveis na cena contemporânea*, Rio de Janeiro: ENSP/Fiocruz (unpublished PhD dissertation).

Benítez Manaut, R. (2002) 'Mexico: Doctrinas de Seguridad y Defensa (del Siglo XIX al XXI)', in J. S. Tulchin (ed.), *Nuevos Temas de Seguridad en América Latina*, Barcelona: CIDOB Ediciones, pp. 57–72.

— (2003a) 'Seguridad y Relaciones Cívico-militares en América Central y México. Escenarios a Inicios del Siglo XXI', in K. Bodemer (ed.), *El Nuevo Escenario de (In)seguridad en América Latina. ¿Amenaza para la Democracia?*, Caracas: Editorial Nueva Sociedad, pp. 75–107.

— (2003b) 'América del Norte; ¿Seguridad Regional en Construcción?', paper presented at the first Congreso de Americanistas en el foro EPS-18, 'Desafíos y Tendencias de las Políticas de Seguridad en Las Américas al Comienzo del Siglo XXI', Santiago de Chile: Universidad de Chile, 14–18 July.

Berkowitz, L. (1993) *Aggression: Its Causes, Consequences and Control,* Boston, MA: McGraw-Hill.

Binford, L. (2002) 'Violence in El Salvador: A Rejoinder to Philippe Bourgois's "The Power of Violence in War and Peace"', *Ethnography*, 3: 201–19.

Bourdieu, P. (2000) *Pascalian Mediations,* Stanford, CA: Stanford University Press.

Bourgois, P. (2001) 'The Power of Violence in War and Peace', *Ethnography*, 2: 5–34.

Bowden, M. (2001) *Killing Pablo. The Hunt for the World's Greatest Outlaw,* New York: Penguin.

Briceño-León, R. (2002) 'Introducción: La nueva violencia urbana de América Latina', in R. Briceño-León (ed.), *Violencia, Sociedad y Justicia en América Latina*, Buenos Aires : CLACSO, pp. 13–26.

Broderick, W. J. (2000) *El Guerrillero Invisible*, Bogotá: Intermedio Editores.

Brown, R. M. (1976) *The Strain of Violence*, New York: Oxford University Press.

Burt, J. (1998) 'Shining Path and the "Decisive Battle" in Lima's *Barriadas*: The Case of Villa El Salvador', in Stern (1998), pp. 267–306.

Caldeira, T. (1996) 'Crime and Individual Rights: Reframing the Question of Violence in Latin America', in Jelin and Hershberg (1996), pp. 197–214.

— (2000) *City of Walls: Crime, Segregation and Citizenship in São Paulo*, Berkeley: University of California Press.

Cambio 16 (1998), 269, 10–17 August; (2002), 468, 10–17 June.

Camel Anderson, E. (2002) 'Venamcham Denuncia Terrorismo de estado contra el Empresariado', *El Universal*, 23 January.

— (2003a) 'Bloquean a Empleados de PDVSA', *El Universal*, 7 January.

— (2003b) 'Reducción de Nómina en PDVSA se Acerca a 50%', *El Universal*, 1 March.

— (2003c) 'Deficit de ONG contra la Pobreza', *El Universal*, 15 June.

Cameron, M. A. (2000) 'Elections in a Hybrid Regime: Civil–Military Relations and Caesarism in Peru', paper presented at the XXIIth International Congress of the Latin American Studies Association, Miami, FL, 16–18 March.

Cammack, P. (1981) *Coronelismo and National Politics in Brazil*, Glasgow: Institute of Latin American Studies, University of Glasgow.

Campos, E. (1988) 'Da Falange Vermelha a Escadinha: o Poder nas Prisões', *Presença*, 11.

Cardona Marrero, R. (2001a) 'Plan Bolívar Manejó 200 Millardos', *El Universal*, 18 August.

— (2001b) 'Recorte de Presupuesto Afecta Aviación Militar', *El Universal*, 31 October.

— (2002) 'Toma de la PM "Fue Impecable"', *El Universal*, 18 November.

Castañeda, J. (1996) 'Democracy and Inequality in Latin America: A Tension of the Times', in J. I. Domínguez and A. F. Lowenthal (eds), *Constructing Democratic Governance. Latin America and the Caribbean in the 1990s – Themes and Issues*, Baltimore, MD and London: Johns Hopkins University Press, pp. 42–63.

Castells, M. and J. Mollenkopf (eds) (1992) *Dual City: Restructuring New York*, New York: Russel Sage Foundation.

Castro, M. and P. Ventura Nicolas (2002) 'Petroleros Responden Otra Vez', *El Universal*, 3 December.

Cavarozzi, M. (1987) *Autoritarismo y Democracia (1955–1983)*, Buenos Aires: CEAL.

Ceballos Melguizo, R. (2001) 'The Evolution of the Armed Conflict in Medellín. An Analysis of the Major Actors', *Latin American Perspective*, 116, 28(1): 110–31.

CEH (1999) *Guatemala. Memoria del Silencio*, vols I–XII, Guatemala: UNOPS.

CELS (2003) *Estadísticas sobre el Cumplimiento de la Ley por Parte de las Instituciones de Seguridad Pública*, Buenos Aires: CELS.

CEPAL (2001) *Panorama Social de América Latina 2000–2001*, Santiago de Chile: United Nations.

Cerigua Weekly Briefs (1997), 26 July.

Chevigny, P. (1995) *Edge of the Knife. Police Violence in the Americas*, New York: New Press.

Clarín, Buenos Aires (2003), 27 April, 15 May, 6 and 28 July.

Clavijo, S. (1998) *Dividendos de Paz y Costos de la Guerra en Colombia: La Fuerza Pública y su Presión Fisca*, Documento Cede 98-15, Bogotá: Universidad de los Andes.

Clawson, P. L. and R. Lee (1996) *The Andean Cocaine Industry*, New York: St Martin's Press.

Coecho, E. C. (1988) 'Da falange vermelha a escadinha: o poder nas prisões', *Presença. Política e Cultura* 11: 106–14.

COFAVIC (2002) 'Venezuela: Democracia y Derechos Humanos', *Informe Semestral*, Jan.–Aug.

— (2003) ' La Democracia en Venezuela está Seriamente Amenazada (Periodo septiembre 2002 a febrero 2003)'.

Cohen, J. L. and A. Arato (1992) *Civil Society and Political Theory*, Cambridge and London: MIT Press.

Collier, D. (ed.) (1979) *Los Nuevos Autoritarismos en América Latina*, Mexico: Fondo de Cultura Económica.

'Colombia: The Forgotten War' (2001) *Latin American Perspectives*, 116, 28 (1).

Comisión de La Verdad y Reconciliación (2003) *Informe Final* (Vol. II), Lima: CVR.

Coronel Aguirre, J. and C. Loayza (1992) 'Violencia Política: Formas de Respuesta Comunera en Ayacucho', in C. I. Degregori (ed.), *Perú: el Problema Agrario en Debate/SEPIA IV*, Lima: SEPIA, pp. 509–37.

Costa, G. (1999) *La Policía Nacional de El Salvador (1990–1997)*, San Salvador: UCA Editores.

Cotler, J. (1970) 'The Mechanics of Internal Domination and Social Change in Peru', in Horowitz (1970), pp. 407–44.

— (1999) *Drogas y Política en el Perú,* Lima: Instituto de Estudios Peruanos.

Cruz, J. M. and L. A. González (1997) 'Magnitud de la Violencia en El Salvador', *Estudios Centroamericanos*, 588: 953–66.

Cruz, J. M. and M. Portillo (1998) *Solidaridad y Violencia en las Pandillas de Gran San Salvador: Más allá de la Vida Loca*, San Salvador: UCA Editores.

Cruz, J. M., A. Trigueros Arguëllo and F. Gonzalez (2000) *El Crimen Violento en El Salvador: Factores Sociales y Económicos Asociados,* San Salvador: IUDOP.

Dagnino, E. (1998) 'Culture, Citizenship, and Democracy. Changing Discourses and Practices of the Latin American Left', in S. E. Alvarez et al. (1998), pp. 33–63.

Dahrendorf, R. (1992) *O Conflito Social Moderno*, Rio de Janeiro: Zahar Editores.

Dammert, L. (2000) *Violencia Criminal y Seguridad Pública en América Latina: la Situación Argentina*, Santiago de Chile: United Nations/CEPAL/ECLAC, Serie Políticas Sociales 43.

Dammert, L. and F. T. Malone (2002) 'Inseguridad y Temor en la Argentina: El Impacto de la Confianza en la Policía y la Corrupción sobre la Percepción Ciudadana del Crimen', *Desarrollo Económico. Revista de Ciencias Sociales*, 42, 166.

Dammert Ego Aguirre, M. (2001) *Fujimori-Montesinos. El estado mafioso. El poder imagocrático en las sociedades globalizadas*, Lima: Ediciones El Virrey.

Degregori, C. I. (1987) *Sendero Luminoso. I. Los Hondos y Mortales Desencuentros. II. Lucha Armada y Utopía Autoritaria*, Lima: IEP/CEPRODEP (Documentos de Trabajo, 4 and 6).

— (1989) 'Sendas Peligrosas: La guerra del Comandante Huayhuaco', *QueHacer*, 58: 26–30.

— (ed.) (1996) *Las Rondas campesinas y la derrota de Sendero Luminoso*, Lima/ Huamanga: IEP/Universidad Nacional de San Cristóbal de Huamanga.

— (1999) 'Reflections', in Arnson (1999), pp. 251–6.

— (2000) *La Década de la Antipolítica. Auge e Huida de Alberto Fujimori y Vladimiro Montesinos*, Lima: IEP.

De la Jara Basombrillo, E. (2001) *Memoria y Batallas en Nombre de los Inocentes. Perú 1992–2001*, Lima: IDS.

Deli Sante, A. (1996) *Nightmare or Reality? Guatemala in the 1980s,* Amsterdam: Thela.

Del Pino Huamán, P. (1993a) 'Los Campesinos Hacen Suya la Organización que Inicialmente Se Impulso', in Starn (1993), pp. 51–3.

— (1993b) 'Tiempos de Guerra y de Dioses: Sendero, Ronderos y Evangélicos: Historia de una Guerra sin Fin', manuscript, IEP/Universidad Nacional de San Cristóbal de Huamanga.

— (1996) 'Tiempos de Guerra y de Dioses: Ronderos, Evangélicos y Senderistas en el Valle del Río Apurímac', in Degregori (1996), pp. 117–88.

Del Toro, M. C. (1995) *Mexico's War on Drugs, Causes and Consequences*, Boulder, CO: Lynne Rienner.

Departamento de Estado de EU (2001) *Apoyo de los Estados Unidos al Plan Colombia*, Washington, DC: State Departament.

Depaz (2000a) *El Proceso de Negociación del Gobierno Colombiano con las Farc-Ep*, Bogotá: Gobernación de Cundinamarca, February.

— (2000b) *Proceso de Solución Política del Gobierno Colombiano con la UC-ELN*, Bogotá: Gobernación de Cundinamarca, April.

DESCO – Centro de Estudios y Promoción del Desarrollo (1989) *Violencia política en el Perú* (vols I and II), Lima: DESCO.

Dew, E. W. (1994) *The Trouble in Suriname, 1975–1993*, Westport, CT: Praeger.

Diamond, L. (1999) *Developing Democracy: Toward Consolidation*, Baltimore, MD: Johns Hopkins University Press.

Diario Oficial (Bogotá) (1989) 10, 11 and 29 January; (1994) 5 July.

Diez Canseco Cisneros, J. et al. (2002) *Balance de la inversión privada y privatización, 1990–2001. Objetivos/resultados*, Lima: Fondo Editorial del Congreso del Perú/Serie Documentos Parlamentarios.

Dirección Nacional de Política Criminal (2000) *Estudio de Victimización. Ciudad de Córdoba 1999*, Buenos Aires: Ministerio de Justicia y Derechos Humanos.

— (2001) *Estudio de Victimización. Gran Buenos Aires 2000*, Buenos Aires: Ministerio de Justicia y Derechos Humanos.

— (2002a) *Estudio de Victimización. Ciudad de Buenos Aires 2001*, Buenos Aires: Ministerio de Justicia y Derechos Humanos.

— (2002b) *Informe Anual de Estadísticas Policiales. Año 2001*, Buenos Aires: Ministerio de Justicia y Derechos Humanos, Sistema Nacional de Información Criminal.

Domínguez, J. I. and A. F. Lowenthal (eds) (1996) *Constructing Democratic Governance. Latin America and the Caribbean – Themes and Issues*, Baltimore, MD and London: Johns Hopkins University Press.

Dowdney, L. (2002) *Child Combatants in Organized Armed Violence: A Study of Children and Adolescents Involved in Territorial Drug Faction Disputes in Rio de Janeiro*, Rio de Janeiro: ISER/Viva Rio.

Echandía, C. (1999) 'Expansión Territorial de las Guerrillas Colombianas: Geografía, Economía y Violencia', in Deas and Llorente (eds), *Reconocer la Guerra para Construir la Paz*, Bogotá: Ediciones Uniandes-Cerec-Grupo Editorial Norma.

Elias, N. And E. Dunning (1992) *Deporte y ocio en el proceso de la civilización*, Madrid: Fondo de Cultura Económica.

Emmerich, N. (2000) *Narcotráfico y Modernización en la Argentina 1989–1999*, Tesina de Graduación, Buenos Aires: Universidad de Belgrano.

Escobar, C. (2002) 'Clientelism and Citizenship: The Limits of Democratic Reform in Sucre, Colombia', *Latin American Perspectives*, 126, 29(5): 20–47.

Escuela Nacional Sindical (2002) *Informes Sobre derechos humanos de los trabajadores Colombianos*, Bogotá: Escuela Nacional Sindical.

Fico, C. (2001) *Como eles agiam: os subterrâneos da ditadura militar: espionagem e polícia política*, Rio de Janeiro: Editora Record.

Figueroa Ibarra, C. (1991) 'Guatemala: The Recourse of Fear', in Huggins (1991).

Findlay, M. and U. Zvekic (1994) *Alternative Policing Styles, Cross Cultural Perspectives*, Kluwer: Deventer.

Fitch, J. S. (1998) *The Armed Forces and Democracy in Latin America*, Baltimore, MD: Johns Hopkins University Press.

Foucault, M. (1977) *Discipline and Punish*, London: Penguin Books.

Foweraker, J. (2001) 'Grassroots Movements and Political Activism in Latin America: A Critical Comparison of Chile and Brazil', *Journal of Latin American Studies*, 33(4): 839–65.

Fumerton, M. (2002) *From Victims to Heroes: Peasant Counter-Rebellion and Civil War in Ayacucho, Peru, 1980–2000*, Amsterdam: Rozenberg Publishers.

Frühling, H. and J. S. Tulchin (eds), with H. A. Golding (2003) *Crime and Violence in Latin America. Citizen Security, Democracy, and the State*, Washington, DC, Baltimore, MD, and London: Woodrow Wilson Center Press/Johns Hopkins University Press.

Gallón Giraldo, G. (1979) *Quince Años de Estado de Sitio en Colombia, 1958–1978*, Bogotá: Editorial América Latina.

Gamarra, E. (2003) 'Has Bolivia Won the War? Lessons from Plan Dignidad', in Vellinga (2003), pp. 24–53.

García del Delgado, D. (2003) *Estado-nación y la Crisis del Modelo. El Estrecho Sendero*, Buenos Aires: Grupo Editorial Norma.

Gaspar, G. (1997) *Guerrillas en América Latina*, Santiago de Chile: FLACSO (Nueva Serie FLACSO).

Gaspari, E. (2002) *A Ditadura Escancarada*, São Paulo: Cia das Letras.

Geen, R. G. (2001) *Human Aggression*, 2nd edn, Buckingham: Open University Press.

Geffray, C. (2001) 'Effects Sociaux, Economiques et Politiques de la Pénétration du Narcotrafic en Amazonie Brésilienne', *International Social Science Journal*, 3.

Gereffi, G., M. Korzeniewicz and R. P. Korzeniewicz (1994) 'Introduction: Global Commodity Chains', in G. Gereffi and M. Korzeniewicz (eds), *Commodity Chains and Global Capitalism*, Westport, CT: Praeger, pp. 1–14.

GHRC / Guatemalan Human Rights Commission (1983) *Boletín Internacional*, 5.

Giddens, A. (1985) *The Nation-State and Violence*, Cambridge: Polity Press.

Giusti, R. (2002) 'El 71% del Pais Rechaza a Chávez', *El Universal*, 3 November.

Glebbeek, M. L. (2003) *In the Crossfire of Democracy. Police Reform and Police Practice in Post-Civil War Guatemala*, Amsterdam: Rozenberg Publishers.

Golbert, L. and G. Kessler (2001) *El Crecimiento de la Violencia Urbana en la Argentina de los 90. El Debate entre la Explicación Económica y la Sociológica*, Buenos Aires: mimeo.

Gonzalez, D. (2003) 'Dispersaron con bombas lacrimógenas nueva marcha opositora en Los Próceres', *El Nacional*, 13 January.

Gosner, K. and A. Ouweneel (eds) (1996) *Indigenous Revolts in Chiapas and the Andean Highlands*, Amsterdam: CEDLA Publications.

Gugliotta, G. and J. Leen (1990) *Kings of Cocaine*, New York: Harper & Row.

Bibliography

Guimaraes, H. and V. de Paula (1992) 'Cotidiano Escolar e Violência', in A. Zaluar (ed.), *Educação e Violência*, São Paulo: Cortez Ed.

Gwynne, R. (2000) 'Globalization, Neoliberalism and Regional Response in the Americas', in M. Vellinga (ed.), *The Dialectics of Globalization: Regional Responses to World Economic Processes*, Boulder, CO: Westview Press, pp. 149–62.

Gwynne, R. and C. Kay (2000) 'View from the Periphery: Futures of Neo-Liberalism in Latin America', *Third World Quarterly*, 21(1): 141–56.

Haan, A. de and S. Maxwell (eds) (1998) 'Poverty and Social Exclusion in North and South', *IDS Bulletin*, 29(1): 1–31.

Hagopian, F. (1996) 'Traditional Power Structures and Democratic Government in Latin America', in Dominguez and Lowenthal (1996), pp. 64–86.

Hammond, J. L. (1999) 'Law and Disorder. The Brazilian Landless Farmworkers' Movement', *Bulletin of Latin American Research*, 18(4): 469–90.

Held, D. (1987) *Models of Democracy*, Cambridge: Polity Press.

Herman, M. (1996) *Intelligence Power in Peace and War*, Cambridge: Cambridge University Press/ Royal Institute of International Affairs.

Hernandez, A. M. (2003) 'Disidentes Exhortan a la FAN Desconocer Autoridad de Chávez', *El Universal*, 13 June.

Hernandez, C. (2002) 'Tarde de Sangre, Noche de Golpe', *El Universal*, 20 April.

Horowitz, I. L. (ed.) (1970) *Masses in Latin America*, New York: Oxford University Press.

Hoy en Planeación (2003), 3 April.

Huggins, M. K. (ed.) (1991) *Vigilantism and the State in Latin America: Essays on Extralegal Violence*, New York: Praeger.

— (1997) *Political Policing*, Durham, NC and London: Duke University Press.

— (1998) 'From Bureaucratic Consolidation to Structural Devolution: Police Death Squads in Brazil', *Policing and Society*, 7.

Huggins, M. K., M. Haritos-Faroutos and P. Zimbardo (2002) *Violence Workers*, Berkeley: University of California Press.

Human Rights Watch (1992) *The Struggle for Land in Brazil*, New York: Human Rights Watch.

— (1993) *Forced Labor in Brazil Revisited*, New York: Human Rights Watch.

— (1996) *Colombia's Killer Networks. The Military–Paramilitary Partnership and the United States*, New York: Human Rights Watch.

— (2000) *The Ties that Bind: Colombia and Military–Paramilitary Links*, New York: Human Rights Watch.

— (2001) *The 'Sixth Division'. Military– Paramilitary Ties and US Policy in Colombia*, New York: Human Rights Watch.

— (2003) *Informe Annual 2003: Venezuela*, New York: Human Rights Watch.

Isaacson, A. and J. Olson (2001) *Just the Facts, 2000–2001, A Civilian's Guide to US Defense and Security Assistance to Latin America and the Caribbean*, Washington, DC: Latin America Working Group.

Isbell, B. J. (1990) 'The Text and Contexts of Terror in Peru', conference paper no. 42, presented at the research conference, 'Violence and Democracy in Colombia and Peru', held at Columbia University, 30 November to 1 December.

IUDOP (Instituto Universitario de Opinión Pública) (1996) 'La Violencia en El Salvador', *Estudios Centroamericanos*, 569: 240–9.

Janowitz, M. (1975) *Military Conflict*, Beverly Hills, CA: Sage.

Jay, A. (1993) *Persecution by Proxy. The Civil Patrols in Guatemala,* Washington, DC: Robert F. Kennedy Memorial Center for Human Rights.

Jelin, E. and E. Hershberg (eds) (1996) *Constructing Democracy. Human Rights, Citizenship and Society in Latin America*, Boulder, CO: Westview.

Johamowitz, L. (ed.) (2002a) *Vladimiro. Vida y Tiempo de un Corruptor. Expediente I*, Lima: El Comercio.

— (ed.) (2002b) *Vladimiro. Conversando con el Doctor. Expediente II*, Lima: El Comercio.

Joyce, E. and C. Malamud (eds) (1998) *Latin America and the Multinational Drug Trade*, London: Macmillan.

Juergensmeyer, M. (2000) *Terror in the Mind of God: The Global Rise of Religious Violence,* Berkeley: University of California Press.

Katz, J. (1988) *The Seductions of Crime*, New York: Basic Books.

Keane, J. (1997) *Reflections on Violence*, London: Verso.

Klarén, P. F. (2000) *Peru. Society and Nationhood in the Andes*, New York: Oxford University Press.

Klockars, K. (1985) *The Idea of Police*, Beverly Hills, CA: Sage Publications.

Koonings, K. (2001) 'Armed Actors, Violence and Democracy in Latin America in the 1990s: Introductory Notes', *Bulletin of Latin American Research*, 20(4): 401–8.

— (2002) 'Civil Society, Transitions, and Post-War Reconstruction in Latin America: A Comparison of El Salvador, Guatemala, and Peru', *Iberoamericana-Nordic Journal of Latin American and Caribbean Studies*, 32(4): 45–71.

— (2003) 'Political Armies, Security Forces, and Democratic Consolidation in Latin America', in G. Crawthra and R. Luckham (eds), *Governing Insecurity: Democratic Control of Military and Security Establishments in Transitional Democracies*, London: Zed Books, pp. 124–52.

Koonings, K. and D. Kruijt (eds) (1999) *Societies of Fear. The Legacy of Civil War, Violence and Terror in Latin America*, London: Zed Books.

— (eds) (2002) *Political Armies. The Military and Nation Building in the Age of Democracy*, London: Zed Books.

— (2003) 'Latin American Political Armies in the Twenty-first Century', *Bulletin of Latin American Research*, 22(3): 371–84.

Kruijt, D. (1996) 'Ethnic Civil War in Peru: The Military and Shining Path', in Gosner and Ouweneel (1996), pp. 241–56.

— (1999) 'Exercises in State Terrorism: The Counter-insurgency Campaigns in Guatemala and Peru', in Koonings and Kruijt (1999), pp. 33–62.

— (2001) 'Low Intensity Democracies: Latin America in the Post-dictatorial Era', *Bulletin of Latin American Research*, 20(4): 409–30.

Kruijt, D. and K. Koonings (1999) 'Introduction: Violence and Fear in Latin America', in Koonings and Kruijt (1999), pp. 1–30.

Kruijt, D. and M. del Pilar Tello (2002) 'From Military Reformists to Civilian Dictatorship: Peruvian Military Politics from the 1960s to the Present', in Koonings and Kruijt (2002), pp. 35–63.

Kruijt, D., C. Sojo and R. Grynspan (2002) *Informal Citizens. Poverty, Informality and Social Exclusion in Latin America*, Amsterdam: Rozenberg Publishers.

Kurtenbach, S. (2003) 'El Nuevo Escenario de (In)seguridad en América Latina: ¿Amenaza Para la Democracia?', in K. Bodemer (ed.), *El Nuevo Escenario de*

Bibliography

(In)seguridad en América Latina: ¿Amenaza para la Democracia?, Caracas: Nueva Sociedad, pp. 11–37.

Labrousse, A. (1993) *La Droga, el dinero y las Armas*, Mexico: Siglo XXI Editores.

— (2000) *Drogues: un Marché de Dupes,* Paris: Editions Alternatives.

Lamounier, B. (1977) 'Formação de um Pensamento Político Autoritário na Primeira República', *História Geral da Civilização Brasileira*, 9, *O Brasil Republicano*, São Paulo: Difel.

Langgut, A. J. (1978) *Hidden Terrors*, New York: Pantheon.

La Rotta Moran, A. (2002) 'Desconocen Gobierno de Chávez', *El Universal*, 23 October.

Latin America Working Group and Center for International Policy (n.d.) 'Presencia Militar de Estados Unidos en Colombia' (<www.ciponline.org/facts>).

Latorraca, M., H. Montero and C. Rodriguez (2003) 'Política y Corrupción Policial', *Le Monde Diplomatique*, May.

Leal, A. and P. Aiquel Garbarini (2002) 'Chávez Admite Errors y Pide Perdón a los Gerents Removidos de Pdvsa', *El Nacional*, 16 April.

Leal, V. N. (1975) *Coronelismo, enxada e voto: o município e o regime representativo no Brasil*, São Paulo: Editora Alfa-Omega.

Leal Buitrago, F. (1994) *El Oficio de la Guerra. La Seguridad Nacional en Colombia*, Bogotá: Tercer Mundo Editores.

— (1995) 'Estabilidad Macroeconómica e Institucional y Violencia Crónica', in F. Leal Buitrago (ed.), *En Busca de la Estabilidad Perdida,* Bogotá: Tercer Mundo Editores-Iepri-Colciencias.

— (ed.) (1996) *Tras las Huellas de la Crisis Política,* Bogotá: Tercer Mundo Editores-Fescol-Universidad Nacional.

— (ed.) (1999) *Los Labirintos de la Guerra. Utopías e Incertidumbres sobre la Paz*, Bogotá: Tercer Mundo Editores.

— (2000) 'Situación política de Colombia', *Anuario Social y Político de América Latina y el Caribe*, 3: 55–64.

— (2001) *La Seguridad Nacional a la Deriva,* Bogotá: Alfaomega Editores-Universidad de los Andes-Flacso Sede Ecuador.

Le Bot, Y. (1995) *La Guerra en Tierras Mayas. Comunidad, Violencia y Modernidad en Guatemala (1970–1992)*, Mexico: Fondo de Cultura Económica.

Lee, R. (2004) 'Perversely Harmful Effects of Counter-Narcotics Policy in the Andes', in Vellinga (2004).

Leeds, E. (1996) 'Cocaine and Parallel Politics in the Brazilian Urban Periphery: Constraints on Local-level Democratization', *Latin American Research Review*, 31(3): 47–84.

Leons, M. B. and H. Sanabría (eds) (1997) *Coca, Cocaine and the Bolivian Reality*, Albany, NJ: University of New York Press.

Lins, P. (1997) *Cidade de Deus*, São Paulo: Cia das Letras.

Linz, J. J. and A. Stepan (eds) (1996) *Problems of Democratic Transition and Consolidation. Southern Europe, South America, and Post-communist Europe*, Baltimore, MD, and London: Johns Hopkins University Press.

Lloyd Griffith, I. (1997) *Drugs and Security in the Caribbean: Sovereignty under Siege*, University Park: Pennsylvania State University Press.

— (ed.) (2002) *The Political Economy of Drugs in the Caribbean*, London: Macmillan.

López, E. (1994) *Ni la Ceniza, ni la Gloria. Actores, Sistema Político y Cuestión Militar en los Años de Alfonsín*, Bernal: Universidad Nacional de Quilmes.

Loveman, B. (1999) *For La Patria: Politics and the Armed Forces in Latin America*, Delaware: Scholarly Resources Inc.

Luppo, S. (2002) *História da Máfia*, São Paulo: Editora UNESP.

McClintock, C. (1999) 'The Decimation of Peru's Sendero Luminoso', in Arnson (1999), pp. 223-49.

McClintock, M. (1985) *The American Connection. State Terror and Resistance in Guatemala*, London: Zed Books.

Maier, J. (1996) 'Breve Historia Institucional de la Policía Argentina', in P. Waldmann (ed.), *Justicia en la Calle. Ensayos Sobre la Policía en América Latina*, Medellín: Biblioteca Jurídica Diké.

Maier, J., M. Abregú and S. Tiscornia (1996) 'El Papel de la Policía en la Argentina y su Situación Actual', in P. Waldmann (ed.), *Justicia en la Calle. Ensayos sobre la Policía en América Latina*, Medellín: Biblioteca Jurídica Diké.

Martín-Barbero, J. (2002) 'The City: between Fear and the Media', in S. Rotker (ed.), *Citizens of Fear. Urban Violence in Latin America*, New Brunswick, NJ: Rutgers University Press, pp. 25-36.

Martinez, E. (2002) 'Referendo Se Realizará el 2F', *El Universal*, 28 November.

Mauceri, P. (2000) 'Unchecked Power: The Presidency under Fujimori and Beyond', paper presented at the XXIInd International Congress of the Latin American Studies Association, Miami, FL, 16-18 March 2000.

Mayorca, J. I. (2002a) 'En Manos del Ejército Comité de Informática de la Industria', *El Nacional*, 7 March.

— (2002b) 'Alianza de Militares Activos Precipitó la Caída de Hugo Chávez', *El Nacional*, 13 April.

Medina, C. (1990) *Autodefensas, Paramilitares y Narcotráfico en Colombia: Origen, Desarrollo y Consolidación*, Bogotá: Editorial Documentos Periodísticos.

Medina, O. (2003) 'Las Mechas del 23', *El Universal*, 15 June.

Melo, J. O. (1990) 'Los Paramilitares y su Impacto sobre la Política', in F. Leal and L. Zamosc (eds), *Al Filo del Caos Política en la Colombia de los Años 80*, Bogotá: Tercer Mundo Editores-Universidad Nacional.

Méndez, J. (2002) 'Problemas de Violencia Ilegal. Una Introducción', in J. Méndez, G. O'Donnell and P. Pinheiro (eds), *La (In)efectividad de la Ley y la Exclusión en América Latina*, Buenos Aires: Paidós.

Méndez, J. G. O'Donnell and P. S. Pinheiro (eds) (1999), *The (Un)rule of Law and the Underprivileged in Latin America*, Notre Dame, IN: University of Notre Dame Press.

Menzel, S. H. (1996) *Fire in the Andes*, Lanham, MD: University Press of America.

— (1997) *Cocaine Quagmire*, Lanham: University Press of America.

Mesquita, M. (1996) 'Homicídios de Crianças e Adolescentes', *Encontro Nacional de Produtores e Usuários de informações*, Rio de Janeiro: IBGE.

Míguez, D. and A. Isla (2003) 'Conclusiones. El Estado y la violencia urbana. Problemas de legitimidad y legalidad', in A. Isla and M. Daniel (eds), *Heridas Urbanas. Violencia Delictiva y Transformaciones Sociales en los Noventa*, Buenos Aires: Editorial de las Ciencias y FLACSO-Argentina.

Ministerio de Defensa Nacional (1970) *Copilación de Disposiciones Legales Vigentes, 1964-65*, 5, Bogotá: Imprenta de las Fuerzas Militares.

— (1995) *Memoria al Congreso Nacional 1993–1994*, Bogotá: Imprenta y Publicaciones de las Fuerzas Militares.

— (1998) *Memoria al Congreso Nacional 1996–1997*, Bogotá: Imprenta y Publicaciones de las Fuerzas Militares.

— (1999) *Colombia. Defensa Nacional,* 450, Bogotá: Ministerio de Defensa.

Ministerio de Seguridad de la Provincia de Buenos Aires (2002) *Estadística Delictual 2000, 2001 y 2002*, La Plata: Centro de Operaciones Policiales, Sección Estadísticas.

— (2003) *Delitos Cometidos con Armas de Fuego. Informe Preliminar*, La Plata: Ministerio de Seguridad de la Provincia de Buenos Aires.

Mollejas, C. (2003) 'Solo 14 Funcionarios Investigan 25 Homicidios en Actos Políticos', *El Universal*, 5 January.

Montgomery, T. (1995) *Revolution in El Salvador. From Civil Strife to Civil Peace,* Boulder, CO: Westview Press.

Morales, J. (1989) *Cocaine: White Gold Rush in Peru*, Tucson: University of Arizona Press.

Morrison, A., M. Buvinic and M. Shifter (2003) 'The Violent Americas: Risk Factors, Consequences, and Policy Implications of Social and Domestic Violence', in Frühling et al. (2003), pp. 93–122

Moser, C. and C. McIlwaine (2000) *Urban Poor Perceptions of Violence and Exclusion in Colombia,* Washington, DC: World Bank.

— (2001) *Violence in a Post Conflict Context: Urban Poor Perceptions from Guatemala*, Washington, DC: World Bank.

Muleiro, V. (2003) 'Los Tiros Zumban en el Oído del Gobierno', *Clarín*, Buenos Aires, 13 July.

Muñoz, H. (1998) 'On Poor Relations and the Nouveau Riche: Shining Path and the Radical Peruvian Left', in Stern (1998), pp. 447–69.

North, L. (1981) *Bitter Grounds. Roots of Revolt in El Salvador,* Toronto: Between the Lines.

Obando, E. (1998) 'Civil–Military Relations in Peru, 1980–1996: How to Control and Coopt the Military (and the consequences of doing so)', in Stern (1998), pp. 385–410.

Observatoire Géopolitique des Drogues (2000) *The World Geopolitics of Drugs 1998/1999*, Paris: OGD.

ODHAG (1998) *Guatemala: Nunca Más,* vols I–IV, Guatemala: ODHAG.

O'Donnell, G. (1999) *Counterpoints: Selective Essays on Authoritarianism and Democratization*, Notre Dame, IN: University of Notre Dame.

— (2002) 'Las Poliarquías y la (In)efectividad de la Ley en América Latina', in J. Méndez, G. O'Donnell and P. Pinheiro (eds), *La (In)efectividad de la Ley y la Exclusión en América Latina*, Buenos Aires: Paidós.

OIM (2001) *Annuario entradas y salidas internacionales de Colombia 2001*, Bogotá: Organización Internacional de Migraciones.

Olivares, F. (2002a) 'La Fuerza Armada Fracturada', *El Universal*, 21 April.

— (2002b) 'El Pánico Se Desató al Mediodía', *El Universal*, 29 April.

— (2003) 'FAN Revolucionaria', *El Universal*, 8 June.

Orozco Abad, I. (1992) *Combatientes, Rebeldes y Terroristas. Guerra y Derecho en Colombia,* Editorial Temis-Universidad Nacional.

Paige, J. (1998) *Coffee and Power. Revolution and the Rise of Democracy in Central America,* Cambridge, MA, and London: Harvard University Press.

Painter, J. (1994) *Bolivia and Coca: A Study in Dependency,* Boulder, CO: Lynne Rienner.

Palacios, M. (2003) 'Diputados Denuncian los Círculos Bolivarianos', *El Nacional,* 14 March.

Pardo Rueda, R. (1996) *De Primera Mano. Colombia 1986-1994: entre Conflictos y Esperanzas,* Bogotá: Cerec-Grupo Editorial Norma.

Payne, L. A. (2000) *Uncivil Movements. The Armed Right Wing and Democracy in Latin America,* Baltimore, MD: Johns Hopkins University Press.

PDH (1994) *Los Comités de Defensa Civil en Guatemala,* Guatemala: PDH/AECI/ASADI.

Pécaut, D. (1999) 'From the Banality of Violence to Real Terror: The Case of Colombia', in Koonings and Kruijt (1999), pp. 141–67.

Peñate, A. (1998) *El sendero estratégico del ELN: del idealismo guevarista al clientelismo armado,* Bogotá: Universidad de los Andes, Centro de Estudios sobre Desarrollo Económico (Working Document 15 of the Programa de Estudios sobre Seguridad, Justicia y Violencia).

Peralva, A. (2000) *Violéncia e Democracia: O Paradoxo Brasileiro,* São Paulo: Paz e Terra.

Pérez Rodíguez, S. (2002) 'Refugiados en la Plaza Altamira', *Tal Cual,* 24 October.

Pereira, A. (2000) 'An Ugly Democracy? State Violence and the Rule of Law in Post-authoritarian Brazil', in P. Kingstone and T. Power (eds), *Democratic Brazil: Actors, Institutions, and Processes.* Pittsburgh, PA: University of Pittsburgh Press, pp. 217–35.

Pereira, A. and D. Davis (2000) 'New Patterns of Militarized Violence and Coercion in the Americas', *Latin American Perspectives,* 27(2): 3–17.

Pinheiro, P. (1991) 'Police and Political Crisis, the Case of the Military Police', in Huggins (1991).

Pinheiro, P. S. (1996) 'Democracies without Citizenship', *NACLA Report on the Americas,* 30(2): 17–23.

Pinto, M. (1994) *Report by the Independent Expert, Mrs Monica Pinto, on the Situation of Human Rights in Guatemala,* Commission on Human Rights, Economic and Social Council, United Nations document number E/CN.4/1995/15.

Pizarro, E. (1991) 'La Insurgencia Armada: Raíces y Perspectivas', in F. Leal and L. Zamosc (eds), *Al Filo del Caos. Crisis Política en la Colombia de los Años 80,* Bogotá: Tercer Mundo Editores-Universidad Nacional.

Pizarro, E. and R. Peñaranda (1991) *Las FARC (1949-1966). De la Autodefensa a la Combinación de Todas las Formas de Lucha,* Bogotá: Tercer Mundo Editores-Universidad Nacional.

PNUD (Programa de las Naciones Unidas para el Desarrollo) (2002) *Indicadores sobre violencia en El Salvador,* San Salvador: PNUD.

Poleo, P. (2002) 'Factores de Poder', *Nuevo País,* 17 April.

Poole, D. (ed.) (1994a) *Unruly Order: Violence, Power, and Cultural Identity in the High Provinces of Southern Peru,* Boulder, CO: Westview Press.

— (1994b) 'Peasant Culture and Political Violence in the Peruvian Andes: Sendero Luminoso and the State', in D. Poole (1994a), pp. 247–81.

Popkin, M. (1996) *Civil Patrols and Their Legacy. Overcoming Militarization and Polarization in the Guatemalan Countryside,* Washington, DC: Robert F. Kennedy Memorial Center for Human Rights.

— (2000) *Peace without Justice: Obstacles to Building the Rule of Law in El Salvador*, University Park, PA: Penn State University Press.

Prensa Libre (2002), 13 July.

PROVEA (2003) *Informe Anual*, 14.

Puex, N. (2003) 'Las Formas de la Violencia en Tiempos de Crisis: una Villa Miseria del Conurbano Bonaerense', in A. Isla and D. Míguez (eds), *Heridas Urbanas. Violencia Delictiva y Transformaciones Sociales en los Noventa*, Buenos Aires: Editorial de las Ciencias and FLACSO-Argentina.

PuntoDoc (2003), Canal América, Buenos Aires, 9 June.

Ramírez, S. and L. A. Restrepo (1989) *Actores en Conflicto por la Paz. El Proceso de Paz durante el Gobierno de Belisario Betancur*, Bogotá: Siglo XXI Editores-Cinep.

Ramos, C. G. (1998) 'Transición, Jóvenes y Violencia', in C. G. Ramos (ed.), *América Central en los Noventa: Problemas de Juventud*, San Salvador: FLACSO.

Rangel, A. (1999) 'Las Farc-Ep: Una Mirada Actual', in Deas and Llorente (eds), *Reconocer la Guerra para Construir la Paz*, Bogotá: Ediciones Uniandes-Cerec-Grupo Editorial Norma.

— (2000) *Colombia: Guerra en el Fin de Siglo*, Bogotá: Tercer Mundo Editores-Universidad de los Andes.

Remijnse, S. (2001) 'Remembering Civil Patrols in Joyabaj, Guatemala', *Bulletin of Latin American Research*, 20(4): 454–69.

— (2003) *Memories of Violence. Civil Patrols and the Legacy of Conflict in Joyabaj, Guatemala*, Amsterdam: Rozenberg Publishers.

Restrepo, L. (2001) *La Multitud Errante*, Bogotá: Ed. Planeta Colombiana.

Reuter, P. (1985) 'Eternal Hope, America's Quest for Narcotics Control', *Public Interest*, 79: 79–95.

Rios, A. (2002a) 'Un Referendo Consultivo Sera Respetado por el Ejército', *El Universal*, 24 October.

— (2002b) 'La Fuerza Armada Espera el Humo Blanco Electoral', *El Universal*, 4 November.

Rivera Campos, R. (2000) *La Economía Salvadoreña al Final del Siglo: Desafíos para el Futuro*, San Salvador: FLACSO.

Roberts, B. (1996) 'The Social Context of Citizenship in Latin America', *International Journal of Urban and Regional Research*, 20(1): 38–65.

Robles, R. (1996) *Crimen e Impunidad. El 'Grupo Colona' y el Poder*, Lima: Asociación pro Derechos Humanos APRODEH.

Rodríguez, G. (2002) 'Terrorismo Estremeció Ciudad', *El Universal*, 26 February.

Romero, A. (1997) 'Rearranging the Deck Chairs on the Titanic: The Agony of Democracy in Venezuela', *Latin American Research Review*, 32(1): 7–37.

Romero, D. (2002a) 'La Historia Secreta de un Fracaso Militar', *Tal Cual*, 16 April.

— (2002b) 'Cacería en la GN Dejó 29 Generales sin Cargo', *Tal Cual*, 22 May.

— (2002c) 'La Estrategiá Militaria después de 11A', *Tal Cual*, 15 October.

— (2002d) 'Intriga en el Alto Mando', *Tal Cual*, 21 November.

Romero, D. and V. Romero (2002a) 'Alas Rotas', *Tal Cual*, 20 June.

— (2002b) 'Fragatas Obsoletas', *Tal Cual*, 21 June.

— (2002c) 'Adiós a las Armas', *Tal Cual*, 25 June.

Romero, M. (2003) *Paramilitares y Autodefensas, 1982–2003*, Bogotá: Instituto de Estudios Políticos y Relaciones Internacionales, Universidad Nacional de Colombia/Editorial Planeta Colombiana.

Rosa, H. (1993) *AID y las Transformaciones Globales en El Salvador*, Managua: CRIES.

Rosada-Granados, H. (1999) *Soldados en el Poder. Proyecto Militar en Guatemala, 1944–1990*, Amsterdam: Thela Thesis (Latin America Series).

Rospigliosi, F. (2000) *Montesinos y las Fuerzas Armadas. Cómo Controló durante una Década las Instituciones Militares*, Lima: IEP.

Rotker, S. (2002) 'Cities Written by Violence: An Introduction', in S. Rotker (ed.), *Citizens of Fear. Urban Violence in Latin America*, New Brunswick, NJ: Rutgers University Press, pp. 7–24.

Roy, J. (2001) 'La Asistencia Europea a Colombia: ¿Una Contribución Virtual a un Plan Virtual de Paz?', *Colombia Internacional*, 51, Jan.–Apr.

Ruiz Pantin, E. (2002) 'Asociación de Alcaldes Rechaza Intervención de la Metropolitana', *El Nacional*, 19 November.

Sain, M. F. (2000) 'Democracia e Forças Armadas: Entre a Subordinação Militar e os "Defeitos" Civis', in M. C. D'Araujo and C. Celso (eds), *Democracia e Forças Armadas no Cone Sul*, Rio de Janeiro: Editora FGV.

— (2002) 'Nuevos Horizontes, Nuevos Dilemas. Las "Nuevas Amenazas" y las Fuerzas Armadas en la Argentina Democrática', *Desarrollo Económico. Revista de Ciencias Sociales*, 42, 166: 263–83.

— (2002b) *Seguridad, Democracia y Reforma del Sistema Policial en la Argentina*, Buenos Aires: Fondo de Cultura Económica.

— (2003a) 'Hay Omisión, Complicidad o Participación', *Página/12*, Buenos Aires, 6 July.

— (2003b) 'Modernizar la Policía Ataca la Ineficiencia y la Corrupción', *Debate. Revista Semanal de Opinión*, 17, 4 July.

— (2003c) 'Seguridad, Democracia y Reforma de la Organización Policial en la Argentina', paper presented at the international seminar 'Políticas de prevención del crimen y la violencia en ámbitos urbanos', organized by the Alcaldía Mayor de Bogotá and the Universidad de Los Andes, Bogotá, Colombia, 22–23 May 2003.

— (2003d) 'Los desafíos de la inteligencia regional en un contexto de globalización', paper presented at the Third Regional Symposium on Security and Defence: *Nuevas tendencias de la seguridad subregional*, Chilean Graduates Centre for Hemispheric Defence Studies (CHDS), Santiago de Chile, 14–17 April 2003.

Salieron, V. (2002) 'La Economia Se Desplomó 10%', *El Universal*, 27 December.

Sánchez, G. (2003) 'Asuntos Internos, Negocios Sucios', *Noticias*, Buenos Aires, 5 July.

Sánchez Gómez, G. (1990) 'Guerra y Política en la Sociedad Colombiana', *Análisis Político*, 11, September and December.

Santacruz Giralt, M. L. and A. Concha-Eastman (2001) *Barrio Adentro: la Solidaridad Violenta de las Pandillas*, San Salvador: IUDOP.

Santacruz Giralt, M. L. and J. M. Cruz Alas (2001) 'Las Maras en El Salvador', in ERIC, IDESO, IDIES, IUDOP, *Maras y Pandillas en Centroamérica*, vol. 1, Managua: UCA Publicaciones.

Sarmiento, T. (2003) 'SONDEO–Economía de Venezuela tendrá contracción récord en 2003', *Noticias Finanzas.com*, 11 June, <www.finanzas.com>.

Savenije, W. and H. F. M. Lodewijkx (1998) 'Actos Expresivos e Instrumentales de la Violencia entre Pandillas Salvadoreñas: una Investigación de Campo', in C. G.

Bibliography

Ramos (ed.), *América Central en los Noventa: Problemas de Juventual*, San Salvador: FLACSO.

Savenije, W. and K. Andrade-Eekhoff (2003) *Conviviendo en la Orilla,* San Salvador: FLACSO.

Scheper-Hughes, N. (1997) 'Peace-Time Crimes', *Social Identities*, 3(3).

Schiray, M. (1994) 'Les Filières-stupéfiants: Trois Niveaux, Cinq Logiques', *Futuribles*, 185.

Schirmer, J. (1998) *The Guatemalan Military Project: A Violence Called Democracy*, Philadelphia: University of Pensylvania Press.

— (2002) 'The Guatemalan Politico-Military Project. Whose ship of state?', in Koonings and Kruijt (2002), pp. 64–89.

Segal, M. W. and D. R. Segal (1983) 'Social Change in the Participation of Women in the American Military', *Research in Social Movements, Conflicts and Change*, 5: 235–58.

Semana (1998) 827, 9–16 March; 844, 6–13 July; (2000), 967, 13–20 November; (2001), 986, 26 March–2 April; (2003), 1,085, 17–24 February.

Shearer, D. (1998) 'Private Armies and Military Intervention', *Adelphi Paper*, 316, London: IISS.

Siglo Veintiuno (1997), 9 May.

Skidmore, T. E. (1998) *The Politics of Military Rule in Brazil*, New York and Oxford: Oxford University Press.

Sluka, J. (2000) *Death Squad. The Anthropology of State Terror*, Philadelphia: University of Pennsylvania Press.

Smith, M. L. (1992) *Entre Dos Fuegos. ONG, Desarrollo Rural y Violencia Política*, Lima: IEP (Colección Mínima 26).

Smith, P. H. (ed.) (1992) *Drug Policy in the Americas*, Boulder, CO: Westview Press.

— (1998) 'The Rise and Fall of the Developmental State in Latin America', in M. Vellinga (ed.), *The Changing Role of the State in Latin America*, Boulder, CO: Westview Press, pp. 51–74.

Smut, M. and J. L. E. Miranda (1998) *El Fenómeno de las Pandillas en El Salvador,* San Salvador: UNICEF and FLACSO.

Soares, L. E. (2000) *Meu Casaco de General. Quinhentos Días no Front da Segurança Pública do Rio de Janeiro*, São Paulo: Companhía das Letras.

Soares, L. E., J. T Santo-Sé, J. Rodrigues and J. and L. Piquet Carneiro (eds) (1996) *Violência e Política no Rio de Janeiro*, Rio de Janeiro: Editora Relume Dumará.

Solomon, J. (1994) *Institutional Violence. Civil Patrols in Guatemala,* Washington, DC: Robert F. Kennedy Memorial Center for Human Rights.

Sozzo, M. (2002) 'Usos de la Violencia y Construcción de la Actividad Policial en la Argentina', in S. Gayol and G. Kessler (eds), *Violencias, Delitos y Justicias en la Argentina*, Buenos Aires: Manantial.

Spence, L., M. Lanchin and G. Thale (2001) *From Elections to Earthquakes: Reform and Participation in Post-war El Salvador*, Cambridge: Cambridge University Press.

Stanley, R. (2001) 'Violencia Policial en el Gran Buenos Aires: ¿Necesita el Neoliberalismo una Policía Brava?', in K. Bodemer, S. Kurtenbach and K. Meschkat (eds) *Violencia y Regulación de Conflictos en América Latina*, Buenos Aires: Nueva Visión / ADLAF / HBS.

Stanley, W. (1996) *The Protection Racket State, Elite Politics, Military Extortion and Civil War in El Salvador*, Philadelphia, PA: Temple University Press.

Starn, O. (ed.) (1993) *Hablan los Ronderos: la búsqueda por la paz en los Andes*, Lima: IEP.

— (1998) 'Villagers at Arms: War and Counterrevolution in the Central-South Andes', in Stern (1998), pp. 224–57.

Stepan, A. (1971) *The Military in Politics; Changing Patterns in Brazil*, Princeton, NJ: Princeton University Press.

Stern, S. J. (ed.) (1998) *Shining and Other Paths. War and Society in Peru, 1980–1995*, Durham, NC: Duke University Press.

Stewart, P. (2002) 'Colombia asks Neighbors to Join Drug War', 15 October (<http://ciponline.org/demilita.htm>).

Storrs, K. L. and N. M. Serafino (2001), 'CRS Report for Congress', 21 December.

Subero, C. (2002) 'Más de 60 Generales Sin Cargo', *El Universal*, 13 May.

Subsecretaría de Planificación y Logística (2003) *Información sobre Secuestros en el Ámbito de la Provincia de Buenos Aires*, La Plata: Ministerio de Seguridad de la Provincia de Buenos Aires.

Táger, A. G. and M. Mérida (2002) *Privatización de la Seguridad en Guatemala*, Guatemala: FLACSO (manuscript).

Tapia, C. (1997) *Las Fuerzas Armadas y Sendero Luminoso: Dos Estrategias y un Final*, Lima: IEP.

Thoumi, F. E. (1995) *Political Economy and Illegal Drugs in Colombia*, Boulder, CO: Lynne Rienner.

Tokatlian, J. (2000) *Globalización, Narcotráfico y Violencia. Siete Ensayos sobre Colombia*, Bogotá: Grupo Editorial Norma.

Toro, M. C. (1995) *Mexico's 'War' on Drugs: Causes and Consequences*, Boulder, CO: Lynne Reinner.

Trinkunas, H. A. (2000a) 'Crafting Civilian Control in Emerging Democracies: Argentina and Venezuela', *Journal of Interamerican Studies and World Affairs*, 42(3): 77–103.

— (2002b) 'The Crisis in Venezuelan Civil–Military Relations: From Punto Fijo to the Fifth Republic', *Latin American Research Review*, 37(1): 41–76.

— (2002) 'The Reemergence of the Venezuelan Armed Forces as a Political Actor', *Journal of Iberian and Latin American Studies*, 8: 165–72.

Tullis, L. M. (1995) *Unintended Consequences: Illegal Drugs and Drug Policies in Nine Countries*, Boulder, CO: Lynne Rienner.

Turner, S. (1985) *Secrecy and Democracy: The CIA in Transition*, London: Harper & Row.

UNDCP (1997) *World Drug Report*, London and New York: Oxford University Press.

— (2000) *World Drug Report 2000*, Oxford: Oxford University Press.

United States General Accounting Office (2000) *Drug Control in Colombia*, Washington, DC: GAO (<http://www.gao.gov>).

US Bureau of Democracy, Human Rights, and Labor (2003a) *Brazil. Country Reports on Human Rights Practices 2002*.

— (2003b) *Guatemala. Country Reports on Human Rights Practices 2002*.

Valderrama, M. and H. Cabieses (2004) 'Questionable Alliances in the War on Drugs: Peru and the United States', in Vellinga (2004), pp. 55–73.

Valencia, L. (2002) *Adiós a la Política, Bienvenida la Guerra: Secretos de un Malogrado Proceso de Paz*, Bogotá: Intermedio Edit.

Vallespin, A. (2002) *La Policía que Supimos Conseguir*, Buenos Aires: Planeta.

Van der Veen, H. T. (1998) 'The International Drug Complex: When the Visible Hand of Crime Fractures the Strong Arm of the Law', European University Institute (<www.unesco.org/most>).

Vélez, M. A. (2000) *Farc-ELN. Evolución y Expansión Territorial*. Documento Cede 2000-08, Bogotá: Universidad de los Andes.

Vellinga, M. (2003) 'Globalization and Neoliberalism: Economy and Society in Latin America', *Iberoamericana: Nordic Journal of Latin America and Caribbean Studies*, 32(2): 34–52.

Vellinga, M. (ed.) (2004) *The Political Economy of the Drug Industry: Latin America and the International System,* Gainesville: University Press of Florida.

Waldmann, P. (2003) *El Estado Anómico. Derecho, Seguridad Pública y Vida Cotidiana en América Latina*, Caracas: Nueva Sociedad.

Weber, M. (1978) *Economy and Society*, Berkeley: University of California Press.

Weffer Cifuentes, L. (2002) 'El Alto Mando Me Traicionó, Cobardes!', *El Nacional*, 17 April.

Wickham-Crowley, T. P. (1992) *Guerrillas and Revolution in Latin America. A Comparative Study of Insurgents and Regimes since 1956*, Princeton, NJ: Princeton University Press.

Williams, R. (1994) *States and Social Evolution, Coffee and the Rise of National Governments in Central America,* Chapel Hill and London: University of North Carolina Press.

Wilson, S. and M. Zambrano (1994) 'Cocaine, Commodity Chains, and Drug Politics: A Transnational Approach', in Gary Gereffi and Miguel Korzeniewicz (eds), *Commodity Chains and Global Capitalism*, Westport, CT: Praeger, pp. 297–316.

World Bank (2001) *World Development Report 2000/2001*, Oxford: Oxford University Press.

World Health Organization (2002) *World Report on Violence and Health,* Geneva: World Health Organization.

Wouters, M. (2001) 'Ethnic Rights under Threat: The Black Peasant Movement against Armed Groups' Pressure in the Chocó, Colombia', *Bulletin of Latin American Research,* 20(4): 498–519.

Youngers, C. A. (2000) *Deconstructing Democracy: Peru under President Alberto Fujimori*, Washington, DC: WOLA.

Zaitch, D. (2002) *Traquetos: Colombian Drug Entrepreneurs in the Netherlands,* The Hague: Kluwer Law International.

Zaluar, A. (1985) *A Máquina e a Revolta*, São Paulo: Editora Brasiliense.

— (1998) 'Para Não Dizer que Não Falei de Samba', *História da Vida Privada no Brasil,* 4, São Paulo: Cia das Letras.

— (2000). 'Perverse Integration: Drug Trafficking and Youth in the Favelas of Rio de Janeiro', *Journal of International Affairs*, 53(2): 654–71.

— (2001) 'Violence in Rio de Janeiro: Styles of Leisure, Drug Use, and Trafficking', *International Social Science Journal*, 3: 369–79.

Zapata, J. C. (2002a) 'Así Cayó Carmona', *Tal Cual*, 15 April.

— (2002b) 'El Hombre de la Chaqueta Morada', *Tal Cual*, 2 May.

Zartman, I. W. (ed.) (1995) *Collapsed States: The Disintegration and Restoration of Legitimate Authority*, Boulder, CO: Lynne Rienner.

Zaverucha, J. (1994) *Rumor de Sabres: tutela milita ou controle civil*, São Paulo: Aica.

Index